OTHER NOTED GUERRILLAS
(Of the Civil War in Missouri)

_____

LARRY WOOD

3rd Edition

Hickory Press
Joplin, Missouri

Published by

Hickory Press
Joplin, MO

ISBN: 978-0-9702829-5-8
LCCN: 2015903128

Table of Contents

Preface

The main difference between this edition of *Other Noted Guerrillas* and the second edition issued last year is that I have added a chapter on Saline County guerrilla leader Jim Rider. When I wrote the 2007 first edition, containing a chapter on Mart Rider, I thought that Mart and Jim Rider were close kin, and, partly because they were often mentioned in Union records by last name only, I mistakenly attributed certain activities to Mart that should have been attributed to Jim. I later learned that the two men were not closely related and that Jim Rider was much more active as a guerrilla leader than Mart Rider.

When the 2014 edition was released, I chose simply to omit the chapter on Mart Rider as the most expedient means of removing the misinformation from the book. However, continued research on Jim Rider has convinced me that he and his extensive activities as a guerrilla leader in Missouri warrant a chapter in the book. Thus, for this third edition, the original chapter on Mart Rider has now been replaced by a chapter on Jim Rider. I have also made minor additions to a couple of the other chapters, notably the chapter on Joe Hart.

The overall premise of the book, however, remains the same: to tell the stories of certain Civil War guerrilla leaders in Missouri who were ignored or given only passing mention in John N. Edwards's 1877 book *Noted Guerrillas*, a romantic account of William Quantrill and his close followers. By implication, a co-purpose of the book is to show that guerrilla warfare in Missouri was more widespread throughout the entire state than the almost exclusive focus on Quantrill, in the Edwards book and in popular culture for a hundred years after its publication, would lead one to believe.

Since 2007, we have seen a continued interest in Missouri's guerrilla conflict during the Civil War and perhaps a greater recognition of the pervasiveness of that conflict. Still, it is worth reiterating that Quantrill, although the most notorious guerrilla leader in Missouri, was far from the only one. It is also worth re-examining, as I do particularly in the last chapter, the dubious stereotypes about the guerrillas, perpetuated largely by the selective focus on Quantrill, which often still persist in the popular consciousness, despite arguments outlined by historians and authors in recent years that would tend to refute many of them.

1
The Rise of Guerrilla Warfare in Missouri

Results from the 1860 presidential election reveal the political makeup of the slave-holding border state of Missouri on the eve of America's Civil War. Out of 165,518 votes cast, Republican candidate Abraham Lincoln received 17,028 or about ten percent of the total, and most of these Republican votes came from the St. Louis area. Southern Democrat John C. Breckinridge received 31,317 votes, or about nineteen percent of the total. Meanwhile, Northern Democrat Stephen A. Douglas claimed a narrow plurality of 58,801 votes over the Southern compromise candidate, Conservative Unionist John Bell, who polled 58,372. In other words, the two centrist candidates received approximately seventy-one percent of the total vote.[1]

In the winter of 1860-1861, after South Carolina and other Southern states had withdrawn from the Union, the three distinct political camps that arose in Missouri in regard to the question of secession tended to mirror the outcome of this recent election. The unconditional Unionists comprised a small group who fully supported the Federal government's attempt to bring the seceding states back into the Union by whatever means necessary. This sentiment tended to predominate around St. Louis, where the state's fiercely loyal German population was concentrated and where the group's most prominent spokesman, Congressman Francis P. Blair, Jr., lived. At the other end of the political spectrum was another relatively small group who felt Missouri should immediately join the seceding states. Governor Claiborne Fox Jackson, although he had been elected as a Douglas Democrat, was a leading exponent of this secessionist sentiment, and it predominated in a few outlying, rural counties. The overwhelming majority of Missouri citizens, however, fell into a group known as conditional Unionists. Although many in this middle group had Southern roots and, therefore, held Southern sympathies, the group maintained a position of "armed neutrality." The conditional Unionists would support the Union as long as the Federal military did not try to reclaim the Southern states by force or try to occupy Missouri. However, they felt the state should be ready to defend its own borders in the event of such an "invasion." Sterling

Price, a former governor and a Mexican War veteran, was the leader of this centrist group. He headed a state convention in St. Louis at which delegates voted almost unanimously in early March of 1861 to stay in the Union.

After the Confederate attack on the Federal installation at Ft. Sumter, South Carolina, on April 12, 1861, however, the chances of compromise quickly faded. President Lincoln called for 75,000 volunteers for service in the Union Army, and Missouri was expected to furnish four regiments as its quota. Governor Jackson refused to comply and declared that the state would not furnish one dollar or one man for Lincoln's "unholy crusade."[2]

Instead, the governor pushed a resolution through the state legislature condemning any attempt by the Federal government to coerce the Southern states, and he also started trying to organize a military force to defend Missouri. The latter effort met a lukewarm reception in the legislature; nonetheless, Southern sympathizers in Jackson and Clay counties captured a Federal arsenal at Liberty on April 20 to supply arms for the budding state militia.

At about the same time, Congressman Blair started recruiting men in the St. Louis area for the Federal military. Drawing on the fervent Union fever of a quasi-military group called the Wide-Awakes that had been drilling in the St. Louis area throughout the spring, Blair quickly enlisted ten regiments, and they began drilling under Captain Nathaniel Lyon, who had arrived from Fort Riley, Kansas, a few weeks earlier with a company of regular infantry.

In early May 1861, about 700 of Governor Jackson's militiamen under General Daniel M. Frost gathered for training at Camp Jackson, not far from the Federal arsenal in St. Louis. Many of Frost's men came from a militant secessionist group known as the Minutemen, who, like the Wide-Awakes, had been drilling for weeks. Having learned that the militia had received arms from the South, Lyon concluded that Frost intended to seize the arsenal, although Frost denied he had such an objective in mind.[3]

On May 10, Lyon, with several thousand Federal troops, disarmed and arrested the militiamen at Camp Jackson. As he marched the prisoners toward the arsenal through the streets of St. Louis, angry pro-Southern demonstrators hurled insults at the Federal troops and pelted them with rocks. During the confrontation, according to Lyon, someone in the crowd also shot at one of his soldiers. At any rate, some of the troops recklessly opened fire on the crowd, and almost thirty civilians were killed.

The incident sparked rioting in the streets of St. Louis, and it enraged citizens throughout the state, driving many conditional Unionists into the secessionist camp. If the vote on secession had been held after the Camp Jackson affair, as various historians have suggested, Missouri very possibly would have joined the Confederacy, but the state convention had been vested with full authority to decide the issue and had already voted to stay in the Union.[4]

Now, though, the Missouri legislature quickly approved Governor Jackson's plan to raise a state military force. It was called the Missouri State Guard, and Jackson issued a call for 50,000 men to fill out its ranks. Sterling Price, one of the conditional Unionists who'd joined forces with the governor, was given the rank of major general and placed in charge of the state force.

On May 21, Price met in St. Louis with Brigadier-General William S. Harney, commanding the Union Department of the West, and reached an agreement to try to keep the war out of Missouri. Price would maintain order within the state, and in return Harney agreed not to make any military movement inside the state. Blair and Lyon, however, viewed the Price-Harney agreement with "great disgust" and considered it a stalling tactic by Governor Jackson to allow his state troops time to arm themselves while he made plans to join the Confederacy. Congressman Blair used his influence in Washington to have Harney replaced by Lyon, who was promoted to brigadier general.[5]

Jackson and Price sought a conference with the new Federal commander in hopes of maintaining the terms of the Price-Harney agreement. Meeting with Lyon in St. Louis on June 11, Jackson proposed to disperse the state militia and try to keep peace within the state if Lyon would disband the Missouri volunteer units that had been recruited for the Union. The zealous Lyon, however, declined to compromise. He felt a Federal military presence was necessary to protect Missouri's loyal citizens from harassment by secessionists and to prevent a Confederate movement into the state. Rising from the negotiation table, he said he would see everyone in Missouri dead before he would let the state dictate to the U. S. government. "This means war!" he declared, and he had Jackson and Price escorted out of St. Louis beyond Union lines.[6]

Jackson's party retreated to Jefferson City, burning bridges and cutting telegraph wires along the way to disrupt the Federal lines of transportation and communication. Lyon, meanwhile, boarded steam boats with his own company and Blair's regiment of volunteers and set out up the Missouri River in pursuit. He also dispatched a force to Springfield to cut off a possible southerly retreat by the state troops and to prevent a juncture between them and Confederate Brigadier General Benjamin McCulloch, who was in northwest Arkansas.

By the time Lyon reached Jefferson City, Jackson had already deserted the state capitol and given orders for the State Guard to assemble at Boonville and Lexington. The Federal troops caught up with Jackson on June 17 at Boonville and routed a detachment of state troops in what afterwards was sometimes called the "Boonville Races" because of the precipitous flight of the raw militiamen.

Jackson and his troops continued their retreat southward as Price rode ahead in search of a suitable location to train and organize the Missouri State Guard and to try to enlist the aid of McCulloch. On July 5, 1861, Jackson's untested army met a force of about 1,100 Federals at Carthage under Colonel Franz Sigel, part of the troops Lyon had dispatched to southwest Missouri. Jackson's army was untrained and poorly equipped, but it numbered over 5,000 men. After a running fight that lasted all day, the state troops finally repulsed Sigel, and he was compelled to retreat toward Springfield. Meanwhile, Lyon was stalled in the northern part of the state by heavy rains and a delay in outfitting his supply train. The Southern forces were left in temporary control of the southwest corner of Missouri, allowing Price time to train and equip his budding command.

After two or three weeks of training, Price's army, reinforced by McCulloch's Confederates and Arkansas state troops under Brigadier General Nicholas Bart Pearce, started toward Springfield, where Lyon had arrived in mid-July. On August 10, the combined Southern forces met and defeated Lyon's Federal army at Wilson's

Creek, a few miles southwest of Springfield, in the first major land battle of the Civil War west of the Mississippi. General Lyon himself was killed early in the day, and the Southern forces eventually repulsed the Federals after a bloody battle that lasted all morning.

After the Confederate victory at Wilson's Creek, McCulloch and Pearce returned to Arkansas, while Price started north to try to break the Federal stronghold on the Missouri River. On September 20, Federal forces at Lexington finally surrendered to the State Guard after a three-day siege. However, Price could not sustain his presence in the northern part of the state, and the State Guard retreated to southwest Missouri a few days later to counter Federal forces that were once again concentrating at Springfield.

In July, the state convention had reconvened to declare the state offices vacant and to elect a provisional government; so Jackson's administration was a government in exile. Nonetheless, this body met in late October at Neosho and voted to take Missouri out of the Union and join the Confederacy. Although the number of legislators present at the session reportedly fell short of a quorum and the state convention had previously been vested with authority to decide the question of secession, Price fired off a hundred-gun salute to the resolution, and many of his men got drunk celebrating it. Many Southern-leaning citizens in the state considered the action legitimate, and the Confederacy readily approved the ordinance.

In early November, Price issued a proclamation calling for 50,000 volunteers from the northern counties of Missouri to march south for the purpose of joining the Confederate Army. Although a Southern fervor had swept through the state after Price's victories at Wilson's Creek and Lexington, the number of men who answered his call was still far short of the requested quota, and by February of 1862 he was forced to retreat into Arkansas in the face of an advancing Federal army under Brigadier-General Samuel R. Curtis.

Curtis pursued the Missouri State Guard into northwest Arkansas, where Price united with Confederate forces under McCulloch and Major-General Earl Van Dorn. The two sides met at Pea Ridge on March 6 and waged a fierce battle over the next three days. Despite superior numbers on the part of the Southern forces,

Curtis's army finally repelled them, firmly securing the state of Missouri for the Union.

After Pea Ridge, Price joined the Confederate Army, and he was sent east of the Mississippi, as the South virtually abandoned the state of Missouri. However, many of Price's men balked at following him into Confederate service. Some chose instead to remain members of the disintegrating State Guard. Others, with the term of their initial six-month enlistment in the State Guard having expired, simply returned home to try to resume their normal occupations. Even some of those who agreed to accompany Price were accepted under the condition that they could return to Missouri whenever they chose.[7]

While Price and the Confederate Army crossed the Mississippi, the State Guard remained in the Missouri area. Most of its members had entered service with the narrow objective of resisting a Federal invasion of their state, and many still saw this as their primary goal. However, the loss of many members to the Confederate Army and to civilian life left the Missouri State Guard with insufficient numbers to fill out an army. If it were to remain a viable military force, the State Guard would need new bodies. Men like Colonel John T. Coffee, commander of the Sixth Cavalry Regiment of Brigadier-General James S. Rains's Eighth Division of the State Guard, were sent back into the state to recruit. Often the recruiting officers were men, such as William Marchbanks, who had been company commanders during the early days of the State Guard but who had been left without companies to command by the re-structuring of Southern forces. Still holding the titular rank of captain, they returned to Missouri searching for men to once again fill out their units.

The rise of guerrilla warfare in Missouri largely coincided with these recruiting expeditions in the late winter and early spring of 1862, because the recruiting officers, now leading mere "bands," were reduced to fighting a war of sabotage. The officers were still nominal members of the State Guard, and they usually paid lip service to the idea of joining the Confederate Army. (Some were more sincere than others in expressing such a purpose.) However, they spent most of their time skirmishing with Federal troops, striking Union targets, and harassing loyal citizens. While many of their comrades were in

Mississippi with the Confederate Army, they were back home still fighting a battle that had already been lost—the fight for Missouri. With neither the means nor the manpower to wage regular war, their futile quest quickly degenerated into an all-out guerrilla warfare that was fueled by revenge and marked by atrocity, and it grew more savage as the war went on.

Major General Thomas C. Hindman no doubt encouraged the rise of guerrilla warfare in Missouri and elsewhere in the Trans-Mississippi when he issued General Order #17 in June of 1862 authorizing Southern citizens to band together in groups of ten or more for the "effectual annoyance of the enemy."[8] However, in the case of Missouri at least, Hindman's order simply lent official sanction to an activity that was already occurring.

As early as the summer of 1861, Union authorities had sometimes used the term "guerrilla" to describe saboteurs like the bridge-burners of northern Missouri or men like Martin E. Green, a colonel in the Missouri State Guard who spent the late summer in the northeast part of the state belatedly trying to fill out his cavalry regiment and occasionally skirmishing with Federal troops. However, the term did not come into widespread use until several months later when the early recruits of the State Guard began returning home at the end of their six-month enlistment and officers were forced to go back into their home districts to recruit.

Although the Southern recruiting officers had more military legitimacy than Federal authorities gave them credit for, they fit the definition of what we normally think of as guerrillas in the sense that they operated independently and usually did not wear uniforms. Thus, the Union usage of the term "guerrilla" has been largely accepted for the purposes of this book, but the author has not, with only one or two exceptions, extended the definition, as Union officials routinely did, to include officers who attained the rank of colonel or above.

The Civil War guerrillas in Missouri varied in renown from the widely notorious like Quantrill to the completely obscure, whose names, if they were ever known, have been long forgotten. What follows are the stories of a few Missouri guerrillas, less noted than Quantrill and his associates, but whose lives and Civil War careers are nonetheless fascinating.

Senator Jim Lane, whose Kansas troops skirmished with Bill Marchbanks and other guerrillas at the Battle of Dry Wood Creek. (J. Dale
West collection)

2
William Marchbanks: As Bad as Quantrill

William Marchbanks was born August 26, 1834, in Overton County, Tennessee, the oldest son of Nathaniel R. and Henrietta Marchbanks. In the spring of 1841, the family migrated to Missouri and settled on a farm in that part of Bates County that later became northwestern Vernon County. In addition to farming, the elder Marchbanks also served the community as a justice of the peace, a role that may have led indirectly to his son's involvement in a violent border squabble prior to the war.[1]

In 1856, a man named James Hardwick settled on the Little Osage River in Bourbon County, Kansas, just across the state line from Vernon County. In addition to the tract of land he settled on, he also purchased two abandoned claims adjoining his property. Early the next year, Isaac Denton, who had been a neighbor of Hardwick's in Alabama, moved to the area, and Hardwick let him settle on one of the abandoned claims. A couple of months later, however, the two men had a falling out, and Hardwick tried to evict Denton from the abandoned claim. When Denton refused to leave, the quarrel was taken to a committee called the Squatter's Court for resolution. Although the disputants were both proslavery men, Denton argued that Hardwick had no right to the land because it actually belonged to a Free State man who had been driven from the territory by border ruffians. Since that man was no longer in the area, Denton said that he, as the person who was actually living on the land, had the best claim to it. The tribunal, composed mainly of Free State men, ruled in Denton's favor.[2]

The decision infuriated Hardwick, and a feud between the two families erupted. They traded threats and accusations until the night of March 30, 1858, when a band of bushwhackers called Denton from his home and shot him dead in the doorway. Hardwick was immediately suspected of the crime, but he fled to Missouri to avoid prosecution. A friend of his named Travis, however, was arrested for complicity in the crime. Travis was tried and acquitted two days after Denton's death, but he was shot and killed on his way home from the trial. (Although not directly related to the Denton-Hardwick feud, several other killings of both free-state men and proslavery men took place along the border near this same time, and the escalating violence culminated in the Marais des Cygnes massacre on May 19, 1858.)

In the summer of 1859, Isaac Denton's son John, who had sworn to avenge his father's death, found Hardwick on the streets of Nevada and took him prisoner at the point of a gun. Denton announced that he planned to take Hardwick back to Kansas to stand trial for the death of his father, but after taking him a few miles northwest of Nevada, he shot him on the spot. When Hardwick's body was found, a warrant for the arrest of Denton was issued, and Justice of the Peace Marchbanks delivered it to Constable H. G. Hicklin.

Hicklin found Denton at Fail's store near the Kansas line. Reluctant to confront the man without backup, the constable tried to enlist the aid of some of the idlers at the store, but no one volunteered until twenty-five-year-old Bill Marchbanks rode up and offered to help serve the warrant that his father had played a part in issuing. Together the two men captured Denton, and he was eventually confined in jail at Clinton, Missouri. After a year, though, he escaped and fled back to Kansas.

On October 25, 1860, Denton was again in Fail's store when Bill Marchbanks walked in. Denton immediately drew his revolver and threatened to kill Marchbanks for his role in Denton's arrest the previous year, but other men at the store reportedly intervened to prevent the shooting. Marchbanks fled the store and informed Constable Hicklin of Denton's presence there.

Marchbanks and Hicklin then returned to the store together to try to apprehend Denton as they had done a year earlier. After dismounting, they took up positions near the entrance. Some of the men at the store alerted Denton, and he stepped out of the building with revolver in hand and pointed it toward Marchbanks. Armed with an army musket, Marchbanks fired immediately, and the bullet struck Denton in the heart. He collapsed and died almost instantly.

Some of Denton's friends swore vengeance on Marchbanks, and he stayed away from Fail's store for a few days. Then, in November of 1860, a threatened invasion of Missouri by Kansas abolitionist James Montgomery prompted the commander-in-chief of the Missouri militia to call up a battalion of men to help keep the peace in Southwest Missouri. Most of the men were from other parts of the state, but Bill Marchbanks was made a lieutenant in one of the three companies that composed the battalion. As luck would have it, his company was stationed at Fail's store. Nothing, however, came of the vow of vengeance on Marchbanks nor of the Montgomery threat, and the militiamen spent a quiet winter consuming "inordinate quantities of 'red-eye whisky.'"[3]

When the Civil War broke out, Marchbanks began recruiting a company for General Sterling Price's Missouri State Guard. He joined the state service on May 10, 1861, and was elected captain on May 14.[4]

On June 27, 1861, a company of men under James Montgomery, who was recruiting a regiment for Federal service, marched from the Mound City area into Missouri to form a junction with another company of Union volunteers. In northwest Vernon County, the Federals left's Fail's store and marched down the Little Osage toward the Nathaniel Marchbanks place. When the advance guard approached the home, the soldiers noticed several armed men, Bill Marchbanks and/or his brother Robert presumably among them, lolling on the grounds. The rebels "made war-like demonstrations," but the Federals opened fire first, knocking one of the guerrillas off a fence. The wounded rebel escaped into a field of grain, while the Federals chased after his fleeing comrades. Two of them were captured and brought back to the house, but what ultimately happened to them is not known.[5]

Around the end of June, 1861, twenty-four-year-old Robert "Bob" Marchbanks enlisted in his older brother's company at Papinsville in southern Bates County. A few days later at Lamar, the company united with the main body of State Guard troops, who were on the move south after being routed at Boonville on June 17 by Federals under General Lyon. Bill Marchbanks's company was assigned to Colonel R. L. Y. Peyton's Third Cavalry of Brigadier General James Rains's Eighth Division.[6]

Bob Marchbanks and most of the other men in his brother's company took no active part in either the engagement at Carthage on July 5 or the Battle of Wilson's Creek on August 10, because they had no weapons. Like many other units in the State Guard, Bill Marchbanks's company was ill equipped and poorly armed.[7]

After the Battle of Wilson's Creek, Rains's division marched to western Missouri in advance of the rest of the State Guard and camped in late August near Montevallo. While there, Marchbanks was attached briefly to Thomas B. Cummings's Bates County regiment, and he led the advance when Cummings's troops skirmished with a Federal force on August 24 at Balltown in north central Vernon County. A week later, on September 2, Price's army met and repelled a detachment of Jim Lane's Kansas brigade at Dry Wood Creek. The state forces then turned north and captured Lexington on September 20 after a three-day siege. Although Bill Marchbanks and his company took a somewhat more active role in these engagements than they did at Carthage and Wilson's Creek, his brother Bob was one man who again stayed on the sidelines, this time because of sickness.[8]

In late 1861, when the six-month term of enlistment of the Missouri State Guard volunteers expired, Marchbanks was among those who declined an invitation to immediately join the Confederate Army. Instead, like many other members of the disintegrating State Guard, he took to the bush to wage a marauding, guerrilla warfare. In late January, 1862, he and Sidney D. Jackman were sent into the Vernon County area by General Rains to recruit for the State Guard with the ostensible purpose of going south to join the Confederacy. Marchbanks was to report to Rains as soon as a company had been recruited or within twenty days if he could not enlist enough men to fill out the company. Marchbanks quickly gathered a band of about twenty men, who mainly haunted the Little Osage and Marais des Cygnes rivers in northern Vernon and southern Bates counties. Sometime in the early part of the year, his and Jackman's combined force skirmished with and defeated a detachment of Union militia in Bates.[9]

Marchbanks might, in fact, have planned to go south, but he apparently had trouble filling out his company. At any rate, he ended up lingering in Missouri too long. On March 3, 1862, he, his brother Robert, and a couple of other guerrillas were spending the night at Pleasant Gap in Bates County when a detachment of the First Iowa

Cavalry swept into the community and arrested the rebels. They were escorted to Sedalia, where Bob Marchbanks gave a statement on March 22, 1862, while the older Marchbanks was sent to the Gratiot Street Military Prison in St. Louis.[10]

Bill Marchbanks was shuffled back and forth between Gratiot Street and the military prison at Alton, Illinois, during the spring and summer of 1862. Then on September 20, he was exchanged at Vicksburg, Mississippi. In Arkansas, he fell in with a recruiting party under his old confederate Sidney Jackman, and in mid-November the group started north from Huntsville. Back in Missouri, Marchbanks recruited a company in the area of Bates and Vernon County and rode south to Batesville, Arkansas, where he entered Confederate service.[11]

The following April, Marchbanks returned to Missouri as part of the First Regiment, Missouri Rangers, a loosely organized outfit commanded by Colonel Benjamin F. Parker, with whom Marchbanks had been imprisoned the previous summer. Near Cassville, Marchbanks had a brush with Federal troops while on his way to his old haunts. According to his own statement long after the war, he killed three Union men in the encounter while losing just one man from his company. On April 20, 1863, Marchbanks passed near Avilla in eastern Jasper County going north with about 150 men (perhaps all of Parker's command), and later in the month he scuffled with some Missouri militia in Bates County. Soon afterwards he had a skirmish with Federal cavalry at Balltown in northern Vernon County, where he lost two men wounded.[12]

On May 8, 1863, Federal Colonel Edward Lynde's Ninth Kansas Cavalry broke up a nest of about twenty guerrillas under Marchbanks on the Double Branches in southeastern Bates County. It was the same general area where he had been captured the previous year. Lynde's soldiers killed a few of the rebels, although most escaped by scattering into the brush. In his report of the affair, Lynde complained that the Double Branches had been a rendezvous for the bushwhackers since the beginning of the war because of the preponderance of Southern families living in the area. He took out his frustration by burning eleven homes along the stream and confiscating all the livestock of the purported rebel sympathizers.[13]

Two weeks later, on May 24, Marchbanks, with nineteen men, was camped south of the Marmaton River a few miles northwest of Nevada when a messenger brought word that a party of six or seven militia were traveling the road from Fort Scott to Nevada on the way to their homes in Cedar County. Determining to attack the small squad of "Feds" where the road crossed Dry Wood Creek, Marchbanks galloped to the spot but found that the militia had already passed. The bushwhackers pursued the Federals east and caught up with them in Nevada.[14]

With Marchbanks and a reckless sidekick named Pony Hill leading the charge, the guerrillas galloped onto the square shouting and firing their pistols. About half the militiamen were captured and put under guard at a hotel, while the others fled. Hill and a companion overtook an unarmed man named Shuey near the entrance of a home, where he was trying to find shelter. Despite pleas for mercy from several female bystanders and from Shuey himself, the two desperadoes calmly shot him to death. Northwest of the square, Marchbanks caught up with a would-be escapee named Whitley and trapped him in a dead-end lane. The two exchanged several errant shots before Marchbanks killed Whitley with a shot to the neck.[15]

At least one militiaman eluded capture, and, meanwhile, those being held in the hotel also managed to escape. The Federals hurried home with news of the guerrilla attack and the killing of Shuey and Whitley, while Marchbanks returned to his camp on the Marmaton. Two days later about a hundred militiamen from Cedar and St. Clair counties returned to Vernon County in quest of revenge. After a token search turned up no sign of Marchbanks, the militiamen rode into Nevada and burned the town.[16]

As Nevada went up in flames, Marchbanks moved north into Bates County. He was not heard from again until July, when he skirmished with a party of Federals from Fort Scott in northern Vernon County near the fork of the Marmaton and Little Osage.[17]

Then on August 2, 1863, Marchbanks was back on the Double Branches in Bates County when Major Alexander W. Mullins and one hundred men of the First Missouri State Militia Cavalry attacked and routed the guerrilla camp. Although forced to abandon several horses and most of their camp equipment, the bushwhackers all managed to escape. The Federals, meanwhile, had one man killed in the melee. The next day, Mullins took up the chase as the guerrillas fled south. He forced them to swim the high water of the Marais Des Cygnes River before finding a safer place to cross his own troops. On the third day, however, he called off the pursuit rather than risk following the desperate guerrillas across the rain-swollen Marmaton.[18]

By the middle of August, Marchbanks had swung back to the north and was in the neighborhood of Germantown in southwest Henry County with about forty or fifty men. On the night of the twelfth, he burned a house in the area, and three days later he alarmed citizens in the vicinity by threatening to devastate the country.[19]

In early September, Marchbanks roamed east into Hickory County. He attacked a detachment of militia stationed at Quincy, killing four, capturing seven, and scattering the remainder. The rebels lost one man killed and two wounded.[20]

Despite having been captured in the vicinity the previous year and despite having already been driven from the area on at least two occasions during 1863, Marchbanks kept returning to his old haunts on the Double Branches. He was camped there on September 22, 1863, when he was once again surprised by a company of the First Missouri State Militia Cavalry, this time under Captain Meredith Morris, and forced to take flight. The Federals captured eighteen horses, eighteen weapons, all the camp equipage, and some private papers belonging to Marchbanks. They once again failed, however, to kill any bushwhackers.[21]

A week later, Marchbanks moved north to the Grand River area of Cass County, apparently to form a juncture with other rebel leaders. By early December, Marchbanks had gone south to rendezvous with the Confederate Army, but remnants of his old company still lingered in the Osage River country of Bates County with the intention of spending the winter there.[22]

The following spring, Marchbanks was first reported back in Missouri when he was supposedly spotted in Bates County on May 3, 1864, with sixty to a hundred men. He was also credited with helping guerrilla leader Henry Taylor burn Lamar on May 28. Later reports suggest, however, that Marchbanks did not actually make his first appearance until early July when he came into northern Vernon

County around Balltown to recruit soldiers for the Confederate Army. He was also implicated in the raid on Barnesville just across the state line in Kansas on the night of July 11, 1864. A few weeks later, Jacob Whalon, who was "known to have officiated with Capt. Taylor and the Marchbanks boys" and who was suspected of participating in the Barnesville raid, was captured and killed by Federal troops.[23]

In late July, Marchbanks and Taylor, with about thirty men, were attacked and routed by a company of the Seventh Provisional Regiment, Enrolled Missouri Militia, in Jasper County just across the state line from Baxter Springs, Kansas. The guerrillas, who lost five or six men killed and several others wounded, continued south after the skirmish, presumably to link up with Price's army.[24]

However, the *Paola (Kans.) Herald* reported that on the night of August 21, 1864, a party of twenty-eight guerrillas under "the notorious Marchbanks" came into Linn County, Kansas, near Potosi. After pillaging the property of citizens, stealing a number of horses and saddles, and taking several Union men prisoner, the gang headed back to Missouri. The next day, a detachment of the Fifteen Kansas Cavalry followed the bushwhackers and attacked them at their camp on the Marais des Cygnes River, driving them in confusion, releasing the prisoners, and recapturing some of the plunder taken the previous night. The leader of this raid may have been Bob Marchbanks rather than Bill, since it is known that Bob was still in the Vernon County area in late August, when he was wounded during a skirmish with Federal scouts on Clear Creek near Montevallo but managed to escape.[25]

During Price's raid into Missouri during the fall of 1864, Bill Marchbanks served as captain of a company in Colonel DeWitt Hunter's cavalry regiment of Jackman's brigade, Shelby's division. During this campaign, according to Jackman, Marchbanks and another officer were "always conspicuous for their gallantry."[26]

In the spring of 1865, Bill and Bob Marchbanks went to visit their father in southeast Nebraska. The elder Marchbanks had moved there two years earlier to escape the harassment of Kansas jayhawkers, who had made his farm in Vernon County a special target

William Marchbanks, in old age, with family members. (Photo courtesy of Susan Hejka)

during the early part of the war, partly because of the bushwhacking activities of his sons. While the Marchbanks brothers were in Nebraska, their presence came to the attention of the deputy provost-marshal at Brownsville, and he wired Colonel Charles W. Blair, post commander at Fort Scott, inquiring about the Marchbanks family. Blair replied, "The two young Marchbanks are the worst sort of bushwhackers. The old man is not. Bill Marchbanks is as bad as Quantrill." He went on to suggest that the Marchbanks brothers and any comrades who might be with them should be arrested and, if possible, sent to Fort Scott. "Iron them heavily," Blair warned, "as no guard-house will hold them."[27]

Blair's opinion, of course, was an exaggerated one. Union officials tended to paint all guerrillas with the same brush, but Marchbanks was obviously not "as bad as Quantrill." According to the compiler of the 1887 *Vernon County History*, Marchbanks, although he fought as a guerrilla, was never known to murder prisoners or private citizens, and he was respected by many who fought against him. After the war he retired to a quiet, peaceful life in the vicinity of Paris, Texas, and became an upright citizen. [28]

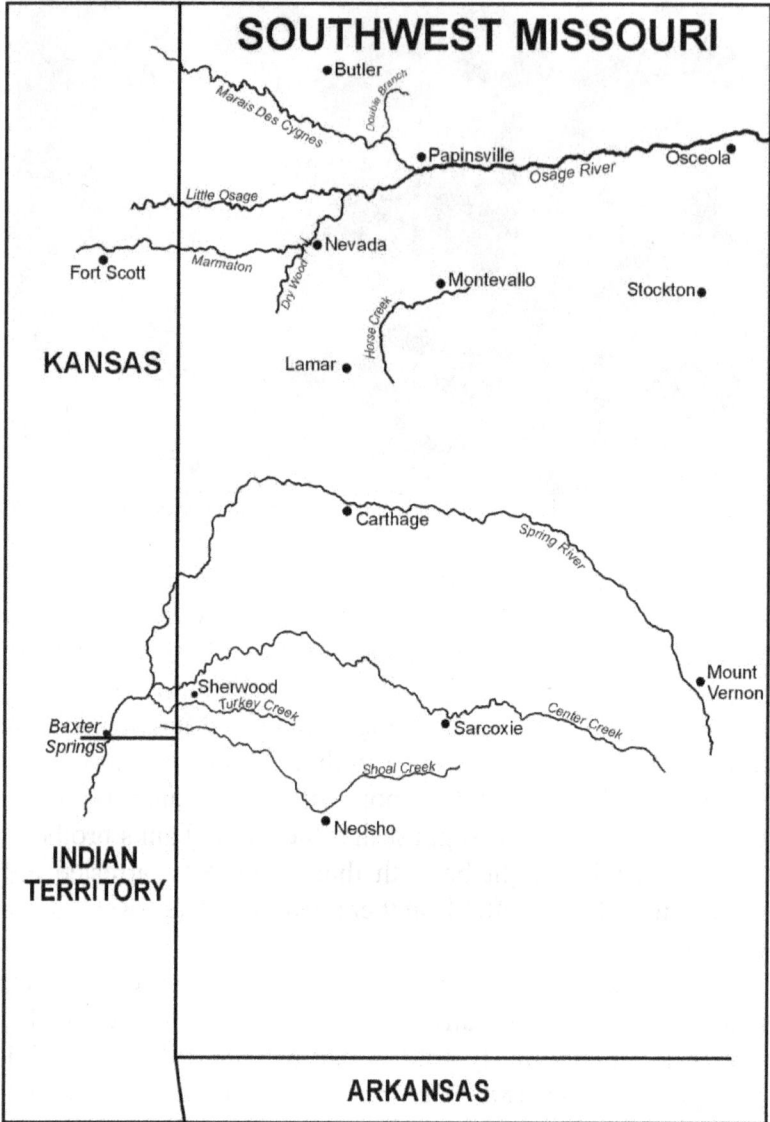

Map of southwest Missouri area showing the haunts of Marchbanks, Taylor, Livingston, and Clem.

3
Henry Taylor, Commanding Bushwhackers in Southwest Missouri

William Henry Taylor, an occasional confederate of Marchbanks, was born October 20, 1831, in Boyle County, Kentucky. He came to Missouri with his parents, Jesse and Elizabeth Anson Taylor, at a young age and settled in Vernon County about 1849. In 1853 he married Emaline Gresham, who died the following year. In 1858, he was appointed sheriff to fill out an unexpired term. Although the *History of Vernon County* says his marriage to Miss Gresham produced one son, Taylor was living alone in Nevada (usually called Nevada City) at the City Hotel at the time of the 1860 census, and his primary occupation was listed as merchant rather than sheriff. In the fall of 1860, Taylor was elected sheriff, the office to which he had earlier been appointed, and soon afterwards he became embroiled in a border dispute with Kansas. In late November of 1860, when citizens of the county petitioned the governor of Missouri for arms and ammunition to protect themselves from a rumored invasion by abolitionists under James Montgomery, Taylor, as the county's chief law officer, endorsed the request and added his own appeal. Considered "as prominent, respected and influential a man as there was in the county," Taylor was still serving as sheriff the following spring when the Civil War broke out.[1]

Taylor, who sometimes went by his initials but more often by his middle name, joined the Missouri State Guard as captain of the Vernon County company in Colonel John T. Coffee's Sixth Cavalry regiment of the Eighth Division. Shortly afterward, this company merged with Colonel DeWitt C. Hunter's Vernon County regiment, the Seventh Cavalry, and Taylor acted as quartermaster of the regiment. On July 20, 1861, he was also elected captain of Company F.[2]

After victories at Carthage on July 5 and Wilson's Creek on August 10, the State Guard started north but took a detour into Taylor's old stomping grounds of Vernon County in response to reports of increased Federal activity in western Missouri. On September 1, 1861, a detachment of Missouri troops that reportedly included Taylor sneaked across the border east of Nevada and stole a hundred Federal mules from a corral near Fort Scott, precipitating an engagement at Dry Wood Creek the next day between Price's army and Senator Jim Lane's Kansas Brigade.[3] The action is sometimes called the Battle of the Mules in tribute to the brash act that instigated it.

On December 16, 1861, Taylor resigned his commission in the State Guard. Returning to Vernon County, he began raising a company from around the Montevallo area for the Southern cause, and he also used the opportunity to take up bushwhacking. Around the 29th of December, he and some of his recruits dashed across the border, raided at least three Union homes near Fort Scott, and carried off several horses, an overcoat, a double-barreled shotgun, and other property.[4]

On January 10, 1862, Taylor took thirty of his men on a scout toward Fort Scott and captured an outpost of fourteen cavalrymen from the Sixth Regiment of Kansas Volunteers on picket duty near the state line. After confiscating horses, weapons and other belongings from the Federals, Taylor released them on parole with instructions to report what had happened to Charles R. "Doc" Jennison, noted Kansas jayhawker who was then at Fort Scott. When the parolees reached the fort, the news of their ordeal "frightened Colonel Jennison and regiment almost into a panic."[5]

Near Dry Wood Creek, as the guerrillas were returning to Montevallo after the raid, Taylor was accidentally shot in the foot by one of his own men. The wound apparently was not serious enough to keep Taylor from riding a horse, however, as he made another dash across the state line near the end of January and briefly skirmished with Federal troops near Fort Scott.[6]

Taylor's company of about seventy men was sworn into service at Montevallo on February 17, 1862, after a rousing speech from Colonel John T. Coffee, who, although still a member of the Missouri State Guard, was recruiting for the ostensible purpose of going south to join the Confederate Army. Coffee's immediate objective, however, was "the protection of the western border."[7]

Taylor and his men set out to protect the border by making a raid along the Big Dry Wood on February 28. They stole two guns from a man named Jim Manes and took other articles from the home of George Strepey.[8]

On March 26, 1862, before organization of his company was yet complete and while awaiting orders to rendezvous with Coffee, Taylor and his men rode east and took part in an attack led by Colonel James M. "Polk" Frazier on Humansville, where several companies of Missouri State Militia were stationed. The rebels were repulsed with six men killed, including Colonel Frazier, and several others seriously wounded. Taylor claimed after the war that his company covered the retreat of the Southern force and saved it from destruction.[9]

On April 11, Taylor and some of his men were eating breakfast at the home of his father-in-law southeast of Montevallo. (Taylor had remarried in 1861 to Sarah Potoroff.) A party of Missouri State Militia recruits, on their way to Springfield to secure arms and equipment, happened on the scene and skirmished with the guerrillas, killing three. Still hobbled by his injured foot, Taylor was captured, along with several of his men. Taylor's brother-in-law, who was at home under cover of a safeguard or protection paper issued by the Union, shot and wounded a Lieutenant Waterhouse of the militia squad and was among those taken prisoner. In addition, the Federals confiscated from the guerrillas a horse with a U. S. brand and several weapons, including two guns that had been taken from the Federal pickets on the border a month or two earlier.[10]

On April 14, three days after Taylor's capture, some of his company, now under command of Lieutenant Joe Woods, skirmished with a detachment of Federals at the Scobey Hotel in Montevallo. The Federals lost two men killed and six wounded, while the rebels had one man, Daniel Henley, mortally wounded and had several others with wounds of varying degrees. In reporting the incident, a Union officer called Henley, also known as Wild Irishman, the "terror of St. Clair, Cedar, and Vernon Counties," while another said he was the "leader of (one of) the most desperate gangs of desperadoes in Missouri."[11]

Meanwhile, Taylor and those captured with him were taken to Lamar and handed over to a detachment of the Second Ohio Cavalry, who, in turn, sent them to Fort Scott. The town "was thrown into considerable excitement" by the arrival of "the notorious Captain

Taylor" and "his banditti" on April 14. After Taylor was lodged in the guardhouse, several prominent men from Vernon County arrived on the scene to protest his incarceration. They swore that the militiamen who had taken Taylor prisoner were jayhawkers who were "playing sharp." In response, Colonel Charles Doubleday of the Second Ohio, commanding at Fort Scott, arrested some of the militiamen, pending an investigation into the matter, and summoned the remainder to the post. One cynical Union observer predicted that Taylor would merely be given the oath and then promptly turned loose.[12]

Instead, he remained a prisoner at Fort Scott, where he continued to receive a stream of visitors. One curious Union soldier stopped by the jail on April 22 to see what the notorious guerrillas looked like. "Some of the party are vicious-looking men," he decided. "Others appear as harmless as men need be."[13]

For the next two months, according to a Fort Scott correspondent of the *Leavenworth Daily Conservative*, Taylor's friends repeatedly tried to show his innocence and win his release. However, "his guilt was so well established that their efforts have been of no avail." Taylor was tried and convicted on charges of robbery, horse stealing, and "violating the laws and customs of war" by being the "captain of a regular so-called 'jay-hawking party'" that was outside the jurisdiction of "any competent civil or military authority." Taylor supposedly even admitted that he was "captain of an irregular band responsible to no party." After his conviction, Taylor was sent to Fort Leavenworth on June 24, 1862.[14]

Around October 1862, he was released on parole under his sworn promise not to take up arms against the Union until officially exchanged, and Major Benjamin S. Henning at Fort Scott employed him as a go-between in an exchange of prisoners between Henning and Confederate guerrilla leader Tom Livingston. Taylor told the compiler of the 1887 *History of Vernon County* that, after securing the parole of the prisoners (about thirty in number), he took them south to join the Confederacy at Huntsville, Arkansas. Taylor, though, had a dispute with General Thomas Hindman and came back to Vernon County in early December to resume the terms of his earlier parole. He moved from Montevallo to Nevada and reported regularly to Union authorities at Fort Scott.[15]

Among the buildings destroyed by fire when a detachment of militia from Cedar and St. Clair counties burned Nevada on May 26, 1863, was the home of Henry Taylor, who was still living there under the terms of his parole. Late in the morning, as the Federals were marching out of town, a squad stopped Taylor on the streets and demanded that he accompany the soldiers. However, as the leader of the squad was examining Taylor's papers, he noticed a Masonic document and, after an exchange of signs with Taylor, allowed him to continue on his way.[16]

In the early summer of 1863, Taylor went to Fort Scott, and Union officials there declared him exchanged. Released from his parole, he returned to Vernon County and "went at once upon the war path."[17]

After rendezvousing with Bill Marchbanks on the Marmaton River north of Nevada, Taylor was given command of a squad of about twelve men, including the desperate Pony Hill (whose killing of the militiaman in Nevada had led to the burning of the town). Taylor's small band marched toward Fort Scott on the night of June 27 and, just across the state line, surrounded the home of a Mr. Beale, where a Federal scout named Tom Whitesides was staying. (The guerrillas may actually have been looking for Jeff Denton, another Federal scout who was married to one of Beale's daughters and was living at the home. Denton, from the same family with whom Marchbanks had feuded before the war, had recently killed a guerrilla named Forbes. However, Denton was away from home escorting a Federal train to Fort Blunt in Indian Territory.) Taylor stationed pickets a quarter mile down the Fort Scott road near a stream. On the other side of the timber that grew along the branch, Union pickets were also posted, and while the guerrillas knew "the precise locality of their opponents," the soldiers were "in blissful ignorance of the close proximity of this precious band of thieves and cut-throats."[18]

Whitesides was dragged from his sleep and placed under a strict guard, while the rest of the Beale household was also kept under surveillance. The guerrillas demanded that the women fix them supper, "which they devoured with keen appetites, indicative of long fasting." It was almost two o'clock in the morning before the rebels finally left, taking with them "considerable plunder in provisions and horses." They released the other members of the household but took

Whitesides along as a prisoner, because he was a noted jayhawker who supposedly had boasted a few weeks earlier of the number of rebels he had killed during the war. A Union report, on the other hand, claimed that Whitesides had intervened on behalf of Taylor at the time of his arrest the previous year to prevent some of the soldiers who had captured him from killing him.[19]

The guerrillas started back to Missouri with Whitesides, intending to hold him as a hostage, Taylor claimed. Inside Missouri, about eight miles due east of the Beale residence, however, the tempestuous Pony Hill rode up beside the prisoner and shot him. The guerrillas left Whitesides dead on the ground and rode back to Marchbanks's camp.[20]

On the morning of July 8, a detachment of the Third Wisconsin Cavalry attacked Marchbanks's camp near the junction of the Marmaton and Osage rivers. The two sides skirmished for about an hour and a half in the brush of the marshy ground before the guerrillas finally scattered. Major Elias A. Calkins of the Third Wisconsin reported one Federal and three rebels killed in the affray. Among the wounded were "Captain Taylor" and "the noted guerrilla Pony Hill."[21]

If Taylor was wounded, his injuries must have been minor, because after the skirmish he promptly rode south and linked up with Tom Livingston in time to accompany the Jasper County guerrilla leader during his ill-fated attack on the Cedar County courthouse at Stockton on July 11. After Livingston's death, some of his men joined Colonel Coffee while others joined Taylor or simply dispersed. Shortly after the Baxter Springs massacre in early October of 1863, twenty-five guerrillas under Taylor, reported to be part of Livingston's old command, encountered a small party of Federal scouts under William Tough on Dry Wood Creek and chased them toward Fort Scott. Later in the fall, Taylor rode south and spent the winter of 1863-64 near Sherman, Texas, in the vicinity of Quantrill's guerrilla camp.[22]

Taylor returned to Missouri the next spring in command of a company of about sixty men. Landing in the southwest part of Vernon County in mid-May, the guerrillas immediately went on a raid toward Kansas, stealing horses and taking Union men prisoner. Around daylight on the morning of May 16, 1864, the raiders reached the vicinity of present-day Garland just across the border with eight captives already in tow. At the nearby home of Lewis Ury, they took three more prisoners, including the homeowner and his son Jo, a former Union scout whom the guerrillas particularly despised. After placing the three men under guard along with those previously captured, the rebels then demanded that the women of the house prepare them breakfast.[23]

Meanwhile, word of the raid had reached a Federal outpost on the west branch of Dry Wood Creek in Vernon County, and a squad of five soldiers of the Third Wisconsin Cavalry, thinking the raiding party was a small one, went out in pursuit. When they realized the considerable force of the guerrillas, two of the soldiers went back to the outpost to report this intelligence, while the other three continued to trail the rebels and caught up with them at the Ury home. Although greatly outnumbered, the plucky soldiers immediately opened fire. The daring display persuaded Taylor to believe that the three soldiers were just the advance of a much larger force, and he promptly ordered his men to mount up and retreat. In the confusion, the prisoners dashed for freedom, and all but Lewis Ury, who was shot and mortally wounded, made their escape.[24]

Taylor and his band struck east across southern Vernon County toward their haunts on Clear Creek in the Montevallo vicinity. Jo Ury raced to the Federal camp on Dry Wood to relay word of what had happened, and as many as 200 soldiers from various points soon joined the chase. The Federal advance came up and skirmished briefly with Taylor in the open prairie just south of present-day Milo. The two sides skirmished twice more in the Clear Creek timber a couple of miles farther east before darkness came on and Taylor drew off to the north, breaking contact with his pursuers. As usual, accounts differ as to the number of casualties, depending on which side was doing the accounting. Colonel Blair, commander at Fort Scott, claimed in his report of the skirmishing that the guerrillas had five men killed and several wounded while the Federals had but two men wounded. After the war, Taylor said he had one man wounded severely and two slightly during the affray and that he saw at least four or five Federals knocked out of the saddle.[25]

On May 27, 1864, less than two weeks after his raid into the edge of Kansas, Taylor and two of his sidekicks had a close call at the home of a Southern sympathizer near Montevallo. When a Union scouting party showed up, the three barely made their escape, and, according to Taylor, the angry Federals burned the home before setting out in pursuit of the guerrillas. Meanwhile, Taylor gathered a few more men and headed south into Barton County. At two o'clock in the morning of May 28, Taylor rode into Lamar with twelve bushwhackers and burned the town, including the county records. Thus, as the compiler of the Vernon County history observed, while the Federal scouting party was still out scouring the countryside for Taylor, he was "busy with his torches" at Lamar. Only women and children occupied the town, because the local militia had departed a few days earlier, and after Taylor's raid, the helpless citizens were left "sitting outdoors" trying to guard the possessions they'd managed to salvage from their homes.[26]

During the early summer of 1864, Taylor had several other minor brushes with Federal scouts as he recruited in the Clear Creek and Montevallo vicinity. By early July, he had gathered about 200 recruits, but at the end of the same month, when he and Marchbanks started south, only about thirty men accompanied the two leaders. On July 31, the rebels were fired on while camped at Turkey Creek near present-day Joplin. The next day near Short Creek on the Kansas line they skirmished with a detachment of eighty Enrolled Missouri Militia on a scout from Mt. Vernon and were put to rout. The guerrillas lost four or five men killed and several wounded, while the Federals reported no loss.[27]

Taylor continued south and joined General Shelby at Batesville, Arkansas. In the fall of 1864, he accompanied Price's army on its raid into Missouri as a member of Elliott's battalion, Shelby's division. On September 30, he sacked a railroad company south of Independence with a force estimated from 80 to 150, stealing blankets, horses, and muskets. A Union scout reported that Taylor was acting in conjunction with George Todd and that both guerrilla leaders were planning to act in concert with Price. If Taylor acted in concert with Price, it must have been as an advance scout, because on the night of October 22, while the main body of Price's army was still occupied at Westport over fifty miles to the north, a gang of about a hundred bushwhackers, supposed to be under Taylor, dashed across the Kansas state line and entered the small village of Marmaton, where they "enacted the sequel to the Lawrence massacre." Six Union men, including merchant Horatio Knowles, were promptly shot down and "left weltering in their own blood." The guerrillas also burned part of the town, including a church and two stores. On their way out of town, they killed three more men, one of them an old man named Squire Reynolds.[28]

After the failed Confederate invasion, Taylor again spent the winter in the neighborhood of Sherman, Texas, as he had the previous year. The following spring he returned to Missouri in company with Archie Clement (leading Bill Anderson's old band), Dave Pool (leading George Todd's old band), and other notorious guerrilla chiefs. When the rebels reached Vernon County in early May 1865, Taylor separated from the other leaders, supposedly after an argument in which he stood up for a local citizen whose property some of the guerrillas had stolen. Colonel Blair sent scouts from Fort Scott into Missouri in pursuit of the rebels, and on May 6 he reported that about 200 guerrillas meant to stay in the border area under Taylor, while the remainder had continued north. Three days later Blair reported that Taylor's men had broken into small bands.[29]

Less than two weeks later, Taylor began negotiating a surrender of all the guerrilla forces in Southwest Missouri. On May 20, 1865, he met with Lieutenant-Colonel David S. Vittum of the Third Wisconsin Cavalry in Nevada and agreed to terms of a surrender calling for him and his men to give up all their arms and turn themselves in at Fort Scott. Given his parole, Taylor went back out to round up his men and make out the rolls for their surrender. The news of Taylor's surrender was quickly conveyed to Union officers all along the border with instructions to end hostilities against the guerrillas as long as they abided by the terms of Taylor's agreement. General Greenville M. Dodge, Commanding the Department of the Missouri at St. Louis, was even moved to celebrate the news. On May 21, he sent a message to Missouri Governor Thomas C. Fletcher that "Henry Taylor, commanding bushwhackers in Southwest Missouri," had agreed to surrender.[30]

After the war, Taylor went to Illinois, where he had earlier sent his family. He then moved to Nebraska for a while before returning to Vernon County, where he was again elected sheriff in 1872. After his term expired, he moved to Dade County and later to

Arkansas, where he helped lay out the town of Eureka Springs. In 1883, he again returned to Vernon County, where he became a merchant and served as postmaster at Montevallo.[31]

4
Tom Livingston, the Chief of Bushwhackers

If Henry Taylor was "commanding bushwhackers in southwest Missouri" during the latter part of the Civil War, as Union correspondence suggested, then Thomas R. Livingston surely would have warranted such an epithet during the early part of the war.

Prior to the war, Livingston and his half-brother, William Parkinson, ran a general store and owned a mine and lead smelter at French Point, Missouri. This was a small settlement on Center Creek in Jasper County about two miles west of Minersville, which is present-day Oronogo. Despite his reputation for whiskey drinking and fist-fighting in the mining camps around Jasper County, or perhaps because of such notoriety, Livingston was considered a prominent citizen in the area. The 39-year-old widower and father of two was described by one observer as "a big, square shouldered man whose weight might have been in the neighborhood of 175 pounds" and who, at least before the war, "was always clean shaven except for his moustache."[1]

When the Civil War came on, Livingston helped raise a regiment in the Jasper County area for the Eighth Division of the Missouri State Guard. It was designated the Eleventh Cavalry, and Livingston was made second in command to Colonel Sanford J. Talbott. As a member of the State Guard, Livingston presumably participated in early actions of the Trans-Mississippi war like the Engagement at Carthage and the Battle of Wilson's Creek.

In early September, Livingston accompanied John Matthews, leader of a ragtag outfit of guerrillas and Confederate Indians, on a raid of Humboldt, Kansas. Upon their arrival, the raiders announced that they had come after John Gilmore and that no women, children, or private homes would be molested. Gilmore, a former merchant at Osage Mission (where St. Paul is now located), had been a business associate of Livingston and was related to Matthews by marriage. However, he did not share their Southern sympathies, and he had recently moved his family and his stock of goods to Humboldt to try to avoid being drawn into the war. The raiders said they were there to take back his merchandise, some of which supposedly belonged to Livingston. They then proceeded to plunder the town.[3]

Then, in mid-October, as part of Colonel Talbott's command, Livingston helped carry out a second raid on Humboldt. On the evening of the 13th, approximately 300 men under Talbott left Preston in northern Jasper County, not far from Livingston's home at French Point, and marched toward Humboldt. Reaching the town the following evening, they swept in and took possession of the place. After putting the men of the village under guard, the Missourians burned the town in retaliation, they said, for the sacking of Osceola by Kansas Senator Jim Lane and his jayhawkers three weeks earlier.[4]

Realizing resistance was futile, a local doctor invited the rebel leaders to take supper with him, and Tom Livingston was one of those who reportedly took him up on the offer. After the raid, the Missouri troops headed back to Missouri in the direction of Sherwood, a small town in the western part of Jasper County not far from Livingston's home.[5]

When the term of enlistment for the Missouri State Guard troops expired in February of 1862, about half of the Eleventh Cavalry entered regular Confederate service, but the other half returned to Jasper County where they hoped to retire to relatively peaceful lives.[6] It was not to be. By the beginning of 1862, the South's prospect of holding Missouri was growing bleak, and the Confederate effort in the state was turning increasingly into a vicious, irregular warfare that often pitted neighbor against neighbor. Partisan bands roved the countryside bent on destroying Union targets, tormenting loyal citizens, and harassing the invading Federal army. It was hard for anyone to stay neutral.

Many of the cavalrymen who returned to Jasper County soon joined Livingston, who was mustering a partisan force in the area.[7] Sometime in early 1862, Livingston took his men and enlisted in the Provisional Army of the Confederate States, and they were assigned to the Confederate Indian Brigade under Brigadier General Albert Pike. Officially designated the First Missouri Battalion, Livingston's command was attached to Colonel Stand Watie's Cherokee regiment and was sometimes called the Cherokee Rangers or other, more colorful, names like the Bloody Spikes. Livingston was given the rank

Livingston was officially part of Stand Watie's command. (Stand Watie #31445 in the collection of Wilson's Creek National Battle-Field, Courtesy of the National Park Service)

of major, but despite the loose Confederate affiliation, his command continued to operate as a roving, independent band most of the time.[8]

Livingston's men, like most guerrillas in the state, were superbly mounted and armed to the hilt, with as many as three or four Colt revolvers thrust into their belts and one or two other weapons carried in saddle holsters or strapped to their backs. They normally wore ordinary civilian clothing, although some occasionally donned

Federal uniforms stolen from the enemy.[9] Livingston himself was said to have sometimes worn a broad-brimmed, white hat, making him a striking figure but also a convenient target.[10]

About the time Livingston joined Pike's Indian brigade, he accompanied the command to Mt. Vernon, where it was temporarily stationed in early February 1862.[11] While lingering in Lawrence County, Livingston and his men went out on a foraging expedition in the Verona area, raided a home, and took three occupants prisoner. They strung one of the captives up to an apple tree before letting him down alive, then, according to the 1888 *History of Lawrence County*, all three "were tied in a bunch and made to travel in that form half way to Mt. Vernon."[12] The next day the unfettered but still closely guarded prisoners were herded to a farm east of Mt. Vernon, where they "were given the work of killing hogs."

About the same time and in the same county, Livingston reportedly made a speech that startled many of his listeners because of its pro-Union slant.[13] Presumably he lashed out at the Confederacy for its indifferent defense of Missouri.

During the spring of 1862, Livingston roamed the "Neutral Lands" of southeast Kansas (present-day Cherokee and Crawford Counties), where he and other officers of Pike's command, "with their barbarous gangs of Indians and scarcely less inhuman whites," found diversion harassing squatters and driving them from the area.[14]

On May 29, Livingston's "scouts" provided Colonel Stand Watie with intelligence of a Federal camp near Neosho in southwest Missouri, and two days later Stand Watie combined with Missouri State Guard Colonel John T. Coffee to attack and rout the Federals. In his report of the affair the next day, Stand Watie credited "Captain Livingston" for informing him of the Federals' location.[15]

Although the irregular partisan bands served a useful role in the Southern effort and their marauding activities received tacit approval if not always official sanction, not all Confederate officers looked upon them with favor. Livingston's band was apparently no exception. In July, the guerrillas roamed into Indian Territory, where Livingston and Colonel Coffee's indiscriminate activities provoked the censure of General Pike. Another Confederate officer later admitted that some of Livingston's men were "no better than thieves and robbers."[16]

Livingston didn't stray for long in Indian Territory before returning to southwest Missouri. In an August 9, 1862 report Union Brigadier General Frederick Salomon, who had just completed a march from Sarcoxie to a camp near Fort Scott, complained to General James G. Blunt, Commander of the District of Kansas, that "Neosho was occupied by the enemy under Jackman and Livingston, on August 6" and that "great rejoicing had been among the secesh population there, dinners prepared for them, etc." Later in the report Salomon groused that "...all Southwestern Missouri is evacuated by Union troops and occupied by a five-times stronger rebel force than all available troops under my command."[17]

In mid-August 1862 Tom Livingston's guerrillas skirmished with a detachment of the Sixth Kansas Cavalry under Colonel W. F. Cloud at Pilot Grove near the northeast edge of present-day Joplin. The following day Cloud discovered part of a large force under Confederate captain (later general) Jo Shelby camped on Coon Creek in northern Jasper County, mistook the rebels for Livingston's men, and was routed as a result.[18]

In late September of 1862, Livingston's band and some of Stand Watie's Indians fell in with Colonel T. C. Hawpe's Thirty-first Texas Cavalry and scouted through Jasper County. On September 20, the combined rebel force came upon and attacked the Federal Second Indian Home Guard (Kansas) under Colonel John Ritchie, who was camped on Spring River in the northwest part of the county at what was known as Shirley Ford (named after the family of Myra Maybelle Shirley—a.k.a. Belle Starr—whose family had settled in the area during Jasper County's early days). Many in the Federal Indian regiment had brought their families with them on the jaunt into Missouri, and when the rebels fired upon the Union picket around eight o'clock in the morning, "...a regular stampede of about 1,500 women and children crowded into camp for protection, making a regular Bull Run retreat."[19]

Ritchie, however, managed to rally his troops and repel the assault, then later in the day mounted a charge of his own. In describing the enemy retreat, Ritchie boasted that "such another skedaddling could not have been beaten, only by the women and children in the morning, and that only because they were more in number." He went on to admit, however, that the number of casualties during the engagement was similar on each side--about twenty dead.

A correspondent from Fort Scott, writing to a Leavenworth newspaper, claimed that some of the Cherokee Indians among the rebels "indulged in the greatest pastime of scalping" several of the dead Federals, while another correspondent from the same place stated that it was Ritchie's Indians who resorted "to all their barbarous modes of warfare, such as scalping," the details of which would be "sickening to humanity."[20]

After Ritchie's initial retreat, the Federal Indians took up defensive positions in some heavy brush, and the Confederates launched several assaults trying to dislodge them but were unable to penetrate the thick scrub on horseback. Finally, according to the *History of Jasper County*, Livingston proposed to the Texas commander that, instead of attacking the enemy head-on, they should charge down the main road and cut the Federals off from their wagon train, which had already forded the river. "Colonel, if you will give me command of your regiment for thirty minutes," Livingston is supposed to have said, "I will capture the whole damn regiment, wagon train and all."[21]

When Hawpe rejected the idea, an argument between the two leaders ensued, and the colonel ordered Livingston and his men to the rear. "Colonel," the hot-blooded Livingston retorted, "you can take your regiment and go straight to hell and I will take my command and go where I damn please."

Without another word, the Texan turned his command north and rode off the battlefield. Livingston waited until the Texans were out of sight, then rode in the opposite direction, leaving the Indians in possession of the field.

Less than a week later, Union patrols spotted Livingston in Kansas. On September 26, Colonel William Weer of the Kansas Second Brigade, citing intelligence from two scouting parties, informed General Salomon that Livingston and Colonel Stand Watie were in the vicinity of Baxter Springs, and Weer fretted that

Confederate forces in the region were amassing for an attack against him at his camp on Jenkins Creek in eastern Jasper County.[22]

On October 15 Livingston was reported on the Dry Fork of Spring River north of Carthage lying in ambush with 200 men for a Union wagon train which was scheduled to pass the location under the escort of Union Captain George F. Earl. The post commander at Fort Scott, Major Benjamin S. Henning of the Third Wisconsin Cavalry, immediately sent Captain Theodore Conkey to reinforce Earl at Carthage, and although Livingston was found to be lying in wait as reported, he declined to launch an attack and let the train pass safely through to Fort Scott.[23]

About this same time Livingston captured a couple of loyal citizens in an attempt to ransom the freedom of several guerrillas being held at Fort Scott. He and Major Henning entered into a negotiation for an exchange of prisoners, with Henry Taylor of Vernon County acting as an intermediary, and three guerrillas, including John Bishop, were released.[24]

In early November, Livingston came across a Union wagon train that was returning from General Blunt's army in northwest Arkansas to Fort Scott for supplies. The guerrillas trailed the train, consisting of about a hundred wagons, for three or four days and made several attempts to capture it, killing three soldiers of the guard during the various skirmishes. The rebels followed the train to within eight miles of Fort Scott on November 7 before retiring to a less taxing endeavor. Withdrawing to western Vernon County, they killed at least two Union men, wounded several others, and took eight or ten prisoners. One of the victims, a man named Howard, was supposedly "shot in cold blood after he had surrendered himself up to them." The Federal wagon train reached Fort Scott on the evening of the 7th, and a few hours later a messenger came in with the news that Livingston was on Dry Wood Creek with a hundred men "murdering and robbing" citizens of the area and "working upstream."[25]

Major Henning immediately sent Captain David Mefford with seventy-five men to intercept the guerrillas. The Union company struck Livingston's trail at Cato just across the border in Crawford County, Kansas, and "pursued him about twenty-five miles to Cow

Creek, and overtook him, making a running fight, and wounding one of Livingston's men and recovering some prisoners."[26]

Because his horses were exhausted, Mefford was forced to break off the pursuit and return to Fort Scott, but in the meantime Henning had sent word to Captain Conkey and Captain Charles F. Coleman, whom he had earlier dispatched to Lamar (in response to Quantrill's attack there), to change course and intercept Livingston at Sherwood. Conkey and Coleman took up the chase and camped the night of the 8th on Spring River above Sherwood. The next morning, "The command then separated, Captain Coleman on the south side of Spring River and Captain Conkey on the north side, and worked down toward Sherwood, and Captain Coleman being in the advance came upon the enemy and charged them, killing four or five and taking four prisoners, including the notorious Captain Baker, who was taken by Captain Coleman himself."[27] (Moses Baker, a captain in Livingston's command, had been a large landowner in western Jasper County before the war.)

A civilian eyewitness to this skirmish, George B. Walker, recalled years later that each side captured about an equal number of prisoners and that Livingston and Conkey, with a Southern girl acting as a go-between, entered into a negotiation for their exchange. According to Walker, Livingston "insisted that in trading prisoners Conkey throw in a gallon of whisky 'to boot.'" After the captain consented to this and delivered the liquor, the guerrilla leader demanded that a Union soldier sample the drink to show it wasn't tainted. "This was done," Walker remembered, "and when the trade was completed, Livingston and his men consumed the whisky and pronounced it good."[28]

On December 8, when a guerrilla band, supposed to be Livingston's men, was spotted on Lightning Creek west of Fort Scott in Bourbon County, the nearby village of Marmaton was thrown into a panic. According to some residents, a couple of Livingston's men had recently made an appearance in the town, and they now assumed that the whole band meant to pay a visit. Messengers quickly carried the news to the fort, and troops went out looking for the rebels but failed to locate them.[29]

Shortly after this episode, Livingston drifted south in search of winter quarters. A Union report on Christmas morning of 1862 placed him in the area of Ft. Gibson in Indian Territory.[30]

Around the 10th of January, 1863, he skirmished with a company of Colonel William A. Phillips's Third Indian Home Guard in Indian Territory about thirty-three miles from Elm Springs, Arkansas. Livingston and his command of about sixty or seventy men "were preparing winter quarters" when their camp was discovered. According to Phillips, the guerrillas "drew up in the woods and offered sharp resistance, which lasted about fifteen minutes, and the enemy fled, leaving several dead and a number taken prisoners."[31] Phillips said the Federals lost but one man dead.

Just a few days later, Livingston had another "spirited little affair" with some of Phillips's men near Maysville. According to Phillips, when the Union force advanced on the enemy in three separate columns, the guerrillas broke and "...ran from the first into the second, and finally into the third. Not less than 25 or 30 rebels must have been killed or disabled."[32]

Livingston had yet another skirmish with Federal troops in the area just a day or so later. Around January 15, Major A. C. Ellithorpe, commanding 500 mounted men on a march from Elm Springs to Maysville, "surprised a party of Livingston's gang" and "...killed nine and captured thirteen of the gentry."[33]

His repeated run-ins with Union forces in the area may have inspired Livingston to abort his southern stay and reclaim the friendlier territory of his home grounds. In any case, his winter visit to Arkansas and Indian Territory proved brief. By February 11 he was back in Missouri, where he was "getting troublesome" in the Neosho area, according to Colonel Phillips.[34]

Livingston and his band continued to move north to the area of Dry Fork. On February 19, from "Camp Crouch" several miles north of Carthage, the rebel chief issued a parole to a Union man named William H. Atkinson whom the guerrillas had taken prisoner. It read as follows:

> Know all men by these presents, that I, the undersigned do solemnly sware before boath God and man, and pledge my

life, property and sacred honor that I will return to my home (Fort Scott, Kansas), as a peaceable and neutral citizen in the present war and difficulty now existing between the United States so-called and the Confederate States of America, that I will not aid nor assist in any way or manner whatsoever in the present difficulty between the two governments, so help me God.

W. H. A.

Witness—Capt. A. S. Humbard.

Sworn to and subscribed before me this,

the 19th day of February, 1863.

T. R. Livingston,

Maj. Com'g 1st Battalion Cherokee Spikes

"His (Livingston's) orthography is not always according to Webster," a Union observer remarked wryly, "but this is not essential to bushwhacking against the 'so-called' U. S."[35]

The same day and in the same area, Livingston, commanding sixty men, skirmished with a company of enrolled militia from Bower Mills. Major Edward B. Eno of the 8th Missouri State Militia Cavalry headquartered at Newtonia was camped at Carthage that same evening and filed a report three days later describing the action. With more than a dash of sarcasm Eno noted that, after fighting with Livingston "a little," the enrolled militia "came charging back through Carthage, swearing because they could not catch him."[36]

The Enrolled Missouri Militia was a Federal home guard force, organized in August of 1862, who were called into service from time to time to repel a particular threat or when other circumstances warranted. All able-bodied men were expected to enlist, and, although most enrollees were staunch Unionists (because the majority of Southern sympathizers had already joined the Confederacy or taken to the bush), the conscription of such citizen soldiers produced many reluctant warriors like those from Bower Mills. Often they were friends and neighbors of the guerrillas they were expected to eradicate and sometimes secretly sympathized with the enemy.

After his skirmish with the enrolled militia, Livingston ranged north toward Lamar, and Eno chose not to pursue him, because he felt the guerrilla band would encounter the Wisconsin Volunteer Cavalry operating in that area. Livingston did run into troops sent out from Fort Scott, but not the Wisconsin Cavalry. Instead, he had a scrape on the North Fork of Spring River with Captain Coleman and a detachment of the Ninth Kansas Cavalry. Coleman succeeded in driving off the guerrillas but lost several men in the process.[37]

Meanwhile, Eno marched below Carthage to scour the thickets around Jones and Jenkins creeks in southeastern Jasper County. Another dose of his sardonic wit clearly shows the secessionist sentiment that predominated in the area. "We took the brush and creek until within a quarter of a mile of that misnomer, Fidelity;" he remarked dryly, "then charged into that place; came upon a small party of the rascals, wounded one and captured three. The balance escaped, our horses being too tired to overtake them."[38] Eno didn't disclose the disposition of the captured infidels.

In his report, he instead turned his attention back to Livingston. "If the Wisconsin scout does not come across Livingston and cut him up, he will go down to the border and harbor at the mouth of Shoal creek again, provided he does not leave the country altogether." Eno then expanded on the latter prospect by asserting that even many of Livingston's best friends were beginning to recognize the damage the guerrillas were doing in the area and were considering presenting the guerrilla chief with a petition to leave.[39]

Eno's intelligence that Livingston might soon leave the area proved to be a bit of wishful thinking. About two weeks later, on the night of March 3, 1863, Livingston and 100 men charged into Granby, where twenty-five of Eno's battalion were stationed. Two men on guard duty were captured and presumed shot to death as nothing was later heard from them. "Two other soldiers," according to Eno, "who were attending a sick family a short distance outside the stockade were captured, and unarmed as they were, begging for their lives, were shot down in their tracks." Livingston then turned and galloped quickly out of town without risking an assault on the stockade.[40]

Union forces clashed with Livingston again less than a week later in western Jasper County. Captain Mefford, with three companies of the Sixth Kansas Cavalry, camped the night of March 8 at Sherwood after a scout through the county along Turkey Creek. Early the next morning, following up a trail located the evening before, Mefford's advance ran into a rebel picket, and shots were fired. According to Mefford, he then "searched the woods and found the camp, which had contained about 70 or 80 men, judging from appearances, which the noted Tom Livingston had left in great haste, cutting halters and ropes...."[41]

Mefford was unable to pursue the guerrillas because of the thick brush but instead moved out onto the prairie at the edge of Turkey Creek and marched about two miles before spotting several men at a stand of timber near the northwestern edge of present-day Joplin. Mefford's advance chased the men about three-quarters of a mile before "they were suddenly turned upon by Livingston's whole force and obliged to fall back to the main command, still pursued."[42]

Seeing his advance repelled, Mefford formed his men behind a stand of trees and brush, dismounted them, and sent them into the timber on foot. Livingston charged to within 90 or 100 yards of the brake and exchanged fire with the cavalrymen for several minutes before retreating rapidly. Mefford reported only one man injured. Livingston's losses were unknown, "but, from the appearance of the woods, must have been considerable in horses." Joel Livingston's *History of Jasper County* says, "The Confederate scouts sustained a severe loss."[43]

Around mid-March, 1863, Livingston and Major Henning entered into negotiations again involving the exchange of prisoners and other matters. Henning sent Livingston a note on March 12 proposing an exchange, and Livingston replied on March 17 from his camp at Brush Creek pressing the terms of the agreement. Livingston demanded the release of J. W. Bryson, "a private belonging to my command, who is confined in Springfield Prison. You will likewise release J. G. Haslet, who is in prison at Ft. Lincoln." Livingston was also particularly concerned that Captain Baker, the man whom Captain Coleman of Henning's command had captured the previous fall near Sherwood, should be released. Henning had previously suggested that Baker might be released, but Livingston had heard nothing of him. "It looks hard," Livingston said, "for you to hold him a prisoner so long as you have held him after the liberality that I have shown you and your men. As I am sure there can be no just charges against Capt. Baker that he should be in prison for and further there is no officer in either army that has acted more honorable to the opposite party than Capt. Baker has. Yet it seems that you still hold him."[44]

Henning's suggestion that Baker might be released was an obvious bit of duplicity, because the major did not share Livingston's high opinion of the "notorious Captain Baker." In fact, Moses Baker was known among Unionists as a "very noted character on Shoal Creek and Spring River," and he had already been executed at the time of the letter exchange between Livingston and Henning. Baker reportedly had attended the hanging of a Union man named John Ireland, and he was accused of having placed the rope around the victim's neck. Therefore, shortly after he was captured, Baker had been sent out from the jail at Fort Scott, supposedly on an errand for water, and shot by his guard.[45]

Livingston continued his letter to Henning by citing a compromise that the two parties had tentatively fashioned. The pact apparently involved an agreement that each side would be entitled to forage unmolested in certain specified territory. "I am under the impression," Livingston added, "if Gen. Cloud, you, and myself could meet, that we could easily come to an understanding, as from what I have heard of both of you, there is very little difference in our views in regard to the present difficulty. I am contending for the old constitution in every particular and down on the Abolitionist Doctrine."[46]

Livingston concluded the note by appending a long list of Federal soldiers that he had paroled without an exchange. He signed the letter, "T. R. Livingston, Major, Commanding 1st Battalion Cherokee Spikes." Then, leaving Captain Andrew J. Pearcy in charge of his band in the Jasper County area, Livingston started the next day toward the headquarters of General Douglas Cooper, who'd succeeded General Pike in command of the Indian brigade, to bring up the balance of his men.[47]

By the spring of 1863 Tom Livingston had become such a vexation to Union leaders in the region that they sometimes falsely sighted him or exaggerated his force. On April 1, Colonel M. La Rue Harrison of the First Arkansas Cavalry reported to General Curtis that Livingston was in southwestern Missouri "with 800 guerrillas."[46]

Despite the date of the correspondence, Harrison's alarm suggests that Livingston had ceased to be an April Fool's joke to Union officials. It hardly mattered that Livingston was, in reality, somewhere off in Indian Territory leading a mere handful of rebels.

Although it is not clear where Livingston was camped at the time, on April 20, 1863, he took up his pen and issued an appeal to the Southern people to join forces with him. It read as follows:

> Attention! Under a commission from the Lieutenant General Commanding, the undersigned is now raising a Battalion or Regiment of Partisan Rangers, to act in advance of the Army, in Northern Arkansas, Missouri, and Kansas. He calls upon all who are willing to spill their blood in defense of the Constitution, as it was understood by our Fathers and its framers, and who are willing to risk their lives in defense of the South against Abolitionism, Fanaticism, and Tyranny in any form, to come forward and lend a willing heart and ready hand. To those whom the oppression of former military leaders has forced to seek an asylum where they could find it, he would say, come on and join me, and you will be treated as men and soldiers.
>
> By inquiring at the Adjutant's office of Colonel Stand Watie's regiment, my Headquarters will always be found.
>
> T. R. Livingston
> Maj. Commanding Cherokee Spikes[49]

When Major Charles W. Blair replaced Major Henning as Post Commander at Fort Scott in the spring of 1863, one of his main charges was the task of quashing Livingston. To this end, troops from the First Kansas Colored Infantry Regiment were stationed at an outpost at Baxter Springs under Colonel James M. Williams.

The previous October, in the first action of the Civil War involving black soldiers, some of Williams' troops had participated in a series of skirmishes with partisans at Island Mound in Bates County and had, according to one Federal officer, heroically answered "the often mooted question of will they fight.'"[50] Confederate sympathizers, of course, deeply resented the enlistment of blacks into the Federal army, and partisans in the Jasper County area especially resented the presence at nearby Baxter Springs of Williams' troops, some of whom were ex-slaves from southwest Missouri.

On May 5 Major Blair sent a detachment from Fort Scott to attack a guerrilla camp that he had learned was established on Center Creek near Sherwood. Reinforced by two companies from the newly organized regiment at Baxter Springs, the Union force "attacked the enemy at daybreak, carrying the camp in gallant style and dispersing the rebels in every direction." The scouting party subsequently broke up another camp in the same area, then headed back to Kansas with several captured prisoners and about fifty confiscated horses and mules. The Union press reported that, although the troops did not succeed in finding Livingston, they "got up a big scare among the rebs."[51]

Some of the rebels at the Sherwood camps might well have been Livingston's followers, but Livingston himself was still resting in Indian Territory at the time. According to his own report of May 28, 1863, to General Sterling Price, Livingston left the Creek Agency on the 6th of May headed for Missouri. On the 8th he skirmished at Cabin Creek with a detachment from Fort Scott, "killing one and wounding one" of the enemy. The Federal squad then took shelter in and around some nearby houses, and Livingston tried unsuccessfully to draw them out before retiring as Union reinforcements approached. Livingston put his own loss at three men slightly injured.[52]

The Union version is somewhat different. Colonel Phillips, Commander of Fort Blunt in the Indian Nation, said that, after fighting with Livingston's men for about an hour, the Union party, which was on its way to Fort Gibson with the mail, "routed them, killing three and wounding several."[53]

While Livingston was absent from southwest Missouri, Southern sympathizers in the area boasted that he would "sweep over this district like a tornado" when he returned. When the guerrilla chief arrived back in the state on May 9, both sides took up the challenge. Around this date, Livingston's men raided into southeast Kansas and, according to a Union report, "committed murders and robberies which always accompany a guerrilla invasion." In response, Colonel Thomas T. Crittenden, post commander at Newtonia, sent Major Eno on a scout into Jasper County in search of his old adversary on May 13.[54]

Eno, in command of 100 men from his own Eighth Missouri State Militia Cavalry and another eighty-four from the Seventh Missouri State Militia Cavalry, proceeded north to Shoal Creek, where Captain Squire Ballew of the Seventh was sent west with orders to scout along the creek, then turn north and rendezvous with Eno the next day at French Point, Livingston's old stomping grounds. Major Eno and the rest of the command camped that evening on Center Creek five miles from Carthage.[55]

The next morning Eno again divided his command, sending Captain Jacob Cassairt of the Eighth Missouri State Militia Cavalry with forty men and Captain M. C. Henslee of the Seventh with thirty-five men down either side of Center Creek toward French Point while Eno and the remainder of the command followed in the middle along the banks of the creek. About 3:00 p.m. approximately a mile and a half east of French Point, Cassairt and Henslee drove in Livingston's pickets and converged on the south side of the creek, where, according to Eno, they encountered the main guerrilla force, "about 100 strong...posted under cover of a log house and dense brush. A severe fight ensued of some fifteen minutes' duration, when our men were obliged to fall back."[56]

Eno blamed the retreat on the fact that Henslee's horse became unmanageable and carried the captain away from his men and the fact that many of Livingston's men were wearing Federal uniforms. Cassairt's detachment mistook the blue-clad guerrillas for Union soldiers and "before discovering their mistake were right among them, had received a galling fire, and were fighting hand-to-hand."[57]

Eno himself was two miles up the creek when the firing commenced, and although he immediately galloped toward the sound of the shooting, he "was not able to reach the ground until all was over." He pressed on after Livingston, hoping to drive the guerrillas into Captain Ballew's detachment moving upstream, but when he reached French Point, he learned to his exasperation that Ballew had merely fired a few times at Livingston's advance and then retreated, allowing the guerrillas to escape.[58]

The partisans broke into small groups, and Eno pursued them over the next four days "almost continually fighting them, starting up scattered squads of from four to ten, chasing and firing on them, when they invariably dashed into the brush and concealed themselves...."[59]

Colonel Crittenden put a slightly better face on the behavior of his men than Eno. He stated in his report of the affray that the scouting party completely routed Livingston, and he made no mention of the initial Federal retreat or of Ballew's dubious effort. Having gotten his hands on a copy of Livingston's April 21 proclamation to the Southern people, Crittenden added wryly in a letter to a Missouri newspaper that his men had "completely whipped...the 'advance guard' of the promised army." Both he and Eno claimed that rebel casualties greatly outnumbered their own--about fifteen guerrillas killed compared to only four Union soldiers. In an addendum to his official report, Crittenden said of the guerrillas infesting his region, "A quick succession of vigorous scouts will destroy and disperse them. Kill Livingston, and there is no one else to mass and congregate these bands. Is a man of much influence."[60]

The Confederate side of the story is predictably quite different in the number of casualties and other details. In his report of May 28, Livingston said that on the 15th (Eno said the 14th) "as I was crossing the timber of Centre Creek, about 10 miles southwest of Carthage, I encountered a scout of the enemy, consisting of 125 Newtonia militia. I immediately got my men in position to receive an assault from him, whom I vigorously repulsed." Livingston then charged and "a sharp firing ensued; the enemy were soon flying before us, being completely put to rout. I pursued him about three miles." The guerrilla chief estimated Union losses at thirteen killed and four mortally wounded and claimed his own loss was just two men slightly injured.[61]

On the 18th of May, Eno gave up his chase after Livingston and went back to Newtonia, allowing the guerrillas to turn their attention to more agreeable pursuits. When Livingston's scouts reported sixty soldiers and a mule train from Colonel Williams' Negro regiment foraging on the Center Creek prairie near Sherwood that very day, Livingston saw a rare opportunity for vengeance on the hated black troops.

He promptly led sixty-seven of his "best mounted men" toward the scene and came upon the Federals at the home of a Mrs. Rader. The foraging party was led by Major Richard G. Ward (the same officer who had commanded the blacks troops in Bates County the previous fall) and numbered, according to Union reports, from twenty-five to thirty-two Negro soldiers and from twenty to twenty-two white artillery men from the Second Kansas Battery. The Federals had driven the woman, whose son was one of Livingston's guerrillas, from her house and were busy pillaging the premises. About twenty of the black troops had stacked their arms in the yard and were in the home rummaging for provisions, with some of them upstairs tossing corn into the five wagons below.[62]

"I charged them at the house," said Livingston in his May 28 report, "flanking them on the right, routed them, and pursued them about 8 miles, to the crossing of Spring River."[63]

Most of Colonel Williams' black soldiers, on foot and unarmed, were shot before they could flee or reach their weapons. The pursuit mentioned by Livingston involved mainly the mounted troops. These were the white officers and some of the "battery boys" who'd come along on the expedition. During the chase, three men from the battery were killed and two captured. A third white soldier and two of Williams' black soldiers were also captured.[64]

Livingston put the enemy loss at "negroes, 23, and 7 white men" while his own command "sustained no loss." The guerrillas also captured the mule train and a good deal of guns and ammunition.[65]

The next day after the guerrillas' attack on the foraging party, Union troops from Kansas came back, 300 strong according to Livingston's report, and burned the town of Sherwood and eleven farm houses in the area. "They put 10 of their dead (negroes) that had been left on the battle-ground the day preceding, and, together with the body of Mr. John Bishop, a citizen prisoner, whom they had murdered, into the house of Mrs. Rador, and burned the premises. They then returned to their camp at Baxter Springs."[66]

Bishop was, in fact, more than a "citizen" prisoner. He was the same man who had been released by Major Henning in the prisoner exchange with Livingston the previous fall. When the soldiers came upon him near the Rader place tending to the Federal

BATTLE OF RADER'S FARM
MAY 18, 1863

IN MEMORY OF 18
U. S. SOLDIERS KILLED IN
ACTION 3 MILES NORTH
OF THIS PARK

Monument at Joplin Museum Complex to soldiers killed by Livingston.

mules that the guerrillas had captured during their attack the previous day, Bishop was taken to the house and killed for violating his parole. Livingston's account of the events surrounding the burning of Sherwood is otherwise essentially confirmed in a letter one of the Union participants wrote to his wife three days after the destruction.[67]

Many of the citizens who had their homes burned fled to Texas, and although some returned after the war, the town, which had been Jasper County's third largest, was never rebuilt.

On May 20, the day after the burning of Sherwood, Livingston and Williams entered into negotiations for an exchange of prisoners. Writing from "Camp Jackson," Livingston proposed trading the three white soldiers he'd captured two days earlier for any Confederate soldiers Williams might be holding. "As for the negroes," Livingston said, "I cannot recognize them as soldiers, and in consequence, I will have to hold them as contraband of war."[68]

Williams responded the next day, May 21, accepting Livingston's proposal for an exchange of the white prisoners, and the

Entrance to Sherwood Cemetery, which is about all that remains of the Civil War community destroyed by Federals on May 19, 1863.

exchange was effected on May 22 with private citizens acting as go-betweens. In answer to Livingston's veiled threat to execute the two prisoners from the colored regiment, however, Williams said he was holding back a similar number of Confederate captives and promised to "follow suit or trump" if Livingston carried through with the threat.[69]

Livingston wrote back on May 23 threatening to kill three Federals for every Confederate captive executed by Williams. The missive was signed, "T. R. Livingston, Major Commanding 1st Battalion Bloody Spikes."[70]

About this time, one of the black prisoners was killed in the guerrilla camp, and the strained negotiations took on an even nastier tone. Livingston claimed a visitor to camp, over whom the guerrilla chief had no authority, shot the prisoner during an altercation between the two men, but Colonel Williams was unconvinced. He told Livingston in a May 26th correspondence that if the guilty party was not delivered to the Federal camp within 48 hours, he'd hang a Confederate prisoner.[71]

Livingston replied the next day from his camp at Diamond Grove, Missouri, that he could not comply with the demand and pointed out that the prisoners being held by Williams did not belong to the guerrilla command. "Consequently," Livingston concluded, "the innocent will have to suffer for the guilty."[72]

Negotiations broke off after this, and each side started killing prisoners.[73]

Toward the end of May, John T. Coffee came up from Pineville to join Livingston, "making a force of 800 to 1,000," according to General Blunt's estimate.[74] The combined rebel force roamed into Kansas and Indian Territory, threatening Williams's black regiment at Baxter Springs, harassing Colonel Phillips's Indian brigade, and disrupting the lines of supply and communication between Fort Scott and Fort Gibson.

On June 8, while most of the Federals from Baxter Springs were out on a scout for Livingston, the rebel chieftain dashed toward the Union camp they'd just left and attacked a small party of soldiers from the Second Kansas Battery who were tending a herd of horses nearby. The guerrillas killed one man, took two prisoners, and also captured the horses. Shortly afterwards, Livingston and Colonel Williams tried briefly to negotiate another prisoner exchange, but the incident at the Rader farm and its aftermath had soured whatever good faith had previously existed. The bargaining yielded no agreement, and Livingston promptly killed the two captives.[75]

Returning to Missouri, the guerrillas carried out a raid on the small settlement of Blytheville, a precursor to the town of Joplin. Then around the middle of June, about the same time that Williams's black regiment marched south into Indian Territory, Livingston moved off to the north. He and Coffee, according to Union Colonel John Edwards's report of the 19th, passed Carthage with about 300 men, a more creditable estimate than Blunt's extravagant calculation three weeks earlier.[76]

Livingston met his end less than a month later leading an assault on a Union detachment at Stockton in Cedar County. On Saturday, July 11, 1863, at about 1:00 p.m., according to the report of Major Charles Sheppard filed four days later, "Livingston, the chief of bushwhackers in this district, with 100 men, surprised and attacked..." a small detachment of militiamen garrisoned in the courthouse. A number of soldiers, who were outside the courthouse lounging on the grounds of the square listening to a political speech in the noonday heat, dispersed at the first sign of the rebels, leaving only about twenty men inside the building to defend the courthouse. These few, however, quickly rallied, barricaded the building, and returned fire.[77]

W. R. Willett, one of the militiamen inside the courthouse, recounted the episode years later. Livingston, he said, "armed with a heavy, breech-loading pistol to which he had attached a rifle stock...," galloped into town and "rode at top speed up to the court house, reined in his horse and fired into the building just as we swung the heavy door into place." During the brief but heated exchange that followed, Livingston "was shot from his horse close to the building as he urged his men on to the attack."[78]

As his men retreated, Livingston tried to rise but several of the Unionists dashed from the courthouse to stop him. One, "who had picked up the fallen man's gun dealt him a terrific blow on the head, and at the same time several others fired into his body."[79]

Sheppard reported the Union loss at four mortally wounded and two slightly wounded, although one of the "mortally wounded," later recovered. The guerrillas left Livingston and three other men dead on the field. After loading about fifteen wounded into a government wagon, they retreated in a southwesterly direction and left the wounded at the small community of White Hare about ten miles from Stockton. News of Livingston's death was heralded in the Union press as far away as Kansas City.[80]

Most of Livingston's guerrillas rode south with Coffee to Cowskin Prairie in McDonald County, where they reorganized later in the month under his command, although some were supposed to have joined Henry Taylor while others, following a Captain Estes, were reported to have joined Quantrill.[81]

Livingston's body was buried in an unmarked grave in a cemetery at Stockton. According to legend, Livingston's men learned of the location, and after the war some of them occasionally returned to visit the grave in secret. Another, less credible story holds that the body was brought back to Sherwood and buried in the cemetery there. Long after the war was over, an old man was regularly seen laying flowers at the grave, which was marked by a big rock with just an "L" crudely etched on it.[82]

Jo Shelby, whose command included many guerrillas, like John Clem, when they were in the regular Confederate Army. (Author's Collection)

5
The Notorious Sheriff Clem

Prior to the Civil War, John W. Clem of Bates County lived on a farm west of Butler with his wife and seven children, and he, like Henry Taylor, served his county as sheriff. When the Civil War broke out, the county court authorized the forty-three-year-old Clem to raise a company of home guards to protect the county's border with Kansas. In mid-July, 1861, this force, which included Sidney Jackman, was involved in a mild skirmish with some Union reserve troops near West Point in northwest Bates county. Clem, however, apparently took little active role in the affray and was later criticized by Jackman for supposedly having proposed a surrender. Almost immediately after this affair, Clem and his company were enlisted into the Eighth Division of the Missouri State Guard as part of Lieutenant-Colonel Thomas B. Cummings's Ninth Cavalry. Cummings, like Clem, had been captain of a Bates County home guard company. Clem was elected captain of Company C on July 22, 1861.[1]

Clem presumably participated in the Battle of Wilson's Creek, but by late August Cummings and his men were back in their home territory near the Bates-Vernon county line. Around August 24 the rebels seized the mill at Balltown in northern Vernon and pressed it into service to feed themselves and other State Guard troops. Jim Lane sent a Federal detachment across the border from Kansas on August 27 to disperse the rebels, and Cummings and his men fled south to the Marmaton. After the Union troops called off the chase, they went back and burned the mill. In contrast to the engagement in mid-July, according to Jackman, Clem "displayed considerable courage" during the retreat from Balltown by staying behind to help save the wagon train after many of the rest of the state troops had fled in disarray.[2]

During the State Guard's fight with Jim Lane's Kansas brigade at Dry Wood in early September, Clem again behaved well, according to Jackman, and through his alertness, prevented an inadvertent attack on Jackman's company by a confused Missouri State Guard force.[3]

When Price started north toward Lexington in September, Clem apparently declined the expedition in favor of remaining in the more familiar territory of Bates County, as he was reported in military records as "absent without leave" from September 12, 1861. Tarrying in his home area, Clem, like many others along the border, was soon drawn into a war of retaliation, involving raid and counter raid. On October 29, 1861, a little over a month after Lane's sacking of Osceola, Sheriff Clem led a "posse" of forty men across the border into southern Miami County under the pretext of recovering property taken from Missouri. In the area of North Sugar Creek, the rebels stole a large quantity of livestock, burned several homes, and reportedly killed at least two men.[4]

Ranging south into Linn County, the rebels arrived at the home of Richard Manning on Mine Creek and "informed him that he had to die." When the frightened Manning sprang for his gun, the gang promptly shot him dead. At the same house, the Missourians also found a young man named William Upton lying in bed. They shot and killed him before he could get up, then robbed the premises of everything of value. They then turned their attention to other homes in the neighborhood, including that of Thomas Speakes. As the gang approached the Speakes home, Joseph Speakes saw them coming and ran to alert his neighbors.[5]

The rebels confiscated about twenty horses and two wagons from the neighborhood, but by the time they started back to Missouri, a party of fourteen Union men had armed themselves in response to Joseph Speakes's alarm and had taken up a position on the road leading out of Kansas. When the rebels approached, the Union men opened fire, killing two and wounding several of the raiders. The Missourians returned fire, killing Joseph Speakes and slightly wounding a couple of other Union men, before making their escape. The rebels were pursued into Missouri but to no avail.[6]

On November 1, 1861, at Cassville, Clem's company was discharged from service, and ten days later their captain's name was stricken from the rolls of the Missouri State Guard. Even though he had taken it upon himself to simply return home without authorization, Clem was evidently never charged with desertion. Around the middle of November, about the time his name was being removed from the rolls of the State Guard, a party of Kansas citizens from the neighborhood of Mound City were on their way to Osceola with wagons and teams to procure their winter's supply of salt when they were attacked near Butler in Bates County by "two companies of secessionists...led on by the notorious Sheriff Clem." The Unionists claimed to have killed nine rebels before making "the best retreat they could."[7]

In early December, Clem made another raid into Linn County leading a band of men estimated between 100 and 300. The gang broke into three groups as they entered Kansas and began committing depredations. One party plundered the village of Potosi, including the store of J. E. Hill. They burned grain and buildings in the area and robbed several private residences, including that of Josiah Sykes. Sykes jerked on his pants, though, and managed to escape into the winter night bareheaded, barefooted, and without coat or vest. During the raid, the gang shot at least one citizen, an old man named Seright whom they ordered to produce a firebrand so that they could burn his stacks of hay. According to a Union report, the seventy-two-year-old man brought out some burning sticks from his fireplace as ordered, but the raiders shot him in the back nonetheless and "burned every thing combustible on the place."[8]

Sykes, meanwhile, made his way "over the frozen ground" to Mound City to report the raid to James Montgomery, commanding a regiment of Kansas troops. Colonel Montgomery promptly sent a detachment of about 700 troops under Major H. H. Williams in pursuit of the raiders. The Missourians had dispersed before they could be tracked down, and Williams discharged his frustration by burning the town of Papinsville on the night of December 13. After the women and children were provided for, "in the choice and expressive language of Jim Lane, Papinsville 'went up.'"[9]

Next, Williams sent Captain John E. Stewart's cavalry fifteen miles away to burn the county seat at Butler. Reaching the place on the afternoon of December 14, Stewart fired the courthouse and all the business section of the town. While Butler was still burning, Sidney Jackman, now captain of a cavalry company in the Missouri State Guard, rode in and drove the Federals out of town, killing at least two of Stewart's men. On their retreat to Kansas, the Federal troops destroyed homes and confiscated stock all along their path, and a number of Unionist refugees followed the caravan out of Missouri.[10]

Although the forty-something-year-old family man had not taken well to regular soldiering on his first go-around, Clem apparently decided to give it another try. On August 18, 1862, during Jo Shelby's recruiting trip into Missouri, Clem signed up for Confederate service at Waverly (although he had probably joined the expedition before it reached Shelby's hometown). On September 8, Shelby gave Clem a commission as a first lieutenant, and Clem was presumably engaged at Newtonia in late September. Then on November 28, 1862, in a reorganization of Shelby's brigade, Clem was re-enlisted at Washington County, Arkansas, by Captain L. J. Crocker, commanding Company K in Lieutenant-Colonel B. Frank Gordon's regiment. On December 10, just after the Battle of Prairie Grove, Clem was again elected first lieutenant, and after Crocker was wounded at the Battle of Hartville in January of 1863, Clem took command of the company. Muster rolls for Gordon's regiment show that Clem drew pay at the end of March, 1863, but there appears to be no record of him afterwards. However, according to Jackman, Clem "went through the war a true friend of the South."[11]

6
The So-Styled Colonel Parker

William Quantrill is usually considered the leading spirit of the guerrilla movement that arose in the Jackson County vicinity during the first part of 1862, but very early in the year Colonel Benjamin F. Parker's importance as a guerrilla chief in the area rivaled that of Quantrill. In fact, the two men seemed to have acted in cooperation during the early months of 1862, as they were mentioned together in Union communications several times during February, March, and early April. Some evidence suggests that Parker may even have held ascendancy over Quantrill at this early stage. Although Union observers sometimes mocked Parker's colonelcy as lacking official sanction, it is probable that he did have some sort of formal Confederate recognition, even at this early phase of the war.

Quantrill is normally mentioned as the leader of the guerrilla party that skirmished with Federal troops at Independence on February 22, 1862. However, at least one Union report named Parker as head of the band and suggested that Parker himself was among those wounded during the affray.[1]

On March 14, 1862, Parker and Quantrill's combined command of about forty men crossed the Missouri River to Clay County and marched into Liberty. The guerrillas spotted an unarmed Union soldier on the streets and demanded to know the whereabouts of the Federal garrison. When the soldier refused to provide the requested information, the bushwhackers promptly shot him down. They soon found the Federal headquarters on their own, and they discovered a recruiting officer and eight or ten other soldiers housed at the location. The guerrillas took shelter behind some nearby houses and began taking pot shots at the Federal quarters. The Union soldiers occasionally answered, and the two sides kept up a desultory gunplay for almost three hours before the Federals finally surrendered under a threat of being burnt out. The jubilant bushwhackers celebrated the victory by tearing down the U. S. flag at the county courthouse before mounting up and riding out of town.[2]

Around the same time as the Liberty raid, Parker also stopped the steamboat *Rowena* on the Missouri River. After examining the manifest, he confiscated about six dozen pairs of boots and some other items before allowing the boat to resume its trip.[3]

Despite the scant mention of Parker in early records, Federal reports of a skirmish in late March, 1862, clearly suggest that Parker had been a noted Confederate leader in the Jackson County area for some considerable time. On the night of March 28, word reached Captain James D. Thompson of the First Iowa Cavalry at Warrensburg that a large body of bushwhackers was camped on the Blackwater River near a mill in northwest Johnson County about twelve miles from the post. The next day the Federals reconnoitered the supposed camp and turned up no guerrillas, but as they started on their return trip to Warrensburg in the afternoon, they happened upon a company of sixty or seventy rebels under Colonel Parker, whom Thompson later identified as a "notorious rebel leader...who has so long been the terror of the more northern counties."[4]

The bushwhackers took to the woods when the Federals charged, and a running fight ensued. One of the pursuing cavalrymen later described the chase in expressive style:

> The Secesh dashed into the brush as usual, and of course we followed through chapparal, brush, bogs, mud, sloughs, gulches and creeks, and over hills, logs, ravines and rocks, for about four miles, they firing as they ran, and we replying with revolvers whenever they permitted us to get within range. They were well mounted and were familiar with the crossings of the creeks, so they had a decided advantage over us, and it was only our best mounted men who were able to keep up with our chivalric but nomadic foes. The chase was a quite exciting one, stirring even the current of my phlegmatic nature. The road, or rather path, through the brush was strewn with hats, caps, blankets, shot-pouches, shotguns, pistols, sabres, Springfield muskets and Enfield rifles, abandoned by the Southern bloods to facilitate their hegira.... After crossing the creek at the old mill the rebels struck across the hill to the river at a point that had formerly been fordable, but now obstructed by drift wood, when

they scattered in all directions except the one they came.... A part of the rebels ran up the river, a part down the river, and a few through the river, but not being able to get their horses up the opposite bank, which was steep and miry, they abandoned them and trusted to the strength of their own legs for the balance of the journey, while not a few of them ensconced themselves beneath logs, sought retirement from this troublous world in tree-tops and tangled underbrush, or courted modest obscurity by sinking quietly into some friendly gutter near by. Of this latter class was the gallant Col. Parker, who was brought back to a consciousness of existence by the announcement that if he didn't "get up out of that he would be shot."[5]

The rebels had at least ten men killed and several others wounded in the fray, while the Federals reported one man dead, one seriously wounded, and one slightly wounded. The Union troops also captured fourteen other prisoners in addition to Parker and confiscated about twenty horses and a lot of arms and equipment.[6]

On March 30, the day after Parker's capture, a detachment of Captain John B. Kaiser's Missouri Cavalry Militia and some of Captain Albert Peabody's First Missouri Cavalry skirmished with a large band of Quantrill's and Parker's men near Pink Hill in southeastern Jackson County on Sni-a-Bar Creek. Although the guerrilla camp was located among an outcropping of rocks on a high bluff, a few Federal volleys soon persuaded the rebels to abandon their fortified position. By the time the Federals scaled the bluff, the guerrillas were long gone, but Captain Kaiser confiscated "ten kegs (twenty-five pounds per keg) of Parker's power." The captain, obviously unaware of Parker's capture the previous day, reported that a great many Southern sympathizers in the area were joining Parker.[7] A lot of them probably ended up joining Quantrill instead.

After his capture, Parker was taken to Sedalia, and a few days later he was sent to the military prison at Fifth and Myrtle Street in St. Louis. His stopover in St. Louis proved brief, as he was transferred to the military prison at Alton, Illinois, on April 8. Union officials listed Parker in prisoner of war records as a "colonel of jayhawkers."[8]

On September 23, 1862, Parker was sent to Vicksburg, Mississippi, to be exchanged. A week later he requisitioned supplies at the Confederate quartermaster post at Monroe, Louisiana, and was issued camp equipage for twenty-six men. Most of these men were presumably those who had been captured with Parker or those like William Marchbanks who had been captured and exchanged near the same time and who now joined his command. If Parker did not already have official Confederate authority as a colonel, he must have received it at Fort Monroe under the Partisan Ranger Act, as his command was now recognized as the First Regiment Missouri Rangers.[9]

In the spring of 1863, Parker was sent back to Missouri to recruit and fill out his regiment. He was first reported in the state in mid-April when he and Marchbanks were spotted going north through the eastern edge of Jasper County. By the first of May, he had established a command center in the Jackson County area and was once again mentioned in association with Quantrill.[10]

On May 3, 1863, from his "Headquarters Confederate Forces" in Jackson County, Parker drew up a letter detailing his grievances against the Federal government. On May 11, he sent three copies of the proclamation to Union Major Wyllis C. Ransom at Westport with instructions that they be forwarded to Major General Samuel R. Curtis at St. Louis, Major General James G. Blunt at Leavenworth, and Lieutenant-Colonel Philip Thompson at Kansas City. Ransom forwarded the first two letters as requested, but since Colonel Thompson had been relieved of his command, the major took the liberty of opening the third copy himself.[11]

The letter read as follows:

> Sir: Having been ordered to this section of the State by the legitimate authorities of my Government to resist any and all invading forces that may have for their object the subjugation of our people, I deem it proper to address you officially of the intention of my Government and the determination of the colonel commanding in the event that the unholy, savage and inhuman war carried on against the people of Cass, Jackson, Lafayette, Bates and Johnson Counties is still persisted in.

Sir, while your soldiers have been treated as ordinary prisoners of war and the Union people respected in person and effect, our soldiers and citizens have been arrested and executed without trial, basing and resting those hellish and diabolical acts upon the testimony of one or two unscrupulous dogs—villains that are sworn to sell and barter away the lives and liberty of men. Your officers in command of regiments, battalions and companies stationed in our border counties have without warrant or justification arrested and shot private citizens, charging as a pretext to that cowardly act that they fed, harbored and gave encouragement to bushwhackers, thereby covering the atrocity of the crime.

The more brutal the act, the stronger the praise awarded by your Government. Your officers with or without your orders have arrested and banished our ladies for vindicating the sacredness of their sex against the slanders and insults of the base and unmitigated scoundrels calling themselves U. S. soldiers. Yes, some have been thus dealt with for refusing to cook, and giving expression to the detestation and abhorrence so justly engendered and borne toward these hireling vandals. What, sir, can you expect from a people whose rights are trampled in the dust--whose property is taken ruthlessly without the least shadow of law and feloniously appropriated--those families have been outraged and subjected to indignities unbecoming the savage--whose friends and kindred have been shot for opposing the unwarrantable and unconstitutional invasion of our rights and country? All this has been done, and now you threaten us with extinction; to extirpate our race and name; to blot out the landmarks of constitutional liberty and reduce to a wilderness the land we once inhabited.

If this is civilized and honorable warfare--if this is the spirit which animates the American people--that people of whom you have so often boasted--then I say, proud and ancient name, how basely lied upon. Now, sir, being vested with authority to operate in this section of the State and protect as far as possible the people claiming citizenship and protection from the Confederate States Government, I therefore make known that I exact the rights of belligerents as ratified upon the first and original agreement between your Government and the Confederate States Government to treat all men in arms, if captured, as prisoners of war, whether they be found in the woods or prairies.

By acts of savage cruelty you have driven our citizens to the woods, forcing them to take desperate steps to protect their lives from the hands of commissioned assassins. The men that are now in arms in this State (with a few exceptions) are Confederate States soldiers fighting to redeem their homes from the desecrating tread of ruffian soldiers and themselves from thralldom.

The unwarrantable seizure of persons and the destruction of property by fire; the carrying off of citizens and imprisoning them in bastilles and felons' dens; the consuming of the people's grain and meat without compensation has precipitated upon the women and children starvation, and their cries are now piercing the throne of Heaven, asking to be avenged. These, sir, are a part of the causes driving men to arms, forcing upon them the alternative of fighting or our reduction to a state of vassalage.

Can these things be tolerated any longer? Can and must the people fold their arms and say, "Oh, Lord, Thy will be done"? Can men stand back and see their families insulted and their property carried off by armed mobs? No! Every impulse that warms the human heart calls upon our people to arms. The blood of our martyred heroes urges our people forward. The bones of our aged citizens bleaching under the midday sun calls for revenge. The tears of the widows and orphans appeal to the sympathy of Southern hearts and ask them to bleed with their comrades that have fallen in defense of their homes and firesides. Outraged humanity bleeds at every pore. The earth is stained with the blood of the innocent, and yet you hunt us with the wild and frenzied madness of the bloodhound. Can you expect willing submission? Can you expect our arms to be surrendered up and we return to our former allegiance? No! Fight is the watchword of our people, and fight we shall until the hordes that now infest our country are withdrawn and our rights acknowledged among the nations of the earth.

We are compelled by the instincts of our nature to resist the enforcement of obnoxious and unlawful measures; hence the sole reason for having our soldiers and citizens put to death. If total annihilation is the intention of your Government, then we are ready. If our lives are required to pay the bond, then we are ready for the struggle. The perversion of the war for the Union to a war of extermination forces upon us retaliation. And if another Confederate soldier or citizen is executed without due process of law, five Union soldiers or citizens shall with their lives pay the forfeit.

This, sir, shall be done independent of the consequences, to take effect from and after the 20th of May, A. D. 1863.

B. F. Parker
Colonel,
Confederate States Army[12]

General Curtis, commanding the Union Department of the Missouri, declined to respond to Parker's decree. Instead, he forwarded it to Brigadier-General Benjamin Loan, commander of the Central District of Missouri at Jefferson City with instructions that Loan "look out for this champion of Southern rights and give him such justice as he merits."[13]

However, General Blunt, Commander of the District of Kansas, replied to the proclamation at some length via a letter dated May 13 at Leavenworth and published in area newspapers shortly thereafter:

Sir: As you do not designate the locality of the Headquarters of the Confederate forces under your command, as honorable belligerents always do, I am compelled to adopt this method of communication with you in reply to your long tirade about Constitutional liberty, etc., about which you appear to have as correct an appreciation as a Hottentot or a South Sea Islander.

I have the honor to say to you, after reading your long lecture, that you need not defer your proposed acts of retaliation until the 20th of May. It is of little consequence to me to know what are the instructions of the "Government you represent." It is sufficient for me to know that you and your motley crew are insurgents and assassins; that you are organizing within the military district of the Federal forces, and are engaged in murdering and plundering unarmed loyal citizens, thereby barring yourselves of all rights and considerations extended to prisoners of war.

I have instructed the officers in command of troops in the border counties of Missouri (and the same rule shall extend to all Territory under my command) that every rebel or rebel sympathizer who gives aid, directly or indirectly, shall be destroyed or expelled from the military District. These instructions will not exempt females from the rule. Experience has taught that the bite of a she adder is as poisonous and productive of mischief as the bite of any venomous reptile. Therefore, all persons known to be in arms against the Federal authorities of this District will be summarily put to death when captured. The only Constitutional right that will be granted them will be the right to make choice of the quality of rope with which they will he hung.

All those who are in sympathy with your cause, and whom the military authorities may not feel justified in putting to death, will be sent south of the Arkansas River. They will do well to avail themselves of this my last friendly admonition.

Trusting that you will fully appreciate the motives which have prompted me to adopt this humane policy toward your misguided friends, I have the honor to remain

Your Obedient servant,
Jas. G. Blunt,
Major. Gen'l.[14]

The exchange of letters between Parker and Blunt is little more than a curiosity except that Parker's letter illustrates the extraordinary level of bitterness that the Federal troops' occupation of Missouri engendered among Southern-leaning citizens of the state and Blunt's reply clearly shows the mounting anger and frustration on the Union side over its inability to quash the civilian resistance.

General James G. Blunt, with whom Parker exchanged letters. (J. Dale
West Collection)

Like General Blunt, Major Ransom also responded to Parker's
communication. On May 12, the same day he received Parker's three
letters, the major wrote a reply and dispatched it via messenger.
Ransom was particularly anxious to protest "the murder of prisoners
as practiced by Todd, Yeager, and Gregg, all of whom profess to be
Lieutenants in the rebel service, and who, in their warfare against us

during the past winter, have entirely disregarded all rules of civilized warfare, and outraged humanity." Ransom told Parker that if he would repudiate the actions of these men and would refrain from murdering prisoners, he (Ransom) would reciprocate by likewise treating any of Parker's men who happened to fall into his hands as prisoners of war.[15]

Parker answered that he was "pleased, to a certain extent, with the tone and gist" of Ransom's letter but that the major's meaning was not entirely clear. Parker admitted that the warfare along the Kansas-Missouri border during the past seven or eight months had degenerated into barbarity, but he was quick to point out that atrocities had occurred on both sides. He went on to imply that the Union was guilty of more than its share. Parker disavowed any connection with George Todd and William Gregg and claimed that he had no jurisdiction over them. He conceded that he had commissioned Dick Yeager as a Confederate officer but only as of May 11. (Yeager, accompanied by Bill Anderson, had just returned from a murderous raid deep into Kansas.) In conclusion, Parker told Ransom that the Union would be able to identify the men Parker was recruiting into Confederate service by a distinctive badge they wore.[16] (This method of identification was also sometimes employed on the Union side by the Enrolled Missouri Militia.)

After Parker's reply to Ransom, the two men broke off further written correspondence in favor of more intimate contact. On the evening of May 14, 1863, Parker's men and Ransom's detachment of the Sixth Kansas Cavalry skirmished south of Westport on the Missouri-Kansas line. "The so-styled Colonel Parker and his gang," as Ransom called the guerrillas, lost two men killed and three horses captured. Ransom dispatched two messengers with news of the skirmish, and one of them was shot from ambush and killed instantly not far from Westport on the morning of May 16.[17]

Later the same night, Ransom took up the chase after a different group of guerrillas who were passing to the east. The next day near Sni-a-Bar Creek in eastern Jackson County he came upon a concentration of men, numbering at least 150, under Parker and Quantrill. Because of the fortified position of the bushwhackers, Ransom declined to launch an assault, although he skirmished briefly with a small party of guerrillas who were delivering flour to the rebel camp.[18]

On May 17, Captain Charles F. Coleman of the Ninth Kansas Cavalry discovered a large camp of bushwhackers on Hog Island (also called Osage Island) in southern Bates County and called for reinforcements before attacking. By the time help arrived in the person of Major Alexander W. Mullins of the First Missouri State Militia Cavalry, the guerrillas had deserted the camp. The bushwhackers reportedly belonged to "one Colonel Parker's command," and Major Mullins rightly discerned that Parker was "organizing a force all along the border."[19]

South of Jackson County, Marchbanks and perhaps others were at work on Parker's behalf, and shortly after his arrival in the Kansas City area, Parker had begun commissioning captains to go into the northern counties with authority to recruit companies of eighty-four men each to be enlisted into the "Line Brigade" for duty in "the Partisan service Confederate States Army." Some of his recruiting officers were Bennet Wood, George W. Calvert, and Joe Hart.[20]

On May 21, a man walked into a saloon in Leavenworth and was quickly identified by the owner, Dick Brown, as "Col. Parker, the rebel who wrote that letter to Gen. Blunt." Brown had previously known Parker in Wyandotte, and one or two customers in the saloon identified the man, too. Also, he reportedly did not deny that his name was Parker. The man was arrested by a local policeman and turned over to military authorities, but he was released after a brief examination. It's not clear, however, whether the incident in the saloon was a case of mistaken identity or the man really was Parker but managed to convince the authorities that he was someone else.[21]

At any rate, Parker was soon heard from again in Missouri. On May 25, 1863, a bushwhacker named Jim Vaughan was arrested at Wyandotte and taken to Kansas City on a charge of being in armed resistance against the U. S. government. About the same time, Colonel Parker captured four Union soldiers who were on their way from Westport to Fort Scott. After a hasty trial, Vaughan was hanged at Kansas City late on the afternoon of May 26 on orders from General Blunt. At midnight of the same day, Parker, unaware that the death sentence had already been carried out, went to the home of a citizen living on the Blue River about fifteen miles south of Kansas City, roused him from his sleep, and compelled him to carry a message to Major Ransom at Westport to the effect that he would kill the four soldiers if Vaughan was executed. When Parker learned that he "was quite too late to be of any use to Vaughan," he promptly carried out his threat by hanging the four soldiers. Ransom, after receiving Parker's dispatch, sent some cavalry out to search the area where the bushwhackers were thought to be camped, but Parker fled before the Federals could come up with him.[22]

Still irate over Vaughan's execution, Parker drew up another proclamation on June 10, 1863, and forwarded it to Major Ransom:

> *To all whom it may concern*:
> Whereas on the 11th day of May A. D. 1863, a communication was addressed to the commanding officer of the Kansas District, to the effect that the Confederate States Government might know the character of warfare waged against the people of Missouri, and the spirit in which it was to be prosecuted; and whereas the State of Missouri being an integral part of the Confederate States Government, separate and apart from, free and independent of the Government of the United States and its civil and military authorities; and whereas the State of Missouri is sovereign in character, ceded to no despotic or arbitrary power, but governed by the will of her people; and whereas by authority vested in her chief magistrate, she did by proclamation sever her allegiance from the United States Government, by reason of the enforcement of despotic, unconstitutional and obnoxious laws; and whereas the General Assembly did by an act ratify the said proclamation, the members thereof being the legitimate representatives of the people; and whereas the United States Government has concentrated troops in the State of Missouri in opposition to the wishes of her people, and in violation of her constitution; and whereas we are to understand by the official reply of Maj. Gen. Blunt, commanding the District of Kansas, that a war of extermination is waged against the people of Missouri; and whereas his reply is taken for granted as the ultimatum of the

United States Government in relation to Missouri; and whereas he, Maj. Gen. Blunt, did by order have one James Vaughan, a Confederate soldier, executed by hanging in violation of the cartel of 1862; and whereas I did by military order No. 2, have executed one United States Major and four privates in retaliation. Now I, Benjamin F. Parker, Colonel commanding Confederate forces in Missouri, do solemnly declare that all men in the U. S. service and belonging to the District commanded by Gen. Blunt, captured in the State of Missouri, shall be treated as assassins and robbers; that all officers under my command are instructed to carry out this, my proclamation, until the inhuman policy inaugurated by him is stopped, and his nefarious and arbitrary orders are revoked.

Done at my Headquarters this the 10th day of June 1863.

BENJAMIN F. PARKER
Col. C. S. A.
Jackson County, Mo.

Parker requested that copies of the proclamation be forwarded to St. Louis newspapers for publication.[23]

His recent renunciation of Todd didn't prevent Parker from joining the Quantrill captain for an attack on a company of Federal soldiers near Westport in mid-June. On the 17th, Captain Henry Flesher was returning from Olathe, Kansas, to Westport with about sixty or seventy men of the Ninth Kansas Cavalry. After a long day's journey, the Federals were about a mile from their destination when they started down a narrow lane that was partially enclosed by a rock fence. Near the end of the lane, Parker and Todd waited in ambush with a large body of guerrillas behind the stone fence and concealed in timber. When the cavalry approached, the bushwhackers opened fire, killing about a dozen soldiers with the first barrage and driving the rest back down the lane the way they had come. The guerrillas gave chase, killing at least another dozen Federals before Flesher was able to form his men out on the prairie beyond the lane and repel the charge. The bushwhackers lost only three or four men during the attack.[24]

On June 29, Parker and three other guerrillas, including Cole Younger, were at Wellington in Lafayette County when four members of the Missouri State Militia rode into town about ten o'clock in the morning. Parker, who was dressed in a full Confederate uniform, ordered the Federals to halt and asked who they were. They replied by asking him who he was.[25]

"It's none of your damn business!" exclaimed Parker as he commenced firing.

The militia returned fire, killing Parker with the second shot. The other guerrillas, two of whom were dressed in Federal uniforms and the third in "orthodox butternut," managed to escape, although one was wounded in the melee.[26]

The Federals confiscated Parker's horse and two pistols, one of which was engraved with Parker's initials. They also took from the body Parker's commission and papers authorizing him to raise a regiment in Missouri. Two days later, the editor of the *Kansas City Daily Journal of Commerce* rejoiced, "B. F. Parker, Colonel C. S. A is dead! He has issued his last Proclamation!"[27]

Not quite! A couple of weeks after Parker's death, Dave Pool, a Quantrill lieutenant, took a Union man named "Colonel Childs" prisoner in Lafayette County and hauled him off to the woods to be hanged. The man's life was spared when some of his former friends among the bushwhackers spoke up on his behalf, but Pool swore that he planned to kill fifty Union men in retaliation for the death of Colonel Parker. It's highly unlikely that Pool killed that many Union men during the entire Civil War, but no doubt Parker would have been happy to know that someone was still issuing proclamations in his name.[28]

Not only did Parker not live long enough to complete the organization of his brigade, but at least two of his recruiters were also killed near the same time that he died. Bennet Wood was killed on June 20, nine days before Parker, just a few miles west of Wellington near Napoleon, and Joe Hart was killed in mid-July in Livingston County. George Calvert, another of Parker's captains, was captured in north Missouri in mid-June shortly after he, too, had issued a stirring proclamation. Thus ended the dream of Colonel B. F. Parker's "Line Brigade."[29]

After Parker's death, Quantrill reasserted his leadership among the guerrillas. As one Union observer noted on August 1, a month after Parker was killed, "Quantrill is now the chief in command of the bushwhacking forces south of the Missouri River."[30] Another three weeks later, Quantrill's standing among the guerrillas reached its terrible pinnacle when over four hundred men under his command carried out the Lawrence Massacre. One is tempted to wonder whether the enormity of Lawrence would still have occurred if Parker had lived. Or was his denunciation of uncivilized warfare mere rhetoric?

Frank James, member of Hart's band in spring 1863. (Author's Collection)

7
The Notorious and Desperate Rebel Joe Hart

As noted in the previous chapter, one of Colonel Parker's prominent recruiting officers was Joe Hart. (William Marchbanks, the subject of Chapter Two, was also loosely affiliated with Parker, although the connection between the two men is not as clear as the link between Parker and Hart.)

Joseph L. Hart, the oldest son of Felix and Rebecca Rentch Hart, was born about 1841 near Bardstown in Nelson County, Kentucky. Ten years later, the family moved to Andrew County, Missouri, a few miles northwest of Savannah near Fillmore.[1]

After the Civil War broke out, the twenty-year-old Hart was sworn into the Missouri State Guard on May 11, 1861, and went into camp near Rochester in Andrew County on August 25 under a Captain Sullivan. Presumably he took part in the Battle of Lexington, but few details of his state service are known. Sometime in the fall, he was commissioned a lieutenant and apparently sent to recruit in his home territory, although Union records suggest that he had simply come home on business and, instead of going back to his command, had turned to bushwhacking when his term of enlistment expired. At any rate, he was captured on December 9 and taken to St. Joseph. The district provost marshal, Lieutenant Stedman Hatch, said at the time that he considered Hart "a bad man" and thought that he had been "engaged in marauding while absent from his command."[2]

Hart was charged with being in arms against the U.S. government, but he somehow escaped before his case came to trial. According to Edwards, Hart joined Quantrill about this time, but the only official record shows that Hart was still serving as a lieutenant in the State Guard when he was recaptured on April 22, 1862, while recruiting in Jackson County. It's unlikely he was a member of Quantrill's command at this time, although he may have been operating in cooperation with Quantrill. Hart was held in the Kansas City area until early August, when he was shipped to St. Louis and committed to the Gratiot Street Prison. After about a week, he was transferred to the Alton Military Prison at Alton, Illinois. On

September 23, he was among the prisoners sent to Vicksburg for exchange at the same time Colonel Parker was also exchanged.[3]

According to Edwards, Hart was enlisted into regular Confederate service sometime in 1862 and was captured in August near Corinth, Mississippi, while serving with Sterling Price's army as a spy in Jo Shelby's command. Hart was taken for interrogation, so the story goes, into the presence of General Grant himself. Later the same night, Hart escaped from the tent where he was being held and returned to the Confederate camp. If such an incident happened, Edwards must have gotten the date wrong, because Hart was in prison in the St. Louis area throughout August of 1862.[4]

What is known for sure is that, by the fall 1862, Hart was back in the Trans-Mississippi as a first lieutenant in Major General Thomas C. Hindman's First Corp, Army of the West. On November 7, Colonel John M. Johnson appointed Hart as a recruiting officer for the Fifth Regiment Cavalry, Second Brigade, Fourth Division and charged him with enlisting a company of eighty-four men. The order was endorsed by Hindman.[5]

Armed with his new commission, Hart arrived in north Missouri around the first of the new year 1863. About the same time, he started keeping a diary that he filled with lyrical musings intermingled with mundane observations. One of his first entries was the beginning of a plaintive verse that read, "The land of my home is flitting,/Flitting from my view--" Presumably "home" was a reference to the Andrew County area where Hart had grown up. Shortly after penning the lines, he went north on a recruiting expedition; so perhaps his thoughts had turned to his homeland in anticipation of the trip.[6]

According to Edwards, Hart fell in with George Todd in January, was captured and chained in a dungeon while on a mission to St. Joseph, but pulled off another miraculous escape. What is known with certainty is that by the advent of spring Hart had been actively recruiting in north Missouri for some time and already had a reputation as a "notorious character." On March 1, a Federal scout went out from Liberty toward Missouri City in pursuit of Hart and captured one of his recruits, a man named Wiley Roberts, who was transferred to St. Joseph and incarcerated. By mid-March, Roberts was still resting in jail awaiting trial, along with another Clay County man who had been arrested and charged with harboring Hart and his guerrillas.[7]

In the Edwards myth, Hart, escape artist nonpareil, continued to amaze and mystify Union authorities during April and May with yet two more remarkable escapades. Again, all that is known for sure, though, is that Hart was still roaming over northeast Missouri during these months. On April 13, he, Bennet Wood, and another guerrilla came upon a party of militia and exchanged a few shots while on their way to the vicinity of Rochester in Andrew County. After spending a warm, pleasant day in the countryside, the budding poet Hart wrote in his diary, "Night comes on apace, throwing her sable mantle o'er the scene...." A few days later, back in Clay County, a squad of local militia surprised Hart and four of his followers and pursued the guerrillas so hotly that Hart lost his coat and pants in the melee.[8]

On May 1, Hart was camped with George W. Calvert and two other guerrillas named Price and Saunders north of St. Joseph in Andrew County not far from his old home. While laying over in the area, Hart sent for his sweetheart, Miss Alverda "Virdie" Kinnison, eighteen-year-old daughter of Davis and Mary Kinnison of Fillmore, and she came out into the country to meet him. It had been over a year since he had last seen Virdie, and the two young lovers spent a pleasant day together. Hart declared it "the happiest so far of my life."[9]

The literary young Hart had been reading the works of Washington Irving. One story, entitled "Broken Heart," made such an impression on him that he resolved the next day nevermore to coquette or trifle with the affections of his beloved Virdie, and when he returned to her arms the following day, May 3, the muse inspired him to new poetic heights:

> I am again in company with my dearest sweetheart, and Time is fast fleeing away on Golden Wings o'er me and her whom I love best of all on Earth. Today is a pleasant day, and the usual stillness of the Holy Sabbath is plainly to be noticed. Nothing breaks its Heavenly stillness except the soft rustling of the young leaves and the mournful cooing of the Turtle Dove, aided by the cheerful notes of many other birds. 'Tis evening

now, and my heart is filled with sadness to think that I and my girl must soon part, and perhaps forever. Still later, and 'tis midnight—Holy Hour! All the world is wrapped in dream and sleep; but I am still sitting by my Virdie's side, my arm is softly around her slender waist—softly I press her to my beating Heart, and one, two, three, yes, half a dozen sweet kisses I steal from her pouting lips, and three o'clock is here! We part! Oh, shall I ever forget this Hour! Shall I ever forget the glance of that dark Eye! the sweet, mournful smile of that Fair Face! the soft thrilling pressure of that Little Hand! the sweet magic of Her Kisses! never! no never! Rather let my right hand forget its cunning—my eye its correctness of vision—or my tongue its Truthfulness! We have parted, and I am lonely, heartsick, and weary of Life....[10]

From the Fillmore area, Hart ranged northwest into Atchison County, where the fickle Joe, putting aside his promise not to coquette, made the acquaintance of twenty-year-old Miss Kessiah "Kate" Rupe, "a lively girl, with whom I passed the entire day very pleasantly." That night, Hart moved off to the east toward Possum Walk in neighboring Nodaway County. He was halted by a party of Federal soldiers but, after talking to them awhile, he was allowed to pass on.[11]

On May 10, Hart, still in company with Calvert, Price, and Saunders, was on Honey Creek in eastern Nodaway County, where a party of Federals drove the guerrillas from their camp. Hart lost his horse in the skirmish, but he promptly re-mounted himself by stealing a horse and a Navy pistol from a Union citizen in the neighborhood.[12]

A week later, May 17, Hart was back in Andrew County, where he once again rendezvoused with his darling Virdie. "I spent a pleasant day with my sweetheart," he told his diary, "and left her sorrowfully. She looked so mournfully sweet, and kissed me with such tenderness that a loving calm has fallen upon my soul." On the same day of his meeting with his sweetheart, Hart had a "difficulty" with a citizen who balked at giving up his horse to the bushwhacking cause, but perhaps the altercation occurred earlier in the day before the tranquilizing effect of Virdie's love had taken hold.[13]

After leaving Virdie on May 17, Hart started south and, on May 20, met up in Clay County north of Liberty with a bushwhacking band that included Frank James and Moses McCoy. The guerrillas had just come from Missouri City, where the previous day they had attacked a party of five Federal soldiers, killing two officers and seriously wounding a third man. Hart told the guerrillas he had come direct from St. Joseph and that, before leaving, he had paid a visit to McCoy's wife, who had recently been transported to the town and placed on parole there after being arrested in Clay County for aiding Hart and his men.[14]

After rendezvousing with his guerrilla friends in northern Clay County, Hart led them into Clinton County and camped at the edge of Plattsburg on the night of the 20th. Early on the morning of the 21st, the guerrillas rode into Plattsburg and took possession of the place. They stole over $11,000 in "commutation money" from the courthouse. Part of the state military fund, this was money and warrants received from men who had purchased exemption from the Enrolled Missouri Militia. The guerrillas burned the warrants, then plundered the stores and dwellings of the town. They also took several prisoners, including Lieutenant-Colonel Charles Porter, but released them on parole, despite the fact that the same gang just two days earlier had summarily executed two captives.[15] (Colonel Porter and his fellow prisoners were probably spared because, unlike the officers killed at Richfield, they were not uniformed Federal soldiers.)

On May 24, Hart and three other guerrillas went to Carpenter's Store in Clinton County not far from Plattsburg and got into an affray with the owner. (No doubt the merchant objected to the impressment of his property for the Southern cause.) Carpenter and his son fired on the bushwhackers, and when the guerrillas returned fire, the merchant was slightly wounded. Unable to plunder the store, the guerrillas stole four horses belonging to Carpenter. They also tried to burn his house, but the merchant's wife and his Negro servants put out the fire. The gang demanded dinner that evening at the home of a man named David Bevins ten miles north of Liberty, but he refused to serve them and somehow managed to turn them away without a shot being fired. Later the same night, the band showed up at the small community of Centreville, where they took three or four horses. The next day, Hart and four sidekicks, while on a "foraging" expedition, exchanged a few shots with a party of militia but still managed to appropriate two more horses and two weapons, among other gear.[16]

Near the end of the month of May 1863, Hart was shot at by Federal troops while checking the whereabouts of a skiff on which the guerrillas planned to cross the Missouri River. While retreating to camp, he was fired on again by another party of soldiers. One bullet went through the brim of his hat, another nicked the shoulder of his coat, and a third grazed him in the head just behind his ear. Later, when the bushwhackers returned to the river, they found it so well guarded that they had to seek another place to cross. Hart and six companions finally managed to get over to Jackson County on a homemade raft, although three of their horses drowned while swimming behind the makeshift craft.[17]

Hart promptly formed a juncture with Colonel Parker and joined the Line Brigade. From his headquarters at the Sni-a-Bar Schoolhouse on May 31, 1863, Parker renewed Hart's commission as a recruiting officer and gave him the rank of captain. The order read as follows:

> I, the undersigned, by virtue of authority in me vested, do authorize and empower Joseph L. Hart to recruit and command one company of troopers for the Line Brigade, as authorized by the Secretary of War, and joint orders issued to Chas. Harrison and Benjamin F. Parker. The company to compose a part of said Brigade, and enlisted for the Partisan service, C. S. Army. The enlistments regulated in accordance with instructions issued by the Col. Commanding—to be mustered in by the commanding officer of said brigade at the time and place by him designated.
>
> Signed,
> B. F. Parker, Colonel
> and charged with Recruiting Partisan Troops.

The order was witnessed by Bennet K. Wood, Captain of Recruits, and it was also signed by Hart, who pledged "to observe and carry out the directions and provisions of the above order to the full extent of my ability."[18]

Parker also issued an addendum to the order, providing additional instructions and authority:

> *To Joseph L. Hart:*
>
> Sir: You are instructed to issue company commissions to five Recruiting Officers, to enlist men in any county in the State of Missouri for the Partisan service, to be mustered into the Line Brigade when filled, or per orders from the Colonel commanding. The companies to muster, rank and file, eighty-four (84) men, unless otherwise determined.
>
> Signed, B. F. Parker
> Colonel Commanding

Hart began recruiting immediately, using the following oath to swear in the new enlistees:

> I, _____, do solemnly swear or affirm, to enlist for during the war in the Partisan service of the C. S. Army, to be attached to, and recruited for, the Missouri Line Brigade; that I will protect, support and defend the Constitution of the Confederate States of America, and resist all invasion of Confederate Territory against Federal arms; that I will obey, and willingly execute all orders of commanding officers of said Brigade, whether written or oral; that I will observe with care and decision the regulations and provisions of all military orders; and, further, by strict adherence to the army rules I will make indispensable the duty devolving upon its ranks.
>
> This, I answer, so help me God.[19]

Some of Hart's first recruits were apparently men who had already been riding with him prior to his commission from Parker. After quickly gathering a small band in the Jackson County area, Hart re-crossed the Missouri River and headed toward his old stomping grounds of north Missouri. Around the third or fourth of June, 1863, the Clinton County militia skirmished with Hart's band and reported

killing five. The same two forces fought again on the sixth, and seven
more guerrillas were supposedly sent "to kingdom come." Hart told
his diary that, although his band was broken up, he "had the
satisfaction of killing the officer in command of the militia." The
following day, June 7, one of the bushwhackers was captured near
Laclede in Linn County while trying to make his escape out of the
state along the line of the Hannibal Railroad. He was taken to
Chillicothe in neighboring Livingston County, and most of the money
stolen at Plattsburg was found on his person.[20]

After the fight in Clinton County, Hart ranged north into
Andrew County, where he visited his old neighborhood, but his
family was nowhere to be found. To the romantic young Hart, his
homeland must have seemed a forlorn place, because his sweetheart,
Virdie Kinnison, had also relocated, having moved into St. Joseph in
late May.[21]

After a few days in the Andrew County area, Hart started
south again. Near the middle of June, he appeared in southern
Buchanan County, where, in an attempt to procure supplies, he went
to the home of a German farmer and presented himself as a Union
soldier. The suspicious farmer balked at the guerrilla's demands and
managed to stall until a company of militia made their appearance on
the scene. When Hart spotted them coming up the road, he took off
running. The farmer retrieved a revolver and fired several shots at the
fleeing bushwhacker. One of them wounded Hart in the leg, but he
reached the brush and was aided in his getaway by five or six of his
men, who'd been lurking nearby. In his haste, Hart had left his horse
tied to a fence, and the farmer handed it over to the militia when they
arrived. It turned out to be the horse that had been stolen from Captain
Sessions, one of the officers killed at Richfield.[22]

Hart's wound must have been superficial because it didn't
stop him from crossing into Clinton County and stealing "by force of
arms" a "fine iron grey mare" from James F. Vaughan to take the
place of the horse he'd just been forced to abandon, and it didn't keep
him from continuing his journey south. Back in Jackson County, Hart
participated in Parker and Todd's attack on the Federal cavalry south
of Westport on June 17.[23]

Later in the month, still in Jackson County, he momentarily put down his guns in favor of a pen and issued a proclamation in the style of his commanding officer and mentor, Colonel Parker. Hart's declaration took the form of a letter written on June 27, 1863, to Captain William Garth, commander of the Union post at Liberty, and forwarded to the *Liberty Tribune* for publication:

> As I have no other means of ascertaining the ultimatum of the Government which you represent and as I am led to suppose from your late actions that you would not respect a flag of truce from me upon any mission whatever, I seize upon this the only means of correspondence which I have left with you for the purpose of ascertaining some facts relative to paroling and exchanging prisoners, important alike to you and I (sic) and to your men and mine. It seems, sir, that your Government, or its representatives at least, yourself among the number, are determined not to regard the Recruiting officer or partisan troops of the Confederacy as soldiers entitled to the privilege and conditions of war usually observed and entered into by civilized Nations for the soldiers of each opposing party. I have ascertained from sources whose veracity cannot be doubted that prisoners captured and paroled by me have not and will not be respected by you or your commanding officers as such, viz. The case of James C. Courtney was not respected by Col. Moss, and again the case of James Vaughan was not respected by you. I do not wish to inaugurate in upper Missouri the savage mode of warfare which has been inaugurated in Jackson and other counties of Southern Missouri by the United States forces, and which I consider as partly inaugurated by your troops, and which is at present devastating that fair portion of our State and entailing the most miserable and frightful consequences upon the innocent and defenseless citizens thereof. But, sir, if the prisoners James Vaughan and James C. Courtney are not respected as paroled prisoners by your authorities and allowed to go to their homes, there to remain until exchanged, they shall whenever (if ever) captured by any forces under my command be immediately executed by shooting. And furthermore all soldiers in the employ or service of the United States

Government shall be immediately shot to death whenever captured by any forces under my command. Unless the above named prisoners shall be respected as paroled prisoners, and all others that shall hereafter be paroled by me, and all soldiers in the employ or service of the C. S. A., captured partisan or Regular troops, shall and must be respected by you as prisoners of war, subject to exchange and all the privileges of war, otherwise the punishment, hereinbefore mentioned shall be extended with the utmost severity to all persons in the United States service, whenever captured by me, or forces under my command. And furthermore if another house should be burned within your command, in consequence of my having been about, or having received comfort thereat, I shall immediately cause two for one to be burned, and if any citizen of Southern sympathies should be murdered in consequence of my having been about, I shall immediately cause two Union citizens to be put to death in the same manner, or if any Confederate soldier should be captured by your troops and by them or you murdered, I will execute by hanging the first five Militiamen or United States soldiers who may chance to fall into my hands.

Hoping sir, that the cases of Lieut. Col. Charles Porter, Col. James H. Birch Jr., and others paroled at different times by me will be taken as evidence of the fact that I do not wish to carry on a warfare of bloodshed wherein no quarter will be shown, but have on the contrary been guided by a wish to avert such a warfare which I deem would be a calamity, both to your soldiers and mine, and I hope that you will appreciate the humane policy and motive which I have shown and wish to extend to all of my foes, who may chance to fall into my hands. And furthermore hoping that you may give me an answer to this through the columns of the next *Liberty Tribune,* therein setting forth the policy which you intend to pursue and thereby preventing a needless effusion of blood,

> I remain most respectfully sir,
> Your most obedient servant
> Joseph L. Hart,
> Captain and Recruiting Officer, Frontier Line
> Brigade, C. S. A.[24]

Hart apparently didn't tarry long awaiting a reply to his tirade, because a week after writing the letter he was back in his old haunts of northern Missouri, again in his home county of Andrew. On the night of July 4, near Savannah, he and his gang killed a man named John Breckinridge for refusing to feed them.[25]

Then on the evening of July 7, 1863, Hart and a band of about fifteen or twenty guerrillas called at the home of a Union man named Harrison Burns six miles north of Savannah not far from where Hart had grown up. (The Hart family had recently left the area and had not returned.) Near the beginning of the war, Hart had been romantically interested in Burns's daughter, but Burns had ordered Hart to leave the girl alone and to stay off his property. Apparently still nursing the old grudge, Hart had now returned to exact revenge.[26]

The daughter was now married to a former Union soldier named George Henry, and, as luck would have it, he happened to be at the Burns home with his father-in-law when Hart paid his unwelcome visit. Another man named George Jenkins was also present, and all three were current members of the Andrew County militia. When the Union men refused to give up their arms, the bushwhackers promptly shot Henry through the head, killing him instantly. Then they grabbed Jenkins by his hair to hold him down and tried to shoot him in the head also. The bullet, however, entered his cheek and passed out through his jaw without fatally wounding him. Next the gang threw Burns to the floor and shot him in the face while he was on his knees. The ball passed through his jaw and lodged in his arm, seriously wounding him.[27]

After confiscating four Navy revolvers from the dead and wounded men, the guerrillas rode to the nearby home of a farmer named Van Horn and ransacked the house looking for money. When the search turned up nothing of value, Hart forced Van Horn to mount behind him on his horse and guide the gang to the house of a neighbor named Graff, from whom the bushwhackers stole sixty dollars. The guerrillas then took to the brush as daylight approached.[28]

A St. Joseph newspaper, in reporting the raid, described Joe Hart as "a fine looking man, about five feet ten, robust, healthy, fair favored and slightly inclined to be erratic in his movements." The editor added that Hart "is a great stickler for the old Constitution, and abhors Lincoln's outrageous violations of that sacred instrument. So great is his hatred of the friends of the U. S. Government that he murders them on sight."[29]

The night following Hart's Andrew County foray, several Southern-sympathizing farmers who lived in the immediate neighborhood of Mr. Graff were called to their doors and shot on the spot by area Union men in retaliation for the previous night's raid.[30]

Moving east from Andrew County, Hart and his men roamed into Livingston County north of Chillicothe. While in the area, Hart took up his pen again on July 13, 1863, and wrote a letter to his parents. He began by reporting on his brothers, both of whom had previously joined the Confederate Army. Hart had some men in his command who had just come from the army, and they told him that they'd seen his twenty-year-old brother George, a first lieutenant in Brigadier General John S. Marmaduke's division, around the 20th of May in southeastern Missouri and that he was well and in good spirits. Joe relayed the message to his mother and dad. Then he broke the sad news that his eighteen-year-old brother John had been mortally wounded at Springfield in January during Marmaduke's first invasion of Missouri. Young Hart assured his parents that John "fell like a hero.... I, with you, will always mourn his untimely death; yet he could not have died in a better cause."[31]

Next, Hart gave his parents an account of his recent raid through Andrew County. He mentioned Harrison Burns and George Henry by name, but he said he didn't know the third victim he'd shot at the Burns home. He said the only reason the three men were shot was that they refused to surrender their weapons, and he apologized for having to shoot them in the presence of women. He further justified the shootings by naming two citizens whom he claimed the three men had helped murder.[32]

Hart then boasted that he planned to bring "the whole Quantrill Regiment" across the Missouri River and "kill off Andrew County--every last devil--and they know it. You bet they fly when they hear of me up here. They say I am a d--d sight worse than Quantrill, and that my men would sooner die than live."[33]

The letter went on to describe Hart's other recent exploits including the raid at Plattsburg and a recent fight with Federals in

Jackson County in which nearly forty Union soldiers and only three rebels were killed. This was presumably a reference to Todd and Parker's attack on Captain Flesher's cavalry below Westport on June 17.[34]

Hart closed the letter by giving instructions on how to address return mail to him and where to send it. Because he didn't know where his parents were, he addressed the current letter to his Cousin Sallie with a request that she forward it to them.[35]

The young bushwhacker never got a chance to mail the letter he wrote to his parents. On the evening of July 13, the same day he'd written the letter, he and a small band of four or five guerrillas were camped near Spring Hill about ten miles northwest of Chillicothe when a party of Enrolled Missouri Militia under Lieutenant David Gibbs came upon them. The bushwhackers broke for the woods, but Hart paused at the edge of the timber, turned, and started shooting as his companions skedaddled into the brush. Taking deliberate aim, a militiaman named William Matthews brought "the notorious and desperate rebel" down with a single shot. The ball passed through his neck, severing the main artery and killing him instantly.[36]

The Federals took from Hart's body two Navy Colt revolvers, a "silk flag of Jeff Davis' kingdom," a field glass (taken at Richfield), and his memorandum book or diary. They also confiscated four horses and several items of clothing. They buried Hart without ceremony on the spot where he was killed. They gave him no coffin and no stone or marker to indicate the location. However, opined the *St. Joseph Weekly Herald*, "if any romantic young female rebel should chance to be smitten with a desire to pay tribute to his memory, the people of the section in which his carcass is rotting will point out the spot."[37]

Hart's papers, soaked with his blood, were brought to St. Joseph, and many of them were published in a local newspaper. Among his papers were the orders under which he had been recruiting, the letter he had written to his parents, and a letter he had received from his "lady love," Virdie Kinnison, written after she had moved to St. Joseph. Also found was a carefully folded piece of paper with the words "We met" written on the outside. On the inside, Hart had copied a poem entitled "We Met, 'Twas in a Crowd," and a dot of blood stained the center of the paper. "Hart wrote a beautiful hand," concluded the editor, "very similar to a lady's chirography, and his papers bear evidence that the author was a man of very fair ability and education."[38]

Less than a week after Hart's death, two of his men, H. F. Cowherd and Thomas F. Campbell, were captured in Caldwell County. They said they had been recruited by Hart in Jackson County in June and that they had been with him when he was killed. They said he had been shot once in the head, and they thought perhaps he had also been shot in the breast, although they couldn't tell for sure since they were "retreating."[39]

In December of 1864, a year and a half after Joe Hart's death, his brother George was wounded and captured by a Federal scout sent out from Stewartsville on the DeKalb-Clinton County line. He was imprisoned at Macon, then given the oath of allegiance and released in early April of the following year.[40] Regardless of political persuasion, one can only hope that he survived the war and went home to a relatively peaceful existence. Having already sacrificed two sons to America's bloody Civil War, Felix and Rebecca Hart had suffered enough.

The Elusive Jim Rider

Although Missouri guerrilla leader James William "Jim" Rider was mentioned in a few Union after-action reports near the end of the Civil War and was remembered by local historians after the war, little was known until recently about his specific activities. New information gleaned from Union documents reveals Rider, who operated as a Confederate partisan in the north-central part of the state from near the beginning of the conflict until its very end, to be one of the more interesting characters of the Civil War in Missouri, but the facts surrounding his origins and his fate at the end of the war remain something of a mystery.[1]

At least one researcher has identified Jim Rider's father as James M. Rider of Macon County, Missouri, but it is clear from Civil War soldiers' service records and other sources that the James H. Rider (often called Henry), who was the son of James M. Rider, was not the same man who became a guerrilla leader. What is known for sure about the origins of Jim Rider is that he was closely related to George Rider of Saline County, Missouri. The preponderance of evidence, including the 1850 Saline County census listing a thirteen-year-old boy named James in the household of George Rider, points to George as Jim's father. However, other evidence suggests that George was, instead, Jim's uncle, while still other evidence points away from George Rider altogether. As we shall see, some of this contrary evidence was left by Jim Rider himself, perhaps planted as a way to deflect Union suspicion away from his family. If this is true, it would add credibility to the idea that George Rider was, in fact, Jim's father.[2]

Regardless of Jim Rider's exact origins, in the late 1850s he took up residence in the Chillicothe area, where Jason C. Oliver, thought to be Jim's uncle, lived. On October 2, 1860, in Livingston County, Jim married fifteen-year-old Tabitha Winkler, daughter of Andrew G. and Millie Farnel Winkler.[3]

At the outbreak of the Civil War, Jim Rider "went off and left" Tabitha, as she later testified, and she went to stay with her aunt Margaret Snead in Livingston County. Signing up to fight, Rider was enlisted into the Missouri State Guard in Carroll County in June of 1861 by General William Y. Slack, assigned to Colonel Benjamin Rives's regiment of Slack's division, and, according to his own later testimony, elected captain of Company B.[4]

Rider did not, however, accompany Rives to southern Missouri, where the state troops met and defeated a Union force under Colonel Franz Sigel at the Battle of Carthage on July 5, 1861. Instead, Rider roamed north of the Missouri River and showed up on July 9, 1861, in Caldwell County, where he confronted Michael West, his wife's stepfather, outside a Breckinridge store owned by J.A. Price. Tabitha Rider's father, Andrew Winkler, had died, and her mother, Millie, had remarried West in December of 1859. Apparently bad blood existed between Rider and West, although the cause of any such animosity is not known. At any rate, the confrontation between the two men on the morning of the ninth quickly turned violent. The storeowner reported hearing gunshots in the rear lot of his store, and, racing outside, he saw West lying on the ground critically wounded and Rider standing over West holding a double-barrel shotgun in one hand and a revolver in the other. Price said that he "spoke sharply" to Rider, ordering him to desist, but that Rider paid no attention and fired two shots from the pistol at the fallen man. Rider then made his getaway, and West died within a few minutes.[5]

Two other witnesses gave testimony similar to Price's, to the effect that Jim Rider knocked West down with one or two shotgun blasts and then continued shooting him with a revolver after he was down. A fourth man testified that he met Rider just outside town shortly after the incident, that Rider "looked frightened and was going in a hurry," that he asked Rider what the matter was, and that Rider told him he had just killed Michael West.[6]

We know from post-war local histories that Jim Rider, operating with the likes of Livingston County partisan leaders Lewis Best and Joseph Kirk, continued to roam through the counties of north-central Missouri during the fall of 1861. Kirk, like Rider, had joined the Missouri State Guard at the outset of the war and received a commission but soon returned home, ostensibly to recruit for the Southern cause. Kirk, Rider, and Best may, in fact, have found time to do some recruiting, but they spent much of their time skirmishing with Federal forces and preying on Union citizens, although the county histories are generally short on detail in describing their exploits. At one point during the fall of 1861, guerrillas under Best, Rider, and John Blackburn gathered in Livingston County near Spring Hill with plans to overrun the federal garrison at Chillicothe, but when a spy sent into town brought back word that such a design could only be accomplished with the loss of life, the mission was abandoned. Another incident, one for which Rider was later charged by Union authorities, was the theft of a span of black horses in November of 1861 in Carroll County from a Union man named Spriggs.[7]

On April 14, 1862, Jim Rider, Thomas Joseph Ballew, William R. King, and Scott Kissinger were captured by Union authorities in Chariton County, presumably while engaged in some sort of guerrilla activity, although the details of their arrest are not known. They were taken to Jefferson City, where they were formally charged with "violating the laws and customs of war." The specification was that they had taken up arms as insurgents against the United States and committed acts of hostility against U.S. military forces while not part of an organized army. Rider and Ballew gave their county of residence at the time as Livingston, while King was from Carroll County and Kissinger from Caldwell County. The men were tried before a military commission convened on May 16, 1862. They were found guilty and sentenced "to be shot to death at such time and place as the commanding general may designate." The proceedings of the commission were forwarded to President Lincoln for his review prior to the sentence being carried out, and he ruled the death sentence "inoperative" in all four cases, as it had not been approved by the officer ordering the court. Lincoln directed that the four men be released from arrest.[8]

The presidential reprieve, however, hardly mattered in the cases of Rider and Ballew, as they had already effected their own sort of reprieve. On the early morning of July 1, Rider, Ballew and a "desperate character" named Charles W. Turpin managed to make their escape during a heavy rainstorm. Lieutenant Charles O. Patier, the provost marshal at Jefferson City, blamed their escape on the storm and the intense darkness of the night, which gave the guerrillas cover for their escapade.[9]

After his escape, Rider returned to his home in Saline County, where in July, according to his later testimony, he received a commission to recruit from Colonel Caleb Dorsey, who was raising a regiment for Confederate service. He didn't stay in the area long, though, because by the end of July he was back in his old territory north of the river. Reverting to the same type of antics for which he had recently been sentenced to death, he went on a rampage in Carroll and Livingston counties, robbing a store in Carroll and preying on Union citizens of both counties.[10]

Phillip Best testified that Jim Rider and five other men came to his store in Carrollton while the Federal troops stationed there were away from their post in late July or early August and "demanded of him his politics." Rider kept his hand near his revolver and partially drew the pistol several times as the rest of the men began ransacking the store for goods. The guerrillas ended up taking several pairs of jeans and boots, some hats, a number of knives, and other miscellaneous merchandise.[11]

On August 1, Jim Rider and about fifteen other men waylaid William Siniard on a road in Carroll County, according to Siniard's own testimony, and took his horses and wagon from him, leaving him stranded five miles from home. Siniard later learned that the gang had been to his house prior to accosting him on the road and had taken an overcoat and $33 in gold. Siniard's wife came home just as the bushwhackers were leaving her place, and she followed them to a neighbor's house, where Rider supposedly bragged to her that he had been caught by Union authorities three times before but that he always escaped.[12]

One of the young men accompanying Rider during the Siniard caper was nineteen-year-old Newton Woolsey, who later testified against Rider. Woolsey said that, during his "scout" with the guerrillas, Rider told him that he was a lieutenant under Captain Logan Ballew, who was recruiting a company for Confederate service. He said he heard Rider tell Siniard that, if he ever heard of Siniard abusing Southern men, he would "ruin him" but that Rider ended up giving back the overcoat he had taken from Siniard.[13]

Near the same time as the Siniard robbery, Rider also went to the home of twenty-one-year-old J.W. Mitchell in Carroll County and robbed Mitchell's mother of a horse, a saddle, a bridle, two pairs of pants, some other clothes, three bed blankets, and sundry other items. As he prepared to leave, Rider told Mitchell that he would take him (Mitchell) with him if not for the fact that the young man had "sore eyes" and he did not want any "blind men."[14]

Sometime in August of 1862, Rider and others came to the house of John W. Stone in Carroll County about eleven or twelve o'clock at night, called him out of bed, and began verbally abusing him and the Federal authorities. Rider, whom Stone called a "notorious jayhawker," told Stone that if he caught the Federal militia scouting around Stone's house, he would kill them. Before leaving, he made the same brag to Stone that he had made to Mrs. Siniard about having escaped from Federal authorities two or three times.[15]

Other citizens whom Rider victimized in the Carroll County area around this same time included Isham Grace and Martin Risener. Rider and his marauders reportedly relieved Grace of a gray mare, and they went to Risener's home and robbed him of goods valued at $65. Risener said that Rider was a "notorious thief" and that he was pretty sure Rider had jayhawked in his neighborhood four or five times before.[16]

Jim Rider's raids, though, were not confined to Carroll County during the summer of 1862. Sometime in early August, Rider ranged into Livingston County and called at the home of Owen Gale, where he helped himself to a horse, a saddle, a bridle, a coat, a pair of boots, and a blanket. According to Gale, Rider admitted that he also had been to the Gale farm two weeks earlier and taken some jewelry, tobacco, whiskey, and other items. After the most recent visit, as Rider started to leave, he warned Gale not to follow him, saying that if he did, one of them would have to "go up."[17]

Later in August, according to Rider's own testimony, he went south with Colonel Dorsey to join the regular Confederate army, but he did not stay long. In late September, shortly before the Battle of Newtonia, Rider came back to his home territory, armed with a commission from Colonel Joseph O. Shelby to recruit for the Southern army.[18]

Back home in the fall of 1862, Rider resumed the marauding activities he had carried out earlier in the year, roaming over Carroll and surrounding counties. In October, according to the 1881 Carroll County history, a scouting party of thirty Union militiamen went out looking for a band of sixteen guerrillas under Logan Ballew and chased them through Carroll County toward Chariton. On the Grand River just across the county line in Chariton, the guerrillas sprang an ambush, killing Judge James Tolson of Grundy County and wounding a second militiaman. The Union soldiers returned fire, killing one bushwhacker, severely wounding another, and capturing sixteen horses. However, Jim Rider, who was thought to be among the guerrillas, made his escape, along with Captain Ballew. During November, according to the county history, rumors occasionally reached Carrollton that Rider was passing through the county at the head of a large party of guerrillas, and the militia "kept up an interest in his movements" but apparently had little inclination to engage him. The local history described Rider as "bold and adventurous but not scrupulously honest and with a fondness for horseflesh" and added that he "was dreaded by many of the Union citizens of the county, and by some of the Confederates." The 1886 *History of Livingston County*, for its part, said that Jackson Township in the northwest part of Livingston was "in a state of war" in 1862 and that the "exploits and hair-breadth escapes of the partisans of both sides," including Joe Kirk, John Blackburn, and Jim Rider on the Southern side, "...were numerous and highly perilous."[19]

On the evening of January 15, 1863, a Union scout sent out from Marshall, Missouri, captured Jim Rider at the home of William Arthur in the bottoms of northwest Saline County, downriver from Waverly. William Evans was captured by the same scout at or near the same time and place. Rider had on his person his appointment from Shelby, a document that Colonel Dorsey had given him, and a forged pass to go to Illinois, made out to "John Wilkes." Evans, who had just returned from the Confederate army, had in his possession twenty-nine letters from Carroll County women written to their husbands, sons, brothers, and lovers who were then in the Confederate army in Arkansas. Evans and Rider had presumably gathered the letters in Carroll County with plans to deliver them or have them delivered to Arkansas. According to Lieutenant-Colonel William A. Wilson, commanding the Seventy-first Enrolled Missouri Militia at Marshall, nearly all the letters expressed "the bitterest feelings against the United States Government, as well as against all Union people."[20]

Rider and Evans were taken to Marshall, where Rider told Wilson that, in addition to his appointment from Shelby, he also held a commission to recruit for the Confederate army signed by General Thomas Hindman but that he had lost the paperwork. Reporting the capture of Rider and Evans to the *Jefferson City Missouri State Times* on January 22, Wilson said that Rider "hails from Carroll County, and from Chillicothe, and I have it on good authority that he has committed, in Carroll County, many bad acts."[21]

While Rider was still being held at Marshall, Colonel Wilson and Union officers at surrounding posts began gathering evidence to be used against him. In a letter dated January 18 at Waverly, J. Walton wrote to Wilson that he had learned, since Wilson's men had been in the Waverly area a few days earlier, that Jim Rider "was what they called the captain of that company that robbed me last September." Walton said he knew Rider was the man because he had it on good authority "by a lady in the bottom." Walton concluded that Rider was "a bad man."[22]

On January 23, Lieutenant Samuel B. Wait, assistant provost marshal at Carrollton, wrote to the post at Marshall assuring Colonel Wilson that he was taking down affidavits against Rider as fast as he could get them but that some of the witnesses lived a good distance away and it might take several days. Wait said, "Rider is a perfect outlaw, and I think I will be able to prove that he killed his father-in-law. Rider made his brag to one of the witnesses that he had been a prisoner three times but was too sharp for the Federals—that he had always escaped before they could make him take the oath." Wait concluded that, if he had control of Rider, he would put him in irons and in jail and double bar the door or else hang the scoundrel.[23]

Over the next week to ten days, Wait and W.D. McDonald, the acting assistant provost marshal at Breckinridge, took a number of statements from witnesses pertaining to Jim Rider's marauding activities in Carroll County and to the killing of Michael West in Caldwell County. On February 6, Wait wrote to Colonel Wilson again exhorting him not to release Rider until all the evidence had been forwarded. Wait said that Rider had been arrested four times and always exchanged and that he always returned to Carroll County upon his release. He further stated that Rider was "a murderous and notorious jayhawker" and that he did not believe he belonged to General Hindman's command.[24]

By February 6, however, Jim Rider was no longer held at Marshall. On February 2, Colonel Wilson escorted him to Gratiot Street Prison in St. Louis, where Federal authorities took his statement two days later. Rider said he was married but had no children and was a millwright by occupation. He gave his age as twenty-eight and his residence as Saline County. However, he said he was born in Troy County, New York (a predecessor of Rensselaer County). This latter assertion was almost certainly not true and appears to be one of several attempts by Rider to misdirect Union authorities concerning his family origins. Unfortunately the misleading facts left by Rider have served to confuse historians and genealogists as well.[25]

Discounting William Evans, Rider said he "had no forces or any party" with him when he was captured. He explained that the pass for John Wilkes he had with him at the time was one he had found in a letter he had picked up along the road and that he had thrown the letter away. Rider admitted that he was in arms against the United States, and he said he had never taken the oath of allegiance to the U.S. Rider added that he was still wearing the same clothes he was wearing when he was captured: a gray overcoat with black buttons and gray pantaloons.[26]

On February 12, Robert S. Moore, the assistant provost marshal for Livingston County, wrote to St. Louis advising Colonel F.A. Dick, provost marshal general for the Department of the Missouri, that Jim Rider was a "notorious bushwhacker" who "ought to have been shot when taken and not taken to St. Louis." Moore said that he had no evidence at the present time but that, if Dick wanted him to procure some in relation to Rider's guerrilla activities, he would do so as soon as possible. About the same time, Wait and McDonald forwarded to St. Louis the evidence they had collected as well.[27]

On March 14, Rider was ordered for trial before a military commission headed by Colonel W. H. Shaw on charges of murder, robbery, and violating the laws and customs of war. On April 18, the order was withdrawn and replaced by a similar order directing that Rider be tried, instead, by a commission headed by Brigadier General John McNeil. The commission was scheduled to convene in June.[28]

While James Rider languished at Gratiot Street Prison in the spring of 1863, sixty-year-old George Rider of Saline County came under suspicion of having fed and harbored guerrillas, and an investigation was launched into the matter. Summoned to Marshall to appear before Union authorities, Rider admitted that he had fed three guerrillas but only because he was forced to and that he only gave them a "cold supper." He was allowed to depart without taking an oath of allegiance because he had already taken a similar oath in connection with his duty as a road overseer; however the investigation into the question of his loyalty continued. A neighbor named James Rickman testified in early June that Rider had admitted to him the previous October that his son had "gone in the brush." Another neighbor, J.C. Rogers, testified that George Rider had expressed himself in sympathy with the rebellion and that he had fed fifteen bushwhackers, not the three he claimed. Rogers also said that Rider had told him the previous fall that "James Rider staid and eat and slept at his house frequently." Rogers added that James Rider was noted throughout the country as a bushwhacker and horse thief. Alfred L. Towles signed an affidavit that he saw George Rider shortly after he had left his meeting with Federal authorities and that Rider seemed "very much satisfied at the way he got off" and that he was "under the influence of spirits."[29]

The Rickman and Rogers depositions would seem to constitute strong evidence that George Rider was, indeed, the father of James W. Rider. However, Rogers did not say that James Rider was George Rider's son, and the fact that he did not seems almost to imply the contrary. It is possible that the son Rickman was talking about was not James Rider.

During the wee hours of the morning of July 23, 1863, James Rider and six other men escaped from Gratiot Street Prison in St. Louis by prying some bricks from a fireplace and wielding them as weapons against their guards. They rushed a sentinel stationed at the front door of the hall where they were housed, struck him a heavy blow on the arm with one of the bricks, and took his musket. They also attacked a guard stationed just outside the door on the front porch and stuck him a couple of blows but were unable to wrest his musket away. A night watchman in front of the prison, hearing the scuffle on the porch, unlocked the front gate and was hurrying with pistol in hand to the aid of the sentinel on the porch when the latter mistook him for one of the prisoners and shot the revolver out of his hand. The desperate half-dozen then rushed toward a porch window near where another guard was sleeping. Aroused by the commotion, the guard started to rise, when he, too, was struck a blow with one of the bricks. The prisoners then leaped through the window to the ground below and made their escape, presumably through the unlocked gate. Reaching the street, they scattered in all directions amidst a whirr of bullets from sentries stationed at various points around the building. Two of the fugitives reportedly fell during the firing and were thought to be wounded, but they sprang back up and kept running. Both the *St. Louis Missouri Daily Democrat* and the *St. Louis Daily Union* chronicled the escape, giving the names of all six escapees and other information about them, but neither newspaper reported the status of the murder and robbery case against James Rider at the time of his flight.[30]

In late July, just a few days after Rider's escape, a band of bushwhackers fired on a man and a boy near Tenney's Grove just across the Carroll County line in northeast Ray County, breaking the man's thigh bone and wounding his horse, and the boy returned fire, wounding one of the guerrillas. According to the *History of Carroll County*, many area residents believed Jim Rider had returned to Carroll, as he was wont to do, and "was concerned in the affair," but little is known with any degree of certainty about Rider's movements in the immediate wake of his escape.[31]

Meanwhile, the case against George Rider was tentatively resolved in August when the elder Rider gave bond and signed an oath of allegiance to the United States. A month later, however, perhaps partially in response to Jim Rider's reappearance on the scene, an order was issued in Saline County holding George Rider, John Rider (an older son of George Rider), and a few other Saline County men suspected of disloyalty as hostages or "vouchers" for the safety of Union citizens in the area. The Union theory that the guerrillas would not molest Union citizens in the county if they knew their loved ones and friends would have to pay for their misdeeds seems to have proved true to some extent, at least in the case of Jim Rider, who generally confined his marauding activities to the counties north of the Missouri River.[32]

In the late summer or early fall of 1863, Jim Rider apparently fell in with Clifton Holtzclaw, who, like Rider, had been commissioned to recruit for the Confederate army but had turned mainly to marauding. During the spring and summer of 1863, Holtzclaw made multiple raids into Linn County, and Rider, a known associate of Holtzclaw later in the war, made a similar raid into the county in November, robbing Henry Prewitt's store at Linneus. A band of four bushwhackers rode into town one evening about dark wearing Federal uniforms and went straight to the store. They robbed both the store and its patrons of about $500 in money and goods, including "a fine gold watch" taken from local judge Jacob Smith. In chronicling the incident, the author of a post-war county history identified the raiders as a portion of Holtzclaw's band and specifically stated elsewhere in the book that Jim Rider was the gang's leader. The local history added that Rider had boarded at a Linneus hotel for a few weeks prior to the raid.[33]

Rider was also reportedly sighted back in Carroll County in early November. According to the *Carroll County Democrat*, two men, "representing themselves to be gentlemen," called at the home of a citizen in Morris Township northwest of Carrollton and demanded supper. The pair reportedly appeared restless while the meal was being prepared and left in a hurry after they'd eaten. It was rumored in the neighborhood that one of the men was "the notorious Jim Rider."[34]

In December of 1863, Rider apparently registered for Federal service in Livingston County. A "James Ryder" appears on a December list of persons subject to military duty in the Twelfth Sub District of the Seventh Congressional District of the State of Missouri, headquartered at Chillicothe. Ryder gave his age as 28, which is the same age that James William Rider had given while being held prisoner a few months earlier. The age, combined with the fact that James W. Rider was a resident of Livingston before the war and haunted the county during the war, makes it probable that the man who registered for the draft at Chillicothe was the guerrilla Jim Rider, despite the fact that the enrollee gave his county of residence as Jackson and his state of birth as Vermont.[35]

The Enrollment Act of 1863, passed by Congress in March, required all able-bodied men in the U.S. to sign up for Federal service. A similar requirement instituted in Missouri the previous year when the Enrolled Missouri Militia was created had resulted in the conscription of many men of questionable loyalty and driven many others to the bush, but by late 1863 most able-bodied, Southern-sympathizing men from Missouri were either already in the Confederate service or had joined guerrilla bands and given up all pretense of loyalty. For some reason, Jim Rider apparently chose or was induced to maintain such a pretense around his home territory of Chillicothe, but he undoubtedly had no intention of actually showing up for Federal service. After registering on December 8, 1863, James Ryder (i.e. James W. Rider) did not appear for muster, and sometime in 1864 a "failed to report" notation was added to his registration record.[36]

During the early months of 1864, Jim Rider was either relatively inactive or temporarily absent from north Missouri, but he showed up in May, when, according to the *History of Carroll County*, he and Charley Turpin (who sometimes went by the name Charley Burton) "ranged over the woods in the northeastern part of the county, each with half a dozen followers." Turpin, of course, was the "desperate character" with whom Rider had escaped from jail at Jefferson City in the summer of 1862.[37]

Sometime in the late spring or early summer of 1864, Tabitha Rider received a letter from Lucinda Rider, twenty-four-year-old daughter of George Rider, asking Tabitha to come to Saline County for a visit. Tabitha went there, stayed a while, and might have reunited with her husband at this time. (In a statement Tabitha later gave Union authorities, she said that she saw her husband in the summer of 1864 for the first time in two years, but she did not specify exactly when or where the reunion occurred.) After her visit with Lucinda Rider, Tabitha started back to her aunt's home in Livingston County. On the way, she stopped at the house of Robert Shannon in Chariton County to rest and to ask him to take her the rest of the way home. Jim Rider showed up two days later, while Tabitha was still there, and told his wife that "it would not do" for her to go home. He sent her to George Cobb's house about ten miles away. She stayed there about a week and saw "Rider," as she called her husband, twice during the stay. According to Tabitha, she then went back to Saline County to help Eveline Rider sew. (This was a reference to George Rider's wife, Anna, whose middle name was Eveline.) From there she went to stay with a Beatty family in Saline County, where she saw her husband on two different occasions. After about a week, Mrs. Beatty grew afraid for her to stay, Tabitha said, "because I was Jim Rider's wife," and Mrs. Beatty took her to Brunswick, from where she made her way back to Mr. Cobb's. Jim Rider met her there the same day and took her to the John Craig residence in Chariton County, where she stayed about a month and saw Rider six or eight times during the sojourn. Rider then sent her to the nearby Samuel Elliott home, where Rider often visited her. After a couple of months, Tabitha said, Rider took her "to his uncle's George Rider in Saline Co."[38]

Tabitha also said that Lucinda Rider was Jim's cousin, and these statements, on the surface, seem to constitute almost irrefutable evidence that George Rider was not Jim Rider's father, but given Jim Rider's proclivity for feeding Union authorities false information, Tabitha's statements might simply mean that her husband had given her strict orders not to reveal who his parents were. If, indeed, George Rider was Jim's uncle, the best explanation seems to be that Jim's parents died young and Jim went to live with his uncle prior to the 1850 census.

After a week's stay with George Rider, Tabitha continued moving back and forth over the next three months among the homes of Southern sympathizers in Saline and Chariton counties at the behest of her husband, who popped in on her from time to time but still declined to let her go home. Her visits included a couple of very brief ones with the John Rider family in Saline County.[39]

Meanwhile, Jim Rider continued to prowl the countryside with his band of followers. In the summer and fall of 1864, prior to and during General Price's invasion of Missouri, guerrilla activity picked up in anticipation of what Southern sympathizers in the state hoped would be a general uprising that would allow Old Pap to reclaim the state for the Confederacy, and Rider, for one, increased his activity to the point that Union authorities began to take notice. One Federal officer reported that Rider occupied Brunswick on October 10 with a hundred men, and another noted that, when Bohannon and Holtzclaw captured Carrollton on October 17, the "guerrilla chief" Rider was among the rebel force.[40]

On October 20, as Price's army moved west on the south side of the Missouri River, Captain Eli J. Crandall of the Enrolled Missouri Militia at Brookfield in Linn County reported, "The only force now left in this locality are our old friends the bushwhackers, supposed to be commanded by Ryder. They have concentrated the bushwhacking element, and this Ryder has assumed command of them in absence of Mr. Anderson." (This was a reference to Bloody Bill.) Two days later, on October 22, Crandall was busy fortifying Brookfield in response to intelligence he had received that about 200 guerrillas under Rider or Anderson were headed in his direction from Carrollton.[41]

Although the raid on Brookfield never materialized, Crandall and his commanding officer, General Clinton B. Fisk, were still fretting about Jim Rider a month later. Fisk asserted on November 14 that, of all the counties in his District of North Missouri, "Carroll, Chariton and Howard are in the most unhappy condition.... Jackson and Ryder, with perhaps 300 guerrillas, are yet roaming over these counties."[42]

In reality, Rider had apparently crossed the river into Saline County, where, according to Crandall, he was making his head-quarters near Miami "with his father and other rebels in that locality." On the night of November 17, Rider and his band of about twenty-five men captured several boxes of clothing and boots that had been shipped from St. Louis by a Saline County judge to one of his Southern-sympathizing neighbors, a preacher living near Miami. The boat simply left the goods ashore at a Saline County landing, and Rider and his men, by prearrangement, rode up and took them. "This is their plan for shoeing and clothing the bushwhacking whelps," Crandall complained. Temporarily stationed at Brunswick, he told Fisk he was tempted to cross the river and clean out the guerrilla nest. Knowing he wouldn't actually be called upon to carry out the assignment, he added tongue-in-cheek that, even though Saline County was not in the District of North Missouri, he could "imagine" that it was.[43]

One of the adventures that Tabitha said she knew her husband was involved in during the fall of 1864, while he was shuttling her from house to house, was a raid on Bucklin. This was almost surely a reference to Clifton Holtzclaw's foray in November, which might have occurred either before or after the boot-stealing episode. Concerning this raid, the *History of Linn County* observed wryly, "Holtzclaw never killed anyone in Bucklin Township. The people were indisposed to provoke him, and he robbed their stables and pocketbooks and generously spared their lives."[44]

Sometime in November or December of 1864, Jim Rider took his wife, under the cover of darkness, to the home of Sam Hibler in Chariton County. He deposited Tabitha there with instructions that it still "wouldn't do for her to go home" and for her to go by the name of "Mrs. James" if anybody suspicious inquired of her identity. While at the Hibler home, Tabitha decided to go to Chillicothe and seek a divorce from Rider "because he was a bushwhacker," but Mrs. Hibler, so Tabitha claimed, would not let her go.[45]

Meanwhile, Jim Rider continued to skulk over north-central Missouri. On January 9, 1865, he paid a return visit to Linneus, riding into town from the west about ten o'clock at night at the head of a band of a dozen men. The guerrillas stopped first at a place where whiskey was sold and "partook freely," according to the *History of Linn County*. Then, John Lane, a Linneus native and recent recruit to Rider's band, went to the home of Judge Smith and stole the judge's horse, while most of the guerrillas rode on to the square. Their unwelcome appearance caused "great excitement and commotion," according to the local history, and a few citizens reportedly fired shots, while "some shouted 'fire!' others cried 'robbers!' and some made as little noise as possible." The looters rounded up a "bevy of prisoners," robbed a number of them, and demanded to know the whereabouts of T.E. Brawner, a captain in the local militia against whom Rider reportedly bore a grudge. Informed that Brawner was in St. Louis, the bushwhackers made a descent on the Brownlee, Trumbo & Dillon Store, where they learned that Dr. B.F. Dillon had the key to the store safe at his home. Several of the guerrillas went to the doctor's house and rapped on the door, but Dillon grew suspicious and fled out the back door. The marauders saw him just as he was scaling the fence in his back yard and fired a couple of shots at him, one of which struck him a glancing blow on the head that knocked him to the ground. Thinking he was dead, the guerrillas marched back to the square.[46]

In the meantime, after having his horse stolen, Judge Smith had armed himself with a musket and posted himself as a lookout, seated on a wood pile in front of a house near the northeast corner of the square. Along came John Lane riding the judge's horse, and Smith raised his gun and fired, mortally wounding the young bushwhacker. Smith then tried to rally his fellow citizens to gather at the courthouse and make a stand against the pillagers, but one of the guerrillas shot the judge through the gut just as he reached the courthouse fence. Hearing the disturbance downtown, William Pendleton, who lived northeast of the square, grabbed his gun and started toward the scene. He was intercepted by two of Rider's men, who took him to their leader. "Here is a man with a gun who is out after us; what shall we do with him?" one of Pendleton's captors reportedly asked. "Shoot him down!" answered Rider. Pendleton made a dash for freedom, but the bushwhackers shot him dead.[47]

The guerrillas appropriated a horse and buggy from the local livery, loaded the gravely wounded Lane into it, and headed out of town. By the time they got a couple of miles south of Linneus, Lane was dead, and his body was left at the house of a Mr. Cox. The bushwhackers supposedly bragged that they had just killed about a dozen men, and they threatened Cox that, if he did not see to it that the people of Linneus gave Lane a decent burial, they would come back and kill a dozen more. Citing a lack of ammunition and effective arms, the county history said the citizens of Linneus chose not to pursue Rider but, instead, to attend to Pendleton's body and to the severely wounded Smith, who died two days later.[48]

Sometime before or immediately after the Linneus raid, Jim Rider showed back up in Chariton County at the home of Sam Hibler's mother, where the Hiblers had temporarily moved Tabitha. Rider finally relented and told his wife she could go home, but he and his men first took her across the Missouri River into Saline County to the home of a man named George (presumably James J. George, the only man with the surname George in the 1860 Saline County census). At the George place, Tabitha told Rider "to go off and let me alone." After Rider and his band left, Tabitha started for Chillicothe to get her divorce.[49]

Meanwhile, Jim Rider lingered in the Missouri River country, making his way upriver to the vicinity of where the Lafayette-Saline county line meets the Carroll County line. On the morning of the January 19, citizens of Carrollton grew suspicious when a known rebel-sympathizer named Horton came into town to buy a large quantity of provisions. The man was arrested, and, after being held throughout the day, he finally admitted that some of the articles he had purchased were for Rider's guerrillas, who were then camped at his home located on a Missouri River island south of Carrollton. The next morning a detachment of Federal soldiers went down to the river in search of the guerrillas and found the narrow tributary between the island and the north bank frozen over. Part of the soldiers crossed the ice to the island while the rest stayed on the north bank and took up a position near the east end of the island. Near Horton's home, the first party of soldiers found the guerrilla campfire still burning and also discovered a large stash of clothing and sundry other articles nearby. However, the guerrillas, eight in number, had already fled to the east end of the island. They started to cross the ice to the north side of the river when they were spotted by the second squad of soldiers stationed on the bank. The soldiers opened fire, reportedly wounding a couple of the guerrillas, but the rebels returned to the island and managed to escape on a raft across the main channel of the river to Saline County. Meanwhile back in Carrollton, Horton was shot and killed when he supposedly tried to escape. A day or two later, a Federal detachment rounded up a number of horses the guerrillas had left on the island, and two saddles were found on the north side of the river. It was supposed that Rider and one other man had crossed to the north side before the soldiers had interrupted the other eight guerrillas in the process of crossing.[50]

In late January, Tabitha Rider reached Chillicothe with plans to file for divorce but, instead, was taken prisoner by Federal authorities on suspicion of aiding guerrillas. Reporting Tabitha's capture to General Fisk, Lieutenant-Colonel J.H. Shanklin, commanding the Sub-District of Chillicothe, mentioned having broken up Rider's hideout on the river island south of Carrollton ten days earlier, and he suggested, "A vigorous and simultaneous effort in Chariton and Saline might result in the capture or killing of this monster." Fisk, in turn, sent a recommendation to the Department of the Missouri headquarters in St. Louis that Tabitha Rider be banished from the state. "The presence of such," Fisk said, referring to Mrs. Rider, "only induces the stay of devils like Rider." An order that Mrs. Rider be banished was issued shortly afterward, but it was suspended because Tabitha was fully cooperating with Union authorities, naming all the members of Jim Rider's gang and all the people who had harbored her and Rider during the time she was with him the previous summer and fall. Nonetheless, in early March, she was sent to the Gratiot Street Women's Prison in St. Louis, the banishment was reinstated, and she was sent south on April 30.[51]

By late May of 1865, treaties had been signed officially ending the Civil War, and many Missouri guerrillas were surrendering, but Jim Rider was among a coterie of holdouts that included Jim Jackson. On May 24, Rider was reportedly spotted with Jackson, along with five other men, near Boonsborough in Howard County.[52]

Then, in the wee hours of the morning on May 27, a Missouri Militia detachment skirmished with some of Rider's guerrillas at Switzler's Mill in southeast Chariton County. The Federals surrounded the bushwhackers, forcing a few of them into the mill pond, and one drowned. Another guerrilla was reportedly injured, but Jim Rider pulled his final vanishing act, escaping in the darkness with his remaining men, never to be heard from again.[53]

The escapade at Switzler's Mill is the last known mention of Jim Rider in contemporaneous records, and what happened to him after May of 1865 remains even more of a mystery than his exact origins. Perhaps he was killed in late May or early June, as some of his fellow holdouts, like Jim Jackson, were, because there is no apparent trace of him in post-war census records or other documents.

More is known about the fate of his wife, Tabitha. She returned to Missouri after the war, remarried in Livingston County on July 16,

1868, to Sebron Sneed, and started a new family. The fact that there appears to be no record of her divorce from Rider adds credence to the idea that her notorious first husband might have died prior to her remarriage.[54]

Jim Jackson and His Infernal Clan

James "Jim" Jackson was one of the most infamous guerrillas in Missouri during the Civil War. Although he has received little attention since, his reputation for villainy during the war rivaled that of Quantrill and Bill Anderson.

According to his own statement, Jackson was born in Texas and grew up in Bourbon County, Kentucky.[1] He rode with Confederate Brigadier-General John Hunt Morgan's cavalry during the mid-part of the Civil War and was captured during Morgan's raid through Indiana and Ohio in the summer of 1863. Imprisoned at Camp Douglas near Chicago, he soon escaped and drifted into the northern counties of Missouri, where he took up bushwhacking.[2]

He first emerged as a guerrilla leader in the summer of 1864 when he fell in with Clifton D. Holtzclaw's band in the Chariton County area. On July 30, Jackson and Holtzclaw, with about seventy-five men, were taking breakfast at a home twelve miles east of Keytesville when they were interrupted by a detachment of the Thirty-Fifth Regiment, Enrolled Missouri Militia under First Lieutenant Louis Benecke. The soldiers charged the house and opened fire, spicing the morning meal "with Federal pepper," as one Union officer suggested wryly.[3]

The bushwhackers sprang to their horses and fled in great confusion. Regrouping, they mounted a charge, but the Federals repulsed it. The rebels rallied again, but they were again driven back. The stubborn guerrillas launched yet another futile attack before finally retiring to count their casualties. They had four men killed and at least a dozen wounded, including Jim Jackson himself. The militia, meanwhile, lost but one man wounded and one horse killed.[4]

If Jackson was severely injured in the skirmish, as reported by the enemy, he must have made a quick recovery, because less than a month later "the devil in human form, in the person of that notorious, villainous scoundrel and thief Jackson" reappeared in eastern Chariton County and went on a murdering spree. On August 23, he and several of his men visited a tobacco factory in the vicinity of the Chariton River forks, threatened to kill the owner, and took a black man prisoner. They escorted the captive about forty yards from the factory and shot him four times, killing him instantly.[5]

The next day, Jackson and five other men went to the home of Albert Carter in the same vicinity as the tobacco factory and found Carter's son, William, a member of a local militia unit, at the house with his mother. He had just come, unarmed, from the militia camp that morning to get a new supply of clean clothes. When the bushwhackers started to kidnap the young man, his mother tried to intervene. Promising the woman they wouldn't hurt him, they took him several miles down the road and stripped him of his clothes, then told him he could go. As soon as young Carter turned to walk away, one of the guerrillas placed the muzzle of a shotgun to the back of his head and blew his brains out, "literally tearing his head off," and "not a piece of skull left was an inch square."[6]

Several of the men accompanying Jackson were Albert Carter's nearest neighbors. One of them was even a cousin to the murder victim, but on this day politics apparently overrode blood. According to a local citizen who reported the incident to an area newspaper the day after it happened, William Carter's "only crime was unflinching loyalty."[7]

Not long after this incident, Jackson fell in with Jim Anderson, brother of Bloody Bill, and the two gangs roamed into the northernmost counties of Missouri. On September 15, the guerrillas, wearing Federal uniforms and numbering about forty, charged into Callao, situated along the Hannibal-to-St. Joseph Railroad in Macon County, and accosted the depot agent, stealing his shotgun. They then went to a local hotel and robbed several citizens of all their money. Taking along two Union men as prisoners, the rebels next went to a private residence, stole a revolver, and compelled the owner to take them to his nearby store, where they carried off $250 in money and $600 worth of goods. They went to another store and took $700 in money and $200 in goods. At a third store they appropriated $12 in cash and $200 in goods. From yet another store, they seized $450 in money and $150 in goods. The rebels took "all description of goods," supplying themselves with shirts, coats, pants, boots, and so forth.[8]

At the end of their three-hour stay, the rebels started off with one of the prisoners they had captured at the hotel, Clem Wright, a recent enlistee in the Federal army. At the edge of town they opened fire on him. Several of the shots missed, but two passed through his head, killing him instantly. One of the guerrillas remarked savagely as he stood over Wright's lifeless body, "There's one damn dog less in the world."[9]

Four nights later, on September 19, some of the guerrillas, dressed in Federal uniforms as they had been at Callao, galloped into St. Catharine thirty miles to the west, killed a citizen, and took three militiamen prisoner.[10]

Then the gang started north. In late September or early October the bushwhackers robbed the small community of Novelty in southwest Knox County and took several horses from the surrounding countryside. After passing through the county to the northeast, they killed a citizen near Luray in Clark County and then entered Iowa, robbing and killing as they made their way west along the southern border of that state.[11]

Around the 11th of October, in Fabius Township of Davis County, they killed a Union man named Thomas Hardee and another named A. Small. Arriving the same day at the home of a furloughed Federal soldier named Captain Bence, they took the man prisoner, and the leader of the gang told him that he had to die. When the captain pleaded that he not be killed in the presence of his wife, he was mounted on one of the gang's stolen horses and forced to accompany the band back into Missouri. About two miles beyond the state line in Putnam County, the guerrilla leader (presumably Jackson), who had fallen to the rear, rode up and shot the captain in the head, killing him instantly.[12]

By early November, George Todd and Bloody Bill Anderson were dead, Quantrill was still in hiding, and some of the other guerrillas had left Missouri for the winter; but Jim Jackson, after his jaunt to Iowa, was still roaming over the Missouri River counties. From the backwoods of Howard County he sent word into Glasgow that he meant to burn the town and to blow up the hospital that housed Union soldiers wounded during General Price's invasion of Missouri. Federal reinforcements arrived, however, to dissuade the tempestuous Jackson from attempting to carry out his threat.[13]

On November 8, near Boonesboro in Howard County, a detachment of Federal cavalry surprised a camp of about twenty men under Jackson, killing five outright and scattering the rest. Afterwards, the Federals found several bloody bandages strewn about the camp, suggesting that some of the bushwhackers were already nursing wounds at the time of the attack. In reporting the incident, a correspondent for the *St. Louis Missouri Democrat* opined, "This man Jackson appears to emulate the brutalities of Bill Anderson. He has already committed excesses of the most outrageous kind, and has threatened many more. He kills Union men whenever and wherever he comes across them--that is, *radical* Union men.[14]

On November 20, a portion of the Sixty-Second Enrolled Missouri Militia skirmished with Jackson near Salisbury in eastern Chariton County, wounding two of his men, while the Federals had one man seriously hurt. The militia also confiscated "a fancy cap worn by Jackson, beautifully decorated with plumes and feathers." Afterwards, Captain Eli J. Crandall, commander of the militia unit, complained that the guerrillas would be able to "keep up their system of bushwhacking so long as the country is full of traitorous men and women, who keep them posted in every move made by our forces."[15]

Sometime in the fall of 1864 Jim Jackson started carrying on with a young woman named Fanny Duffy of Glasgow. One day, while staying with a family named Hackley near Fayette, Fanny slipped out of the house and was gone some time before returning. That evening Jim Jackson and three other "armed men" came to the Hackley home and stayed for about an hour. When Mrs. Hackley finally ordered both Fanny and the guerrillas to leave, Jackson reluctantly complied but threatened to come back and burn the house down.[16]

Jackson didn't carry out his threat, perhaps because he was too busy cavorting with Fanny Duffy, as nothing was heard from him for the next month or so. Then, on Christmas Eve of 1864, Jackson and his band of about six or eight bushwhackers celebrated the holiday by killing several men in the neighborhood of Westville in northern Chariton County. The day after Christmas, General Fisk, commanding the District of North Missouri, ordered fifty of his best men sent out in pursuit of Jackson. He told his assistant adjutant general to send an officer who would "not rest day or night until Jim

Jackson and his infernal clan are exterminated," and a company from Macon were quickly "on the war path" trying to carry out the order.[17]

The detachment from Macon or another Federal party caught up with Jackson a few days later near Bynumville in northeast Chariton County. Union communications in early January of 1865 reported Jackson severely and probably mortally wounded in the skirmish.[18]

The Union intelligence of Jackson's grave condition was obviously mistaken. On January 10, just a few days after the erroneous reports, General Fisk assigned Major Samuel A. Garth to the Sub-District of Howard, Randolph, and Chariton counties for the express purpose of rooting out the guerrillas. Fisk was especially anxious to eradicate "Jackson and his desperadoes," who, he indicated, were still roaming over the whole sub-district.[19]

Indeed, Union soldiers of the sub-district were out scouring the countryside for Jackson that very day. Around midnight the previous night, Captain Alexander Denny, commanding the Enrolled Missouri Militia at Roanoke, got word that "the notorious Jackson" had been spotted in eastern Chariton County. Gathering ten men, the captain set out at once to try to intercept the guerrilla band. Near the East Fork of the Chariton River, he sent a dispatch to sub-district headquarters at Glasgow requesting reinforcements, then took the Keytesville road. Very shortly Denny and his detachment came upon a small group of men in the timber of a creek crossing about six miles north of Glasgow. Unable to see clearly in the darkness, Denny hailed the unidentified men several times. When he got no response, the militia greeted the tight-lipped campers with a volley of lead.[20]

The guerrillas sprang to their horses and returned fire as they galloped away. Jackson's horse was shot out from under him as he retreated, and a guerrilla named Gray Brown was knocked from the saddle mortally wounded. Jackson quickly mounted Brown's horse and made his escape through the woods along with a bushwhacker named John Robinson. Denny sent a second dispatch to Glasgow and waited until daylight.[21]

At sunup on January 10, Lieutenant Thomas Gannon arrived with a detachment of twenty soldiers from Glasgow, and the Federals promptly took up the chase again. They pursued the guerillas south throughout the morning and crossed the Glasgow to Fayette road into the Boones Lick Hills area. Around one p.m., Lieutenant Gannon and a squad of eight men came upon Jackson and Robinson at a home about ten miles below Glasgow. The two guerrillas raced from the house and leaped to the saddle, but Robinson had to dismount to open a gate. While the guerrillas were stalled at the fence, Gannon and a lieutenant of Captain Denny's command raced ahead of the poorly mounted privates and exchanged about eight shots with Jackson and Robinson. When the rest of the Federals came up, Gannon ordered a charge.[22]

Robinson, who had gotten the gate open but was unable to recover his horse, raced into the woods on foot, while Jackson galloped away nearby. The two bushwhackers formed a junction in the brush and hurried through the woods with the Federals in close pursuit. After about a mile, Gannon caught up with the guerrillas as they were crossing a ravine and forced another shootout. During the exchange, Robinson was shot in the head and killed, but Jackson escaped. The lieutenant trailed the elusive bushwhacker all afternoon until darkness forced him to call off the hunt.[23]

Jackson was once again reported as severely wounded. Civilian witnesses told Gannon that Jackson had blood running down his left leg and that he could scarcely use his right foot. He was also reported to be barefooted and bareheaded. Sure enough, back at the house where Robinson had been killed, the Federals found Jackson's hat and boots. They also took seventy-two dollars, six revolvers, two pocket knives, one compass, one gold pen with silver holder, and the pictures of two young women off the body of Robinson. Gannon divided the booty among his men before heading back to Glasgow.[24]

The emancipation of slaves and the enlistment of Negroes into Federal service during the latter part of the Civil War brought out a particularly vicious streak in Jim Jackson. The previous summer he had killed at least one black man, and now, in the early part of February, 1865, he rode through eastern Boone County putting up posters notifying Negroes that they would be killed if they did not leave the county by the 15th of the month. The announcements also proclaimed that farmers who hired black workers would be killed, too. The threats drew little attention until, five days after the mid-month deadline had passed, Jackson actually began carrying out his "hellish menaces."[25]

About ten o'clock on the night of February 20, Jackson and three other men went to the home of Dr. John W. Jacobs, six miles east of Columbia. Jackson and a sidekick named Abe Rumans went into the house while the other two guerrillas stayed outside. Jackson asked for a sheet of paper, which was provided. He scribbled a note on the paper and stuck it in his pocket. While he and Rumans tarried inside, the two men on the outside were busy with a gruesome work.[26]

The two desperados took Lewis, a former slave of Dr. Jacobs, and hanged him from a beam that stretched from one gatepost to another near the lawn. The horrible deed was accomplished so quietly that it aroused no suspicion inside the house, and Jackson and Rumans soon took their leave.[27]

Lewis's body was not discovered until the next morning. Pinned to his coat was the note Jackson had written inside the house: "Killed for not going into the Federal Army. By order of Jim Jackson." The lynching caused great alarm among blacks in the area, and they thronged into Columbia, seeking the protection of Federal troops.[28]

The reason Jackson gave for killing the ex-slave was obviously facetious. He didn't kill blacks for *not* going into the Union Army but, more likely, to express his outrage over the fact that some *were* enlisting. One officer speculated, in reporting Lewis's murder, that perhaps Jackson had left the note "for the interest of the substitute brokers." These were agents whose job was to find substitutes for men who had the inclination and wherewithal to avoid military service by paying someone else to take their place. Since civilian job opportunities for emancipated blacks were limited, ex-slaves made good candidates for such substitute service.[29]

At noon on February 24, less than four days after Lewis' hanging, Jackson struck again at Switzler's Mill near Roanoke on the Howard-Randolph county line. He and his band of seven bushwhackers hanged two more Negroes, killed a local militiaman named Poe, and robbed another citizen. Later the same day, the guerrillas showed up at Salisbury in eastern Chariton County, where they robbed a local merchant of about $300.[30]

Going north from Salisbury through the eastern edge of Chariton County, Jackson was thought to be headed to Iowa, but instead he turned east and resumed his killing spree. On February 26 he killed "an estimable Union citizen" named John Goddard in the northern part of Randolph County. The gang then marched into nearby Jacksonville and robbed the town of all the money they could find and all the goods they could carry off, including six revolvers and two other guns. Continuing their rampage, the murderous crew next went to Milton in eastern Randolph County, where they lynched another black man on Sunday morning, February 27. They also robbed several citizens and stores and kidnapped a doctor (perhaps to treat their wounded) before retreating south through Allen and Renick.[31]

Telegraph wires buzzed throughout the day with Union messages giving the latest news on Jim Jackson's movements as Federal troops tried to run him to ground. At sundown, a detachment of the Ninth Missouri State Militia Cavalry finally came up with the bushwhackers near Sturgeon in northern Boone County at a home where they were taking dinner. The two sides skirmished for nearly an hour before the guerrillas made their escape in the gathering darkness and continued south toward the Perche Hills. The guerrillas left behind five horses and several weapons, and they had one man wounded. The Federals had two men seriously wounded, both of whom later died.[32]

Jackson's murderous binge stirred Union citizens into a frenzy. A few days after the spree, a resident of Mexico in Audrain County reported that many of the loyal, rural people in his and neighboring counties were either moving into towns or leaving the state altogether because of the outrages of a handful of thieves and bushwhackers under Jim Jackson. He complained that the offenses had been committed only upon Union men and lukewarm Southerners, declaring, "In no case have any notorious rebels been molested."[33]

Jackson's activities and the citizen complaints they spawned also aroused the dander of General Fisk. Piqued by widespread grumbling that troops in the Howard County area were not doing enough to eradicate Jackson, Fisk, on March 5, ordered Colonel

Edward A. Kutzner, commander at Glasgow, to "go after Jackson, and stay after him day and night until he is killed."[34]

The insinuation that his men were not active enough apparently annoyed the colonel. Replying to Fisk the next day, he claimed his troops had just come in from a very tiring chase after Jackson that took them through six counties. Nevertheless, Kutzner promptly sent Captain John D. Meredith back into the Perche Hills for the purpose of hunting down Jackson, but all Meredith accomplished was to kill a citizen accused of harboring bushwhackers and to burn several homes belonging to Southern-sympathizing residents (actions for which Meredith was later arrested).[35]

The mission did little to assuage Fisk's concern over Jackson. On March 13, the general ordered a concentration at Sturgeon of Ninth Missouri State Militia Cavalry troops and sent Captain Henry N. Cook to take command of the regiment there. He made it amply clear to Cook that the troops were not being sent there to do post duty "but to be sent into the brush forthwith on a vigorous, continued, and protracted hunt after Jim Jackson.... When they strike a track, tell them to follow it day and night until Christmas, if necessary.... Stop not short of Jim Jackson's grave...."[36]

General Fisk's fervor to eradicate the bushwhackers scarcely deterred Jackson, though. To avoid the stepped-up Federal scouts, Jackson simply moved northeast of his usual area of operations and resumed his crusade against blacks. Sometime in early to mid-March, he sent "general orders" to a farmer near New London in Ralls County outlining his Negro phobic policy. "My garrilis is heard that you have a cople of famallely of negros settle on your plase.... If you don't make dam negroes leve there ride away I will hang the last negro on the plase and you will fair wors for we cant stand the dutch and negros both." Jackson and his gang, like most of the bushwhackers, hated Germans, whom they called "Dutch," almost as much as they resented the freed blacks.[37]

Jackson soon started back toward Boone County, where on Friday, March 17, he and "three of his co-workers in crime" went to the farm of Thomas Stone about twelve miles north of Columbia. After stealing a horse from the barn, the gang went to a sugar camp on the farm and found two Negro men, a Negro woman, and Stone's young son making sugar. The bushwhacking outfit promptly hanged one of the black men from the branch of a tree within a few feet of the camp. They then took the other black man about fifty yards and also hanged him to a tree. The victims had previously been slaves in the neighborhood, and Jackson threatened Stone's life for having hired them. He then left a piece of paper pinned to the coat of one of the victims and rode away without molesting the woman or child. Scribbled on the piece of paper was the name "Jim Jackson."[38]

Four days later, on March 21, Jackson, with two cohorts, went to the community of Ashland south of Columbia on the Jefferson City road and took over the town. They rounded up all the men in the town, and while one of the bushwhackers stood guard over the fourteen prisoners, the other two robbed postmaster and storekeeper P. T. Christian of $100 in cash and sundry other items. "The whiskey was then passed around, and all hands took a drink, whereupon the bushwhackers departed."[39]

Fortified with liquor, Jackson resumed his homicidal campaign against Negroes that evening not far from Ashland. The bushwhackers lynched a black man and pinned a piece of paper to his coat that said he was hung for not living at home with his former master, an area resident named Austin Bradford.[40]

Punishing blacks for exercising their newfound freedom was, of course, the real reason for Jackson's campaign of murder against former slaves. "Slavery dies hard," General Fisk observed a few days after the latest atrocity. "...I have no doubt but that the monster, Jim Jackson, is instigated by the late slave owners to hang or shoot every Negro he can find absent from the old plantations."[41]

As Jackson's maniacal crusade escalated, the Federal army came under increasing criticism for not stopping it. In response to the criticism, General Fisk blamed the Union's failure to destroy Jackson on "a pretty strong sympathy...with the bushwhacking fraternity" among civilians in the Missouri River counties.[42]

At the same time, the general stepped up the pressure on his subordinates to hunt the notorious guerrilla leader down and organized what he called "a Jim Jackson exterminating corps." He ordered acting Brigadier General Daniel Draper, commanding the newly-formed Sub-District of Mexico, to keep two hundred men on a constant move after Jackson and to "occupy and possess the Perche Hills country back and forth until the friends of Jim Jackson wish he would die to relieve them of the presence of your troops."[43]

To avoid the increased Federal patrols, Jackson again moved his center of operations farther east. In early April, a disciple of Jackson named Warren Martin, calling himself the "Young Hellion of Callaway County," killed two Negro men in the vicinity of Cote Sans Dessein on the Missouri River in the extreme southern part of that county. He also frightened an elderly black woman so much that she fell or ran down a steep embankment on the river and presumably drowned, as she was not heard from afterwards. In addition, Martin stole $100 from a militiaman named Charles Foy and robbed several other citizens in the neighborhood, threatening to shoot them if they didn't fork over the amount he demanded.[44]

On April 29, at ten o'clock in the morning, Jim Jackson, Warren Martin and two other bushwhackers stopped a stage south of Centralia as it was on its way to Columbia. The only passenger inside the stage was Congressman James S. Rollins. The highwaymen searched the stage and found a fancy gold watch that Rollins had hidden when he noticed their approach. They also searched his person and took a pocketbook containing about $75 dollars. The bushwhackers then demanded to know the congressman's name and occupation. Employing what the *Columbia Missouri Statesman* called "the old Centralia dodge," Rollins said his name was Johnson and that he was a farmer who lived a few miles south of Columbia. (Rollins had invoked the same alias the previous fall in Centralia to avoid the wrath of Bill Anderson's gang just prior to the Centralia massacre.)[45]

The stage driver went along with the congressman's ruse by pretending not to know his name. Although seemingly unconvinced, the bushwhackers didn't press the matter of Rollins's identity. Martin traded hats with the lawmaker, and then the bandits let the stage go on its way. Congressman Rollins donned the guerrilla hat, which had part of the brim cut off, for the rest of his journey, and he "presented quite a bushwhacker appearance" when he reached Columbia. After a fiery speech from Rollins, a party of citizens and soldiers from Columbia went out in search of Jackson's gang but lost the trail when darkness and rain came on.[46]

Around midnight on May 2, 1865, six bushwhackers under Jim Jackson rode into Millersburg in western Callaway County. Claiming to be soldiers, they went to the home of Thomas Adams and demanded that he let them in and that he hand over the key to his nearby store. Adams replied that he wouldn't let anyone into his home at that time of night unless he knew their precise business. One of the bushwhackers promptly kicked in the door, but the well-armed Adams stood his ground, ready to shoot the first man who stepped through the entrance. The bushwhackers retreated, and after a few moments Adams went to the doorway to look out. Seeing but one man on horseback near a fence about twenty yards away holding the other guerrillas' horses, Adams raised his shotgun and fired. The bushwhacker, Jim Neal, let out a groan and fell from the saddle mortally wounded. When the other guerrillas rushed to Neal's aid, Adams, realizing he was outnumbered, made his getaway through the rear of his house.[47]

Denied the satisfaction of killing Adams, the guerrillas took out their fury on his property (but did not hurt his family). They burned his home and its furnishings, then broke into his store and took what they wanted before setting it ablaze, too. The guerrillas also sent a house next door to Adams up in flames. Leaving Neal's body in Millersburg with instructions that he should be given a decent burial, the bushwhackers then mounted up and rode out of town.[48]

By May of 1865, the Civil War was winding down, as treaties had already been signed ending hostilities in the East. Although General Kirby Smith had not yet officially surrendered his Confederate command west of the Mississippi, Union success was assured, and the network of civilian support the guerrillas had enjoyed during the war began to weaken.

In north Missouri, the prospect of imminent victory emboldened many Union sympathizers, who had endured indignities at the hands of the bushwhackers throughout the war. In early May a party of Union men, posing as guerrillas and led by two nephews of the man Jim Jackson had killed near Jacksonville in late February, infiltrated a band of bushwhackers in Boone County and killed four of them in their sleep. Jim Jackson himself was a primary target of such intrigue, but the spies failed to penetrate his gang.[49]

In mid-May, with Confederate defeat certain and civilian support deteriorating, many guerrillas in Missouri started surrendering, but Jim Jackson held out. Around the 17th of the month, he and a band of five bushwhackers skirmished at a home in the Blackfoot Hills of Boone County with a squad of seven men from the Howard County Volunteer Missouri Militia, but there were no casualties on either side. On May 23, a detachment from the same militia unit again caught the scent of Jackson in Boone County and tracked him into Howard County. Here the Federals learned that Jim Anderson was camped nearby, and they called off the chase after Jackson to concentrate on Anderson. The next day it was reported at the Howard County Militia's headquarters at Fayette that Jackson was just a few miles away near Boonesboro, but all available mounted troops from the post were already out on other details.[50]

On May 27, the militia at Keytesville in Chariton County skirmished with Jackson and killed his horse out from under him. Jackson and his men, however, escaped.[51]

By mid-June, most of the bushwhackers had given themselves up, and Union officials started losing patience with the holdouts. On June 13, General Fisk ordered Colonel Denny, commanding at Glasgow, to undertake a vigorous pursuit after Jackson and Arch Clement, who was now commanding most of Bill Anderson's former guerrillas. "If they are found, kill them at once. Hold no further parley with them under any pretext, but destroy them whenever found."[52]

On the very day that Fisk issued his order, however, Jackson was already in the act of surrendering. At 11:00 a. m. on the morning of the 13th, he and Bill Stephens, another guerrilla leader in the area, marched under a flag of truce into Camp Switzler at the fairgrounds near Columbia with fourteen followers and surrendered to Captain Henry N. Cook. Jackson sported a pair of gray Confederate pants with a black stripe down the side and a finely embroidered shirt, while the rest of the gang wore ordinary civilian attire. Among the bush-whackers were Abe Rumans, who'd accompanied Jim Jackson to Dr. Jacobs' home in February when the gang had lynched the ex-slave named Lewis, and Warren Martin, the young hellion of Callaway County. After turning over their weapons, giving up their horses, and taking an amnesty oath, the guerrillas were allowed to depart under the stipulation that they leave the state.[53]

Jim Jackson didn't make it out of Missouri, though. After their surrender at Columbia, Jackson and fellow bushwhacker William Farley took time to secure new weapons and horses, then started desultorily toward Illinois. On Sunday morning, June 18, they aroused suspicion when they skirted the small town of Santa Fe in southeast Monroe County rather than riding through the village on the main road. Captain Tanner of the local militia decided to follow the two guerrillas to try to determine their identity and, after gathering twenty men, struck their trail near Florida about ten miles to the north. As the bushwhackers made their way east toward the Missouri River, another militia unit joined the Santa Fe squad, and the Federals began to press the chase. Near the Pike County line, Jackson and Farley realized they were being pursued and took to the woods, but, riding the nags they had procured since their parole, they were quickly overtaken.[54]

They surrendered without firing a shot, and a search of their persons turned up two pistols, three silver watches, sixty dollars in gold, the same amount in bills, and a considerable amount of clothing, including a guerrilla surtout that one of the captors later suggested should be "sent to the cabinet of curiosities and preserved as a 'rare specimen' for the benefit of after ages." The bushwhacking pair claimed they had purchased their horses, and they showed the parole papers they had been given at Columbia. Nevertheless they were brought back to Santa Fe, pending a determination of the validity of the paroles. News of the capture soon spread, and numerous people came in from the countryside to see the prisoners. Several of them recognized Jackson as the leader of a band of bushwhackers who had committed various murders and other atrocities in the area.[55]

While Captain Tanner awaited word from Columbia on the authenticity of the bushwhackers' paroles, a squad of militia from the Littleby Creek area of Audrain County came to Santa Fe on Monday evening, June 19, and, upon hearing the testimony of the witnesses against Jackson, promptly took him out to be executed. The twenty-six-year-old Jackson, standing six feet two inches in height, faced his

Arch Clement, who, like Jackson, was a guerrilla holdout
during late spring 1865. (Author's Collection)

fate with equanimity as the Federal firing squad lined up in front of
him. Described as lean and freckled, the veteran bushwhacker had
many scars on his body from wounds he had received in his numerous
skirmishes with Federal soldiers. "Exhibiting the greatest coolness
and bravery," he requested only, according to one observer, "that he
might be shot by a brave man."[56]

Thinking that Farley would be spared, Jackson took photographs of two young women from a breast pocket and asked that they be given to his fellow guerrilla. He also handed over for delivery to Farley some photographs he had taken of himself earlier that day in Santa Fe. Then he rolled up one of his sleeves, took a bandage from around his arm, and handed it to Captain Tanner. It contained $110 dollars in greenbacks, and Jackson told Tanner he could have it as a gift.[57]

Jackson denied committing many of the outrages that had been charged to him. He claimed that Warren Martin, the young hellion of Callaway County, had perpetrated many of them under his name. As the firing squad took aim, Jackson added, "I have fought, bled, and now I am about to die for my country."[58]

Thus ended the life, opined the nearby *Paris Mercury*, of "one of the most notorious and wicked bushwhackers that ever infested this country." After Jackson was shot, Farley was also taken out and executed, but unlike his leader he "met his fate very reluctantly, exhibiting some feeling on the subject."[59]

10
Clifton D. Holtzclaw: A Fiend in Human Form[1]

Clifton D. Holtzclaw, one of Jim Jackson's confederates during the summer of 1864, was the son of James and Lucinda Holtzclaw. The couple were early settlers of Howard County, Missouri, where all their children were born.[2]

When the Civil War broke out, thirty-one-year-old Clifton Holtzclaw raised a company for the Missouri State Guard. It was assigned to Colonel Congreve Jackson's Second Regiment of Brigadier General John B. Clark's Third Division and designated as Company B. On June 17, 1861, in one of the first skirmishes of the Civil War, Federal soldiers routed the inexperienced State Guard troops at Boonville, and Holtzclaw was captured. He missed the battles at Carthage and Wilson's Creek but rejoined the state troops in time for the Siege of Lexington in late September. On March 2, 1862, his company was sworn into Confederate service at Cove Creek, Arkansas, and it took part a few days later in the Battle of Pea Ridge, where Holtzclaw was wounded.[3]

After Pea Ridge, Holtzclaw's company marched east with Price's army to Mississippi, where in May it merged with a company from Platte County, Missouri, to form Company G of Colonel Eugene Erwin's Sixth Missouri Infantry. Twenty-seven-year-old William W. Holtzclaw, who had been a first lieutenant in his brother's State Guard company, was elected second lieutenant in this company. William was killed at the Battle of Corinth in October of 1862, while two other brothers, Benjamin F. and John W., were killed at Vicksburg the following spring. Yet another brother, James P. Holtzclaw, was also a member of Company G. He, like Clifton, survived the war. Presumably because of the wound he sustained at Pea Ridge, Clifton served only briefly in Company G and held the rank of private. Shortly before his brothers were killed at Vicksburg, he received a Confederate commission and returned to the Howard County area to recruit.[4]

Edwards says in *Noted Guerrillas* that he won the assignment in order to tend to his aging parents, but he also used the opportunity to take up bushwhacking. Around April 12, 1863, he and a band of guerrillas made a raid into Linn County harassing and robbing Union citizens. One man whose home they called at was Peter Smith. The guerrillas stole a gun, some ammunition, and a horse and threatened to kill Smith if he tried to have them arrested.[5]

Three months later, Holtzclaw paid a return visit to Linn County. Now numbering about thirty, his gang called at the home of James Callaway at daylight the morning of July 8. When the rebels demanded the man's weapons, he handed over a rifle. According to Callaway, the leader of the group identified himself as Holtzclaw and said he'd come into Linn County "to give us our orders (meaning our company of E.M.M.). He said when we went out scouting we *must* live off of our own friends and let his sympathizers and rebels alone." Holtzclaw told Callaway that, during his previous visit to Linn County, his band had lived off their own friends and that "if we did not do the same, he would come up here again."[6]

The rebel leader added that some of his friends had been choked and otherwise mistreated and that this had to stop. Holtzclaw claimed he did not interfere with Union men except "to take the contraband of war from them--that is, all property used in the militia." He then added that he had recruited a lot of Callaway's neighbors' sons and that "this was his business—to recruit for the C.S.A."[7]

The same day and in the same area Holtzclaw's band also robbed William T. Prouther of a horse, saddle, and bridle. When Prouther tried to protest the assessment, the gang opened fired on him, wounding him in three places.[8]

On the night of July 11, a detachment of the Ninth Missouri State Militia Cavalry called at the home of John Watson near Switzler's Mill in Chariton County and took the man's son prisoner as a suspected guerrilla. Young Watson escaped during the night, however, and made his way to Holtzclaw's camp. At six a. m. the next morning, Holtzclaw, with a band of sixty to a hundred guerrillas, attacked the militia at the Watson home, where the Federals had spent the night. The two sides exchanged fire for nearly twenty minutes before the guerrillas retreated. The Federals had one man gravely wounded and four slightly, while the bushwhackers left one man on the field seriously hurt.[9]

Around the end of August, 1863, Holtzclaw captured a soldier of the Ninth Missouri State Militia Cavalry, and it was reported that the guerrillas intended to kill the prisoner. On September 1, a detachment from the soldier's regiment under Lieutenant Joseph M. Street went out from Fayette to the home of James Holtzclaw and demanded that he pilot them over the country in search of his son's camp. The elder Holtzclaw, under suspicion no doubt because of the Confederate service of his five boys, had been compelled to take an oath of loyalty a year and a half earlier, but he probably never dreamt that his allegiance would be put to so severe a test as being expected to help Union soldiers hunt down his own son. According to the *Howard County Advertiser*, the cavalrymen and their guide were supposedly in the act of starting out when one of the soldiers "accidentally" shot Holtzclaw, with the bullet "entering the head of the old man, killing him instantly."[10]

Nothing further was heard from the younger Holtzclaw, however, until the following spring when his band roamed through Boone County in early May robbing Union citizens.[11]

Then on June 3, 1864, Holtzclaw, with fourteen men, made a raid on Keytesville, the Chariton County seat. The guerrillas rode into town from the east at about six o'clock in the evening and stopped at the house of John S. Dewey, whom they took prisoner. Proceeding to the main street, they arrested L. A. Cunningham, a Captain Ward, and a number of other Union men who happened to be on the sidewalks. The gang relieved the captives of money, pistols, and other possessions, and they also robbed some of the stores of money and supplies.[12]

Meanwhile, two of the bushwhackers galloped to the residence of County Clerk E. A. Holcomb and dismounted with their pistols drawn. Holcomb and his younger brother ensconced themselves in an upstairs room and opened fire on the menacing pair. Several shots were exchanged, and one of the guerrillas was wounded in the leg. Five more guerrillas then appeared on the scene escorting three of the men who had been taken prisoner. The rebels compelled the Holcomb brothers to hold their fire by threatening to kill the captives. During the lull, the younger Holcomb dashed from the house and was greeted by a hail of bullets, but he managed to make his escape unscathed. The guerrillas then forced an entry into the house and, under a renewed threat of killing the prisoners, demanded the surrender of the older brother. Holcomb refused at first but finally agreed to give himself up after receiving assurance that he would be protected.[13]

After disarming Holcomb and stealing a horse from him, the guerrillas marched him and the other prisoners to the courthouse, where they destroyed county tax records from the previous three years. Back outside, they forced Cunningham and Ward, against whom they nursed special grudges, into the street and threatened to shoot them. The guerrillas held Cunningham in singular contempt because he was a member of the Union League and they considered the county office he held bogus. Also, his father, as a provost marshal for the district, had helped recruit colored soldiers for the Union Army. Their particular complaint against Ward was that he had supposedly protected a black man who had shot a Southern citizen the previous winter. The two prisoners were saved only by "the earnest appeals and entreaties of a few Southern men" who spoke up on their behalf. Finally, with a threat to lay waste the county and to drive out all Union men, Holtzclaw and his bushwhackers rode out of town without further damage.[14]

A few days later, a Union party under notorious Kansas jayhawker and Federal scout J. W. Terman (alias Harry Truman) came into the Keytesville area in search of Holtzclaw. After briefly skirmishing with the guerrillas a few miles outside town, the Federals went into Keytesville and started robbing and killing Southern-sympathizing citizens in revenge for the Holtzclaw raid. One of the men killed, a lad named James Starks, was hanged specifically for being a member of Holtzclaw's band after he supposedly admitted his part in pillaging Keytesville the previous week.[15]

On Saturday, June 18, Holtzclaw retaliated by sacking Laclede in Linn County. About five o'clock in the evening, he rode into town with sixteen men and took possession of the place. He ordered all the citizens to come out of the stores and line up on the public square. Most complied, but two managed to escape and started toward the Union post at nearby Brookfield to sound the alarm. Another citizen, a discharged Union soldier named David Crowder, opened fire on the rebels from the window of a store building, seriously wounding bushwhacker Jim Nave, who had recently joined Holtzclaw after escaping from a St. Joseph jail. The guerrillas returned fire, killing Crowder.[16]

A lawyer named Jonathan H. Jones hurried from a building and was shot and killed when he kept running after being ordered to stop. Holtzclaw expressed regret for Jones's death but told the captives that his orders must be obeyed.[17]

The work of plunder than began. One party of rebels proceeded immediately to the store and post office of John F. Pershing (father of future General John J. Pershing of World War I fame) to secure the arms and ammunition kept there by the local home guard. While there, they tried in vain to break open a safe containing between five and seven thousand dollars that served as the town's bank. The remaining guerrillas relieved the captive citizens of their money and valuables and then robbed the other businesses, seizing over $1,200 in goods and cash from one store alone. At the office of the American Express Company, the bushwhackers tried with an ax to break open a second safe but once again failed. Still, they fared well enough, as their total take was valued at considerably over $3,000.[18]

While the pillaging was going on, Holtzclaw made a brief speech to the prisoners lined up on the street. He told them he held no grudge toward anyone simply because he was a Union man but that his visit was in retaliation for the Union raid on his friends at Keytesville. In a statement that rather belied his declaration of goodwill, he added that there were a few abolitionists in the Laclede area that should be killed. He told the citizens that, if he heard of any of his Southern friends being abused or killed, he would pay the town a second call and would treat the people less kindly. He vowed to kill two Union men for every Southern man who was killed. He then closed with a warning that the citizens should not try to follow the guerrillas when they left town.[19]

Toward the end of his visit, Holtzclaw impressed a driver and mail hack and loaded the injured Nave and a good deal of loot into the rig. He then started it out of town to the west with an escort of three guerrillas, while the main body of bushwhackers rode south out of Laclede.[20]

When the two citizens who had escaped at the outset of the raid reached Brookfield, several Union soldiers immediately headed toward Laclede on a train engine while another party of about twenty-five went by horseback. The Federals on the train overtook the mail hack west of Laclede, because the road ran beside the railroad track for a good distance out of town. The Federals opened fire on the makeshift ambulance, killing Nave and wounding both the civilian driver and the guerrilla who was riding in the cab with the injured man. They also overtook the two mounted guerrillas, killing one and wounding the other, and they recovered from the hack much of the plunder that had been taken at Laclede.[21]

The Federals on horseback had less luck than those on the train. They galloped after Holtzclaw and the main body of guerrillas but failed to overtake them before nightfall. The next morning they went back out in search of the bushwhackers and scoured the countryside all day, but they again failed to come up with any of Holtzclaw's band.[22]

On July 1, 1864, Holtzclaw and twenty-five of his men were taking breakfast at the home of a Southern sympathizer in Howard County about six miles from Fayette when they were discovered and attacked by a squad of fifteen soldiers of the Ninth Missouri State Militia Cavalry under Sergeant Dewitt C. Koontze. The guerrillas lost two men killed and one wounded in the skirmish, while the Federals lost one man killed and one wounded.[23]

Federal officials held a meeting in Fayette on July 9 to organize area citizens under the provisions of General William S. Rosecrans's Order Number 107, a directive for resisting and driving the bushwhackers out of the general's Department of the Missouri. After the meeting, five or six prominent Union citizens of Glasgow, including Clark H. Green, started for home in buggies. Four miles out of Fayette they were stopped by Holtzclaw and a band of twenty guerrillas. The bushwhackers took the captives into the woods and seated them on the ground while Holtzclaw decided what to do with them.[24]

Meanwhile, General Fisk and an escort of twenty soldiers under Captain Henry S. Glaze left Fayette on the Glasgow road about an hour behind the private citizens. Riding with Fisk in his buggy was Benjamin W. Lewis (whom Bill Anderson tormented and abused at Glasgow three months later). When Fisk's party reached the area where Green and his friends had been abducted, a woman who lived on the road came out and told the soldiers what had happened. Captain Glaze formed his men and advanced into the brush in search of the bushwhackers and their captives. Two or three hundred yards deep in the woods, the soldiers spotted the guerrillas, and the two sides started shooting.[25]

At first fire, Holtzclaw released all the prisoners except Green, whom he meant to kill. The guerrillas held a special grudge against Green, because he had been a colonel of the 46th Enrolled Missouri Militia at Glasgow and had been a recruiting officer for colored troops. As the freed prisoners scattered into the woods, one of the bushwhackers snapped his gun at the still-seated Green. When the weapon misfired, Green sprang up and started running, but one of the guerrillas brought him down with a shot to the arm.[26]

The skirmish lasted several minutes before the guerrillas retired deeper into the woods. They had one man seriously wounded and one or two others with lesser injuries. Clark Green got up off the ground and hobbled out of the woods with a shattered arm bone, while Captain Glaze had three pellets of buckshot in his body.[27]

From the Glasgow area, Holtzclaw moved north, ranging through Linn County and into the southeast edge of Grundy. On the morning of July 15, he rode into the village of Lindley, leading a band of twenty-six guerrillas, and cleaned out the place. The bushwhackers robbed the citizens of all the money, horses, and weapons they could find. Afterwards, a party of enrolled militia pursued the guerrillas and caught up with them about eight miles from town. In the ensuing skirmish, Holtzclaw's band wounded five of the poorly-armed Federals, but the dogged home guardsmen kept up the chase and overtook the rebels again in the afternoon. This time the militia had one man killed and another mortally wounded, a result that persuaded them finally to quit the game.[28]

After the Lindley raid, Holtzclaw returned south through Linn County. So, when a man named Stratton was killed and had his house burned near Brookfield on the night of July 17, Union officials supposed it was the work of Holtzclaw. In truth, at the time of Stratton's death, Holtzclaw and his band of twenty-five guerrillas were already back in Howard County, where they spent the night of the seventeenth southeast of Glasgow. Two days later they were still in the same vicinity, although their number had swelled to near fifty.[29]

Toward the end of July, Holtzclaw began recruiting in eastern Chariton County, where he was joined by Jim Jackson. On July 27, Captain Joseph Stanley of the Enrolled Missouri Militia at Keytesville went out on a scout in search of Holtzclaw and found the guerrillas near Union Church in the Chariton River forks area. When the bushwhackers split into small squads and took to the brush, Stanley called off the chase, claiming he was outnumbered by the combined force under Holtzclaw and Jackson and that the guerrillas were trying to lead him into an ambush. He went back to Keytesville and requested reinforcements.[30]

The next morning, July 28, some of Holtzclaw's men stopped a stage coach near Salisbury in eastern Chariton County that was on its way from Brunswick to Allen with three passengers and a cargo of mail. The bushwhackers did not molest the passengers, and after opening up the mail and taking $45 that was found in some of the letters, they put the ransacked mail back in its pouch and let the stage go on its way.[31]

On the same day, Captain Stanley got his requested reinforcements in the form of a company of dubious warriors from Brunswick. Their captain, Thomas E. Brawner, told Stanley that many of the men in his enrolled militia company were sympathetic to the rebellion. They would fight bushwhackers, he said, but would not fight Confederate soldiers. Stanley declined to employ such reluctant fighters against Holtzclaw, because the guerrilla leader was operating under a Confederate flag.[32]

From his camp east of Keytesville, Holtzclaw sent a letter to Stanley on July 29 protesting the mistreatment of Southern citizens by Stanley's troops:

> Sir: Through this medium I wish to inform you that you must restrain your troops or I shall be compelled to retaliate for every violation of the rules of civilized warfare. I am determined to kill two Union for every Southern sympathizer that you or your party may kill (that is, peaceable citizens), and also will kill a Radical for every house that is burnt. I regret that these things are necessary, but you or the men with you give me no choice. Unless your course of conduct is changed Bee Branch had better look out. I will state that I am only repeating my instructions from the Confederate Government.
>
> Yours, respectfully,
> C. D. Holtzclaw, Confederate States

Stanley replied the same day, directing his epistle to "Captain
C. D. Holtzclaw, In Brush":

> Sir: Yours of the above date is at hand and contents
> noted. I am a Federal officer. Expect to deal with thieves,
> robbers, and murderers with rigor. Peaceable citizens will be
> treated with respect as such. Upon exhibition of commission by
> leaders of bands of Southern men, they will be treated as
> Confederate soldiers.
>   Respectfully,
>   Joseph Stanley,
>   Captain, Commanding Post
> P. S. Commission that may be exhibited by citizen as dispatch
> bearer will be safely returned.[33]

Instead of sending his commission to Keytesville for Stanley's
perusal, though, Holtzclaw turned to a more sympathetic ear to voice
his complaint about the mistreatment of Southern citizens. On July
29, the same day as his correspondence with Stanley, Holtzclaw
received a visit from Edwin W. Price, son of Sterling Price. A former
brigadier general in the Missouri State Guard, Price had been captured
a year and a half earlier and had taken the oath of loyalty. He was now
living at home in Chariton County and serving as a corporal in
Colonel William E. Moberly's enrolled militia at Brunswick. After
making a speech to the guerrillas in which he noted that he had sworn
Holtzclaw into the Southern Army three years earlier, Price returned
to town with Holtzclaw's assurance that the bushwhackers would
leave the county in three days if left unmolested. Price also said that
Holtzclaw's men were Confederate soldiers who had been driven to
the bush by Stanley's company. A Union citizen of Keytesville
promptly wrote to General Fisk defending Stanley's company and
complaining of the questionable loyalty of all the other local enrolled
militia. He said that when the men of Stanley's company had signed
up for service, they had done so with the understanding that they
would not have to answer to rebel sympathizers like Moberly and
Price.[34]

Early the next morning, July 30, the undeterred Stanley sent out a scout of forty-three men under First Lieutenant Louis Benecke in search of Holtzclaw. The Federals once again found the guerrillas, about seventy-five strong, in the vicinity of Union Church taking breakfast at the home of a Southern citizen. When the soldiers charged the house, the bushwhackers sprang to their horses and fled but then regrouped and mounted a charge of their own. The guerrillas were finally repelled with a reported loss of four men killed and as many as a dozen wounded. The Union loss was reported as just one man slightly wounded. Three days after the skirmish, Captain Stanley said he had heard nothing more from any of Holtzclaw's men except for six or seven enrolled militiamen who had returned to the fold after deserting to join the guerrillas a few days before the fight.[35]

After the skirmish near Union Church, Holtzclaw moved off to the south into Howard County. On the morning of August 3, his band scuffled briefly near Fayette with a party of Federals under Major Reeves Leonard of the Ninth Missouri State Militia.[36]

On the night of August 9, Holtzclaw stole a horse from a citizen named Earickson living two miles south of Glasgow. He also requisitioned $100 from the man for the guerrilla cause. When Earickson protested that he didn't have that amount in his possession, Holtzclaw told him to leave it on a certain tree stump about a mile from his home the next day, and the man complied.[37]

By the middle of August 1864, Holtzclaw's activities had become enough of an annoyance to draw the attention of Major General Rosecrans. On the 14th the general began wiring his subordinates demanding that something be done about the guerrilla leader. "Why do you not hunt out and whip Holtzclaw…?" he asked Captain Joseph Parke, stationed at Boonville. On the same day, he suggested to General Fisk that the troops from Glasgow should be able to destroy Holtzclaw, and he instructed Fisk to "infuse energy and enterprise into our poor commanders."[38]

On the evening of August 16, a detachment of ninety-one men under Captain Hebard of the Seventeenth Illinois Cavalry from Glasgow was camped in Boone County about ten miles northwest of Columbia near Dripping Spring. Around eleven o'clock, Holtzclaw fired on the Federal pickets from a cornfield, mortally wounding one sentinel and seriously wounding another. The next morning,

Holtzclaw's guerrillas, numbering almost a hundred, renewed the attack, and a lively skirmish took place. According to Union accounts, eight bushwhackers were killed and seven wounded, while the Federals had one man killed and nine wounded, in addition to the two casualties from the previous night.[39]

Holtzclaw was still licking his wounds from the morning skirmish with the Illinois troops when a company of the Third Missouri State Militia under Captain George W. Carey came out from Columbia and collided with the guerrillas, sparking another brisk engagement. In the second skirmish the guerrillas reportedly lost three or four more dead and about fifteen wounded, while the Federals had just nine soldiers slightly wounded.[40]

On the night of August 20, Holtzclaw's band rode into Rocheport and took possession of the place after Jim Anderson's gang had already plundered the town and held it for several hours.[41]

The next night, August 21, Holtzclaw exchanged a few shots with a camp of the Seventeenth Illinois Cavalry on the road between Glasgow and Boonesboro. After the brief skirmish, one of the Federal soldiers found on the field the letter Captain Stanley at Keytesville had written to Holtzclaw almost a month earlier outlining the terms under which he would recognize the guerrillas as Confederate soldiers, and the post commander at Glasgow forwarded it to General Fisk, who briefly investigated the matter before apparently deciding that Stanley had done nothing wrong.[42]

Sometime in late August, Holtzclaw fell in with Bill Anderson, who, like his brother Jim, had been making himself at home in Rocheport and roaming throughout the area of Howard and Boone counties. About the same time, Captain Joseph Parke of the Fourth Missouri State Militia Cavalry finally got around to taking up the task of tracking down Holtzclaw that General Rosecrans had admonished him to undertake almost two weeks earlier. On the 26th, Captain Parke crossed the Missouri River from Boonville into Howard County in search of the guerrillas. His detachment of forty-four soldiers came up with two of Holtzclaw's men about four miles east of Rocheport and gave chase. One the guerrillas was wounded in the running skirmish, but unbeknown to Parke, they were leading the soldiers into a trap. Lurking in the wooded hills overlooking the road was Holtzclaw and Anderson's combined force of a hundred men.

After a pursuit of about a mile, the Federals passed the spot where the guerrillas lay in ambush, and the bushwhackers charged out of their hiding place and swept down on the startled troops, killing eight and wounding a few others. Afterwards, some of Anderson's men scalped and otherwise mutilated the dead soldiers.[43]

Bloody Bill Anderson, an occasional associate of Holtzclaw. (Author's collection)

On September 9, 1864, A. J. Bowyer, who had been captured a few weeks earlier, was hanged at St. Joseph for being a member of "Holtsclaw's band of guerrillas, outlaws, insurgents and robbers, rebel enemies of the United States" and for accompanying the guerrilla leader during his raids through Linn County in April and July of 1863. "A crowd of near 2,000 people, including those of every age and sex," turned out to witness the spectacle of the execution.[44]

The next day, September 10, Holtzclaw skirmished with a detachment of the Sixth Missouri State Militia Cavalry near Roanoke in northern Howard County. During a running fight of five miles, the guerrillas had six men killed, several wounded, and five captured, while the Federals had but two wounded, one severely. General Fisk promptly wired his congratulations to Major Austin A. King, Jr. at Fayette on the successful engagement, and he instructed the major to maintain the campaign against Holtzclaw. Citing intelligence gained from two of Holtzclaw's men who'd been taken prisoner (Bowyer perhaps being one of them), Fisk told King to keep a special eye on Hackley's farm and on Holtzclaw's mother's residence. "He is home almost daily," Fisk said of the guerrilla leader, "and his sisters are great comforters of the bushwhackers."[45]

The five members of Holtzclaw's band captured in the Roanoke fight were taken to St. Joseph and lodged in jail the next week, awaiting trial by military commission. Their names were Elias Brewer, John Bunton, Elias Cottrill, Watson Cottrill, and James Maloney. Holtzclaw promptly sent a message to General Fisk requesting an exchange of prisoners, but, the editor of the *St. Joseph Morning Herald* predicted, "From present indications we presume the general will adopt another method of releasing Union men who have fallen into the hands of the bold outlaw."[46]

One of the "present indications" was the recent hanging of Bowyer and a second was the impending execution of H. A. Griffith, another Holtzclaw man who had previously been taken prisoner and who was sentenced to death on the same day the other five bushwhackers arrived in St. Joseph. Fisk apparently had no intention of negotiating with Holtzclaw. On September 23, a few days after the arrival of the five new prisoners, Griffith was hanged on schedule from the same spot where Bowyer had been launched into eternity two weeks earlier.[47]

In late September, as General Price made his way north after invading Missouri on the 19th, the partisans of northern Missouri began concentrating in anticipation of linking up with the Confederate Army. Holtzclaw, Anderson, and other guerrilla leaders had been operating in the Howard County area for some time, and when Todd and Thrailkill arrived from the eastern part of the state on the 23rd, the total guerrilla command swelled to almost 400 men. After camping that night in southern Howard County, the combined force started north the next day and attacked the Union post at Fayette. After being repelled there, the guerrillas continued north into Randolph County and threatened the town of Huntsville before moving off to the east.[48]

On the morning of September 27, Bill Anderson's gang left the guerrilla camp and went into Centralia in northern Boone County. When a train arrived carrying over twenty furloughed Union soldiers, Anderson marched the soldiers off the train, lined them up, and shot them. He then reunited with the main body of guerrillas a couple of miles southeast of town. A company of the Thirty-ninth Missouri Volunteer Infantry under Major A. V. E. Johnston came into Centralia shortly afterwards and, discovering the atrocity, pursued the guerrillas to their camp. Johnston rode right into the trap set for him by the guerrillas and was cut to pieces. Approximately 125 soldiers out of a total command of about 150 were killed, including Johnston himself, while the rebels lost just three dead. Although Holtzclaw took part in the battle with Johnston's troops, there's no evidence that any of his men participated in Bill Anderson's execution of Union soldiers earlier in the day.[49]

After forming a brief junction with Price in early October south of the Missouri River, Holtzclaw and many of the other guerrillas re-crossed the river under Confederate authority to resume their marauding. Bill Anderson, for example, was sent across the river to disrupt Union lines of communication and transportation, and Holtzclaw was acting under Price's orders as well.[50]

On October 17, Holtzclaw and former Missouri State Guard Lieutenant-Colonel Louis Bohannon, in company with a regiment of Shelby's division, surrounded the town of Carrollton and demanded its surrender. After a parley with the Confederates, Major George Deagle, commander of the local Enrolled Missouri Militia, surrendered his command of about 160 men, gave up his arms, and turned over the town to the Confederates. The rebels swept in and looted the town, then marched the prisoners to nearby Waverly, where most of them were paroled. A few, against whom the Confederates held special grudges for having previously killed some Southern officers, were shot.[51]

After Price's failed invasion of Missouri, many of the already loosely-organized guerrilla bands began to fragment even more. This seems to have been the case with Holtzclaw, as little else was heard from him after the fall of 1864. In early January of 1865, a former Holtzclaw lieutenant named Hines was captured and killed near Rocheport.[52]

Holtzclaw himself, however, left the state not long after Price's invasion and spent the winter in Pike County, Illinois, under the assumed name of Miller. In early March, he and a few other former guerrillas left Illinois for Council Bluffs, Iowa. A month later, they were spotted across the Iowa state line in the Nebraska City, Nebraska, area, the same general vicinity where the Marchbanks brothers took refuge near the end of the war. Holtzclaw and his party were last reported getting ready to head west across the plains.[53]

Instead, Holtzclaw came back to Howard County and took the oath of allegiance at Glasgow on June 29, 1865. In his affidavit, he listed himself as captain of a company of Confederate "rangers" and stated his intention to become a farmer. After the war, Holtzclaw lived at least briefly in California, but at the time of the 1880 census he was living in Linn County, Kansas, following his chosen occupation of farming. In the early 1900s he attended Confederate reunions in Missouri.[54]

The Other Anderson: Bloody Bill's Brother Jim

Around eight or nine o'clock on the evening of July 3, 1862, brothers Bill and Jim Anderson, their cousin Lee Griffin, and two other men lurked in the gathering darkness near the home of Judge A. I. Baker at Rock Creek about five miles east of Council Grove, Kansas, on the Santa Fe Trail. On May 12, Baker had killed the Andersons' father, William C. Anderson, in a confrontation at the Baker home when the elder Anderson arrived with a loaded shotgun to protest a charge of horse stealing the judge had brought against Griffin. Afterwards, the Anderson brothers, who also were under suspicion for horse theft, had fled the area and taken up a marauding existence along the Missouri-Kansas border near Kansas City, but now, less than two months later, the gang was back at Rock Creek in quest of vengeance.[1]

One of the gang members who was unknown to the judge lured Baker from his home under the pretext of procuring whiskey and provisions for a wagon train. Baker and his sixteen-year-old brother-in-law, George Segur, led the stranger from the house toward the judge's roadside store. Suddenly the other four gang members stepped from the shadows and opened fire. Two shots wounded Baker, but he managed to pull his revolver and return fire, grazing Jim Anderson in the thigh. The judge staggered into the cellar beneath the store, and his brother-in-law was also shot and driven into the cellar. The Anderson gang slammed shut the cellar door, piled heavy barrels on top of it, and then set the store ablaze. (Baker perished in the inferno, while Segur managed to escape but died the next day.)[2]

With their murderous work complete, the Anderson gang mounted up and rode for Missouri, terrorizing citizens along the way. Shortly before midnight, the gang reined to a halt at the way station of O. F. O'Dell, twelve miles east of Rock Creek. O'Dell, C. H. Withington, and two other men were playing cards, drinking beer, and anticipating the gala Fourth of July celebration scheduled at Council Grove the next day when the Anderson gang barged in and took possession of the place.[3]

The marauders took the occupants hostage and began ransacking O'Dell's store, looking for tobacco and other goods.

Intoxicated with rage and still bleeding from the gunshot wound he had received during the ambush of Judge Baker, nineteen-year-old Jim Anderson boasted openly of Baker's killing and described the details of the crime to O'Dell and the other captives. Brandishing his revolver, Jim threatened to shoot Withington for the role he had played two months earlier in bringing the horse-stealing charges against the Anderson gang, but, according to the *Emporia News*, Bill intervened on behalf of the prisoner and dissuaded his hot-headed younger brother from carrying out the threat. After herding the captives into a stable located on the grounds of the way station, the bushwhackers tried unsuccessfully to set the store on fire. Frustrated that the green logs would not fire, they stole three fresh horses, mounted up, and set off at a gallop for Missouri.[4]

Although the bloody reputation William T. Anderson later earned as a notorious Confederate guerrilla chief casts a dubious light on the newspaper report of his peacemaking intercession at the O'Dell store, the later life of his younger brother suggests just as strongly that Jim Anderson was fully capable of making and carrying out a threat on the life of C. H. Withington or any other man who happened to cross him. Although often overshadowed by the dark legend of his older brother, the younger Anderson upheld the family legacy of violence both before and after Bloody Bill's death in October 1864, and two years after the close of the Civil War, he, like Bill, met a violent end.

When the Andersons landed in Missouri in July of 1862 after avenging their father's death, they were returning to the state where they'd grown up. The family had moved to Missouri from Kentucky around 1839, about the time of Bill Anderson's birth. After a brief residence in Iowa, where Jim was born, the family came back to Missouri and settled at Huntsville in Randolph County. In 1857, the Andersons moved to Kansas, where their mother, Martha Anderson (nee Thomasson), was killed by lightning in 1860. Bill rode south with Judge Baker in the fall of 1861 to join the Missouri State Guard but had come back home without signing up. Shortly afterwards, the Andersons had a falling out with Baker, resulting in Baker's shooting of the elder Anderson and the brothers' murder of Baker. Now the Andersons were back home leading a free-booting existence. It would not take long for them to be drawn into the bitter partisan warfare that gripped Missouri.[5]

Although the Andersons' initial devotion to the Southern cause was token at best, the gang soon became immersed in the guerrilla conflict, and their indiscriminate pillaging quickly took on political overtones.[6] The partisan fighting provided a cloak of legitimacy for their marauding existence, as they began preying almost exclusively on Union sympathizers.

After returning from Kansas in July, the Andersons drifted east into Lafayette County, where, according to the *Lexington Weekly Union*, the gang killed seven Union men and "robbed every loyal man" in the county south of Lexington during the summer and fall of 1862. The editor identified five members of the gang and emphasized that it was a different band from that of William Quantrill, the notorious guerrilla leader from neighboring Jackson County. Despite Quantrill's infamy, the newspaperman proclaimed the Anderson gang "the basest robbers ever left at large in a civilized community."[7]

In the spring of 1863, the small Anderson group fell in with the larger Quantrill band, and the Andersons rode with Quantrill in August during the infamous sacking of Lawrence, which, according to some of the guerrillas, was carried out in retaliation for the collapse of a military prison in Kansas City in which one of the Anderson sisters and four other Southern girls were killed. The Anderson brothers also rode with Quantrill during the massacre at Baxter Springs in October, but the Quantrill command disintegrated in Texas the following winter.

Bill Anderson then returned to Missouri in the late spring of 1864 at the head of his own small guerrilla band and promptly went on a spree of violence. The gang raided through Cooper County on June 4, killing one Union citizen and robbing several others.[8] Shortly afterwards, Anderson fell in with guerrilla leader Dick Yeager, and on June 12 the combined force attacked a squad of soldiers west of Warrensburg near the Johnson-Cass county line, killing twelve of the fifteen-man squad.[9] The next day Anderson and Yeager rode down on a wagon train south of Lexington and killed nine more Federal troops.[10]

Jim stayed with his brother throughout the remainder of June and most of July as the guerrilla band sashayed back and forth across northern Missouri, skirmishing with Federal troops, killing Union sympathizers, and disrupting lines of communication. On July 12, the gang killed nine Union men in Carroll County.[11] On the 24th they killed and scalped two Union soldiers in Randolph County.[12] The size of the guerrilla command swelled as brash, Southern-leaning boys and young men learned of Anderson's exploits and flocked to join the rising leader.[13]

In late July, after a raid into Shelby County, the bushwhackers, over sixty strong, dropped back down into Randolph County near the Anderson brothers' childhood home southeast of Huntsville. On the morning of the 30th the gang went to the home of Colonel Alexander F. Denny, commander of the local militia, and took the colonel's seventy-two-year-old father captive. Seeking to draw the citizen soldiers into a trap, Anderson put a rope around Denny's neck, hung him up until he was nearly dead, and then dispatched a Negro man to Huntsville two miles away to report the news. According to the *Columbia Missouri Statesman*, "…it was with difficulty that the Colonel could be prevented from rushing to the rescue of his father."[14]

About this time, Bill Anderson divided his command. He placed his brother Jim in charge of most of the guerrillas while he took a small squad of about ten men west through Carroll, Chariton, and Ray Counties and into Clay County to rendezvous with fellow guerrilla leader Fletch Taylor. Meanwhile, Jim Anderson and the rest of the command tarried in the Randolph County area.

On Sunday evening, July 31, the younger Anderson led his men into northwest Randolph County, where they surrounded a schoolhouse, interrupting a divine service, and took thirty-two young men and boys prisoner. They took the captives north into Macon County to Hebron Church and forced them to "cast lots," according to the *Missouri Statesman*. They lined the men up and ordered all them who would be willing to fight for the South to step forward. All but eight did so, and they were immediately released. The eight steadfast Union men, however, were subjected to all manner of insult and indignity such as being stripped of their clothing. Two of the party were lashed with a whip, four had their heads shaved, and the other two were forced to kneel and pray under threat of execution. After stealing two horses from the prisoners, the bushwhackers finally released the eight Union men as well.[15]

A week later, around ten o'clock on the morning of Sunday, August 7, Colonel Denny, with his Forty-Sixth Infantry Enrolled Missouri Militia and a small detachment of the Ninth Cavalry Missouri State Militia, struck the trail of Jim Anderson and thirty bushwhackers about five miles south of Huntsville. The Federals pursued the trail for two hours before losing it and then spent another two hours scouring the woods for any sign of the guerrillas. Around 2:00 p.m. Denny came out on the Huntsville to Fayette road in Silver Creek Township near the home of Owen Bagby, where Anderson and about ten of his men were holed up. Denny sent four men to reconnoiter the residence, and as they approached the house, Jim Anderson shouted for them to identify themselves. Cursing the guerrillas, they yelled back that they were Kansas Redlegs, and the bushwhackers opened fire.[16]

Denny dismounted his men and ordered a charge. Punctuating the attack with boisterous yells, the Federals rushed the house and quickly dislodged the guerrillas. Behind the house, the bushwhackers sprang to their horses and made their escape through gates that had been left open at the rear of the property for just such a contingency. Denny and five or six soldiers whose horses were near the house gave chase while the rest of the Federals raced back to remount. The guerrillas reached the cover of woods about 300 yards ahead of their pursuers, but Denny and his small party charged in after them and exchanged random gunfire with Anderson's gang as the bushwhackers fled through the thick brush.[17]

When the two sides reached a long lane through the woods, "the chase became fierce and rapid," according to Denny. The Federals overtook two guerrillas who were mounted double and shot the horse out from under them. The bushwhacking pair leaped a nearby fence and started across a field on foot. Denny rode after one of them, engaging him in a running pistol fight until another Federal came up and shot the man dead with a rifle. A third soldier pursued the other dismounted guerrilla and wounded him in the neck but was forced to retire after he fired his last shot.[18]

When the remainder of the Federals arrived, Denny renewed the pursuit, but the soldiers could not overtake the well-mounted guerrillas. After outdistancing their pursuers over the course of about three miles, the Anderson band took to the brush and dispersed. On the ride back to Huntsville, however, Denny struck Anderson's trail again. The Federals gave the bushwhackers another run but called off the chase after about ten minutes when the guerrillas again scattered into the woods.[19]

Denny reported one rebel killed and another mortally wounded (the two men who had been riding double) as a result of his skirmish with the guerrillas. He claimed Jim Anderson himself had been shot through the nose. In addition, the Federals seized a half dozen weapons, killed or captured two rebel horses, and confiscated a number of feathered hats. They took almost $400 in gold, silver, and currency from the body of the dead man and also found on the corpse some letters written by parties in Dallas, Texas. The militia, meanwhile, lost but one horse in the melee.[20]

On the morning of August 20, a detachment of the Ninth Missouri State Militia Cavalry under Major Reeves Leonard started from Rocheport on the Glasgow road. As the Federals passed a wooded area half a mile west of Rocheport, a band of about 30 guerrillas under Jim Anderson opened fire from the brush, wounding three or four of Leonard's men. The militia promptly returned fire, killing one of the bushwhacker's horses, and the guerrillas scattered back into the woods. Leonard pursued the rebels in various directions throughout the day but without success. That evening he went into camp a couple of miles down the road from the scene of the ambush, while Anderson's men, having regrouped, paraded into Rocheport and took possession of the place.[21]

Most of the guerrillas retired quietly to a hotel, where Anderson set up a command post. However, five bushwhackers, who had arrived in Rocheport ahead of the main group and got drunk, accosted a local citizen named Henry Turny, who ran a saddler's shop in town. They demanded $2,500 from the fifty-two-year-old man but finally agreed to settle for $450. In the meantime, someone informed Anderson of what was happening, and he sent word to Turny that, if he would come to the hotel, he would be protected. The robbers, though, told their captive they would "blow his brains out" if he tried to go to Anderson; so Turny set off to round up the money and came back with $411, which pacified the drunken crew.[22]

Shortly afterwards, Jim Anderson and a man known only as "Wild Irishman" went to the home of Moses Barth, a local merchant, where they made Barth's maid, Sarah, "do just as they pleased." When Barth's nephew, eighteen-year-old Charlie Meyer, arrived on the scene, Wild Irishman pulled out his revolver and greeted the newcomer with a pistol blow to the head, knocking him down. Anderson caught Charlie as he was falling and told Wild Irishman to quit, but the bushwhacker gave Charlie another lick or two on the arm before obeying.[23]

Anderson then ordered Charlie to open up the stable because he wanted a horse, but after examining the animals, Anderson decided he did not want any of them because they were "no count." When the pair returned to the house, Anderson made Charlie fetch some water so that he and Wild Irishman could wash up. Then the two bushwhackers "left without further damage."[24]

Late that night, having possessed the town for several hours, Anderson and his band mounted up and rode out of town as the gang of C. D. Holtzclaw rode in.[25] Fresh from his raid into western Missouri, Bill Anderson also returned to the Rocheport area about this time and promptly made the place his headquarters.[26]

Jim Anderson was next heard from when he crossed the Missouri River below Brunswick in Chariton County on September 7 with a large band of bushwhackers. The next day, one report suggests, he re-crossed the river into Carroll County with nearly a hundred men and harassed a Union detachment under Major Austin A. King, Jr., of the Sixth Cavalry, Missouri State Militia, who were scouting for guerrillas.[27]

On the night of September 19th, a small party of bushwhackers, clothed in Federal uniforms, dashed into St. Catharine in Linn County and killed one citizen, wounded another, and took three militiamen captive. The culprits, reported as "a portion of Anderson's gang," were likely a part of Jim Anderson's band, because Bill Anderson's men were then gathering in Howard County over fifty miles away.[28]

About this time, Jim Anderson fell in with fellow guerrilla leader Jim Jackson, and the two gangs roamed into the northernmost counties of Missouri. Jackson made a foray into Iowa in mid-October, and a few days later he and Anderson were reported just below the state line. By late October, though, the two bands were back in the Missouri River country.[29]

On October 27, 1864, a month after directing the infamous Centralia Massacre, Bill Anderson was killed while leading a wild charge against a company of Federal militia near the small community of Albany in Ray County. His body was taken to Richmond that evening. About midnight on the night of the 28th, Jim Anderson showed up in Richmond at the home of his cousin, Tom Bayless, who ran a hardware store in the town. He departed about 11 o'clock the next morning, the same day his brother was buried in a Richmond cemetery.[30]

Back in the bush, Jim Anderson continued to roam the counties of north-central Missouri for another month, making his headquarters in the Saline County area just south of the river in company with several other guerrilla leaders, including Jim Rider, Jim Harris, and Jim Jackson. Late in the year, Anderson and most of the veteran bushwhackers, except for a small party who accompanied Quantrill on an ill-fated expedition to Kentucky, slipped out of Missouri and headed for the Sherman, Texas, vicinity in search of winter quarters. (Anderson's surviving sisters, Mollie and Mattie, were arrested and sent to Gratiot Street Prison in St. Louis in early December 1864.)[31]

While the Missourians rested in Texas, the fortunes of the Confederacy grew increasingly bleak, and defeat appeared imminent. Around the first of April 1865, the guerrillas debated the merits of going to Mexico with General Jo Shelby, and a few decided to do so. Most, though, chose instead to return to their old haunts.[32] Even though the agreement at Appomattox was signed in early April, effectively ending the war in the East, the guerrillas apparently did not learn of the Confederate surrender before leaving Texas. Archie Clement, at the head of Bill Anderson's old band; Dave Pool, now commanding the remnants of Quantrill's gang; and Jim Anderson, in charge of his own small band, struck for home about the 18th of the month and landed in central Missouri three weeks later.[33]

In the pre-dawn hours of May 7, the bushwhackers, either as a single group or in concert, struck Holden and Clement's hometown of Kingsville, both in Johnson County, just hours apart. They killed one man and robbed two stores at Holden; killed eight men, wounded two others, burned five houses, and robbed indiscriminately at Kingsville; and cut telegraph wires between Holden and Warrensburg.[34] Circumstances suggest that it was probably Clement's and Dave Pool's men, numbering about 100, who struck Kingsville, while Anderson with a smaller force of about forty guerrillas made the raid on Holden and cut the telegraph wires east of that community. This smaller band, which included a squad under Bill Pool (Dave's brother), passed north of Warrensburg headed toward Lafayette County on the 7th. Colonel Chester Harding, Jr. sent out a party of cavalry from Warrensburg in pursuit, and the Federals managed to kill three stragglers. However, the rest escaped, and the next day, May 8, Anderson and Bill Pool were reported with certainty in Lafayette, where they threatened a Federal encampment of twenty men but declined to launch an attack.[35]

When the guerrillas learned of the Confederate surrender in the East upon their arrival in northern Missouri in early May, they sneered at the report at first as nothing but "a damned Yankee lie."[36] Disabused of their fantasy, they grew dismayed at the attitude of resignation among Southern-sympathizing citizens, who had sustained the bushwhackers throughout the war. Many of the guerrillas, including Dave Pool, expressed a willingness to surrender if they would be treated as prisoners of war, but, according to one report, "They do not speak for Anderson's men."[37] This may have been a reference to Bill Anderson's former men who were then with Clement, but the sentiment held true for Jim Anderson and his band, too. Leery of the treatment they might receive at the hands of Federal authorities if they surrendered and accustomed to life in the bush, Anderson and Clement meant to hold out to the bitter end, bedeviling Union officials and terrorizing Union supporters in the meantime.

While Dave Pool moved off east to the Sni Hills and soon began negotiating a surrender, Anderson, despite a Federal effort to prevent his passage, crossed the Missouri River. With no apparent intention of giving himself up, he ranged north into Livingston County, where his squad reportedly killed two men on May 20.[38] Some doubt exists as to whether Anderson actually committed the murders, though, since a Union officer suggested a few days later that Anderson was being blamed for depredations committed instead by Harry Truman, the notorious Union scout who had clashed with

Holtzclaw the previous summer. Truman ironically had been sent into north Missouri for the express purpose of securing the surrender of the bushwhackers.[39]

What is known with certainty is that Anderson turned east toward his old stomping grounds of Randolph and Howard counties shortly after crossing the river. With a band of eleven men, he arrived in Howard County on May 23 and spent the night at the home of the Elias Thompson family, about six miles from Rocheport, his brother's old "capital." The next morning about 7:30, while still at the house, the guerrillas were attacked by a detachment of Howard County Volunteer Missouri Militia under Sergeant Robert Diggs. The Federals killed four bushwhackers, wounded several others, and captured four horses and a number of pistols and other equipment. Anderson's men killed one soldier and two horses. After the skirmish, Diggs's superior officer, Captain Warren W. Harris, crowed that he hoped "the warm welcome" the bushwhackers received would "admonish them to stay away" from Howard County.[40] He received his wish, at least temporarily, as Anderson's dwindling band, prompted in part, no doubt, by the reception they received in Howard, were quickly back on the trail toward western Missouri.

The heady scent of victory put many Federal soldiers, who had endured the torment of bushwhackers throughout the war, in a swaggering mood. Lieutenant David M. Freeman of the Carroll County militia, after a May 26th chase after Clement in which his men killed or wounded three guerrillas, turned his attention to Anderson. "Now general, if you want Jim Anderson captured," he told Brigadier General Isaac V. Pratt the next day, "send me and thirty of my men and I will bring him in soon, so my men say they can track the bushmen like a dog will a deer. They are anxious to get the job of catching Jim and gang."[41]

Jim Anderson, though, had already passed through Carroll County a day or two earlier headed west, and on the 26th he was spotted in Platte and Clinton counties near the Kansas border.[42] His stay in western Missouri was short lived, however, and a few days later he was back in his old haunts of Randolph and Howard where he and Clement managed to form a junction, despite Federal efforts to prevent such a meeting.[43]

By this time, guerrillas were surrendering in northern Missouri almost on a daily basis. In late May, Dave Pool surrendered at Lexington with forty men and volunteered to go out and round up more bushwhackers.[44] Mart Ryder also surrendered at Lexington about the same time.[45] In early June, Jim Jackson gave himself up.[46]

Rumors circulated that Arch Clement and Jim Anderson would follow suit any day, and Colonel Denny was put in charge of negotiating the surrender of his old nemeses.[47] Captain Harris, a subordinate of Denny, received several of Anderson's and Clement's men at Fayette, but the two guerrilla leaders themselves held out, pressing the conditions of their surrender. Federal authorities resisted their demand that they be treated as prisoners of war and be protected from civil as well as military prosecution. Union officials sought instead their unconditional surrender. So, while the two guerrilla leaders spoke daily of giving themselves up, neither Anderson nor Clement came in. Finally, Brigadier General Clinton B. Fisk, Commander of the Department of North Missouri, ordered Colonel Denny to break off negotiations with the recalcitrant pair and go out in pursuit of them. "If they are found, kill them at once," Fisk's assistant adjutant general instructed.[48]

Despite the Federal determination to track down Anderson and Clement, they managed to elude capture. However, guerrilla activities virtually ceased during the summer as the armistice ending the war took hold in Missouri. The return of relative peace to the state cooled the Federal fervor to round up the bushwhacking holdouts, and most of the guerrillas either left the state or went back to their homes to try to resume their ordinary occupations.[49]

For some of the guerrillas, though, the war did not end in 1865. Embittered by four years of bloody conflict and intense political division, they continued the marauding existence they had known throughout the war and used their rancor to justify a life of crime. On February 13, 1866, a dozen former bushwhackers held up the Clay County Savings Bank in Liberty, stealing $60,000 and killing a college student named Jolly Wymore in the process when the young man gave an alarm.[50] Jim Anderson and Clement were suspected of being among the robbers.[51]

A few weeks later, on March 8, Anderson and another former guerrilla named Isaac "Ike" Flannery turned up in Rocheport, where

Flannery tried to sell the merchants of the town some military bonds that presumably had been taken in the Liberty bank robbery. Finding no buyers, he and Anderson left town on the Boonville road. About two or three miles from Rocheport, where the road led into the Salt Creek bottom, they were ambushed by five men, according to Anderson's account of the affray. Flannery was killed at first fire while Anderson made his escape without a scratch and went to a nearby home to report the incident.[52]

Some of the members of the family who lived at the house accompanied Anderson back to the scene and found Flannery dead with a bullet to the head and no other signs of a fight. Missing were a fine gold watch and chain, about $2,000 in currency and bonds, and a pair of Navy revolvers that Anderson said Flannery had been carrying when he was shot.[53] At least one observer showed little sympathy for the dead man, suggesting, "Flannery ought to have been killed for associating with Anderson."[54]

Anderson's story of the melee was met with almost immediate skepticism. William F. Switzler, editor of the *Columbia Missouri Statesman*, thought it strange that "the notorious Jim Anderson" escaped unscathed and was the only survivor of the affair, and Isaac N. Houck, editor of the *Howard County Advertiser*, reported the episode with the following disclaimer: "These are the particulars as reported by Anderson himself, and we give them for what they are worth." Anderson did not stay around long enough, though, for the suspicions to turn to accusations but instead crossed to the south side of the Missouri River two or three days after the incident.[55]

By March 19, though, Anderson was back in Howard County in the Franklin area, and Missouri Governor Thomas Fletcher sent a letter to an unnamed colonel (presumably Colonel Denny, commanding the post at Glasgow) expressing his concern that Anderson and his men should be brought to justice. The governor authorized a platoon to be called into active service to hunt the desperadoes down. "If they can be captured or killed, it would be the best thing for the state I know of," Fletcher declared.[56]

Anderson, however, again eluded capture and later in the year, following the bushwhacker ritual established during the war, headed for the Sherman, Texas, area to spend the winter. Among the other former guerrillas wintering in the area was Ike Flannery's uncle

George Shepherd.[57] He, like the newspaper editors, was unconvinced by the tale Anderson had told about Flannery's death. Shepherd suspected that Anderson and Jesse James had killed Flannery for his money, which, according to the story Shepherd later told, Flannery had inherited from his father.[58]

GEORGE SHEPHERD.

Sketch of George Shepherd, who claimed to have killed Jim Anderson. (Author's collection)

When Anderson saw Shepherd in Sherman one evening in 1867, according to the yarn Shepherd later told author J.W. Buel, Anderson greeted Shepherd pleasantly, and the two shared a few drinks together in a saloon on the town square. About eleven o'clock, as the bar was closing, Shepherd asked Anderson to go across the street to the courthouse yard with him, because he wanted to talk with him in private. When the two men reached the dark shadows of the courthouse lawn, Shepherd drew a knife, placed it at Anderson's throat, and accused him of killing Ike Flannery. When Anderson did not deny the charge, Shepherd slit his throat and left him dead on the courthouse grounds.[59]

A rumor, or "satisfactory information" as one newspaper called it, did indeed reach Missouri in May of 1867 that Jim Anderson had been killed in Texas, but Bill Pool, who also was spending the winter in Sherman and who'd had some disagreement with Anderson, was the supposed killer. Pool, however, fled the state, and no charges were brought in the case. Years later Shepherd claimed in an interview with Buel that he was the real killer of Jim Anderson, and he provided details of the crime.[60]

The only problem with the newspaper report and with Shepherd's claim is that Jim Anderson got married in Grayson County, Texas, in late 1868, and he his wife (nee Mary Erwin) were still living in Texas at the time of the 1870 census. He died in 1871, but details of his death are not known. So, it's possible he was killed in a revenge attack by one of his former comrades, but if so, it didn't happen in 1867 or thereabouts as the newspaper reported and as Shepherd later claimed.[61]

Some of the Missouri guerrillas gained such notoriety that their legends would not die quite as easily as the men themselves. Kept alive in myth by the wistful yearning of Southern-leaning citizens who saw the guerrillas as avenging angels and by the lingering fear of Northern citizens who viewed them as fiendish bogeymen, some of the more renowned bushwhackers became the subject of recurrent false sightings even after their deaths. William Quantrill, for example, was supposedly seen in Washington, D.C., six months after he died in Kentucky, and similar claims continued to surface years later, including a report that he was serving as a Methodist minister in Huntsville, Alabama.[62] Bill Anderson, whose savage exploits earned him the posthumous sobriquet "Bloody Bill," was reportedly living out his old age in Texas in the early 1920s.[63]

Jim Anderson was immortalized in similar fashion but to a lesser extent. He was implicated in the robbery of the Daviess County Savings Bank at Gallatin, Missouri, in December 1869, and he was suspected of helping the James gang kill a Pinkerton agent near Kearney, Missouri, in March of 1874, several years after his death.[64] Like his older brother, Jim Anderson had become, in the public imagination, a ubiquitous devil that even the grave could not vanquish.

John Thrailkill: A Desperado of the Worst Class

John Thrailkill, the son of Jacob Thrailkill and Eleanor Ann Canoy, was born in Missouri about 1838 in that part of Livingston County that later became Gentry County. Sometime in the mid-1840s Eleanor died, and Jacob Thrailkill returned to Saline County, where he had wed his first wife, and married Sarah Furgerson. The family then moved to Polk County, Iowa. By 1860, however, John Thrailkill was back in his native Missouri living with the George Cooper family at Oregon in Holt County and working as a printer.[1]

When the Civil War broke out, Thrailkill joined the Missouri State Guard as a private and was assigned to Company B of the Fifth Regiment, Third Division. He was engaged at Carthage, Wilson's Creek, Dry Wood, and Lexington. Around the end of November 1861, he was elected captain of a company.[2]

A month later, Thrailkill was enrolled into Confederate Service on Christmas Day at Springfield, Missouri, by Major Robert R. Lawther and assigned to Colonel Elijah Gates's First Missouri Cavalry regiment, which was being organized at the time. Five days later Thrailkill was elected captain of Company F.[3]

Thrailkill was slightly wounded in the action at Sugar Creek, Arkansas, on February 17, 1862, but not enough to keep him from also participating in the action at Bentonville the next day. He was also engaged at the Battle of Pea Ridge in early March and then went east with Price's army and took part in the engagement at Farmington, Mississippi, on May 9, 1862. Five days later at Corinth, Thrailkill was re-elected captain, and he was wounded at the Battle of Corinth on October 4, 1862.[4]

In early March of 1863, Thrailkill was sent back to the Trans-Mississippi in charge of a group of recruiting officers. Reporting to General Price at Little Rock, he was ordered to accompany General John S. Marmaduke on his expedition into Missouri. Although Colonel Gideon W. Thompson, commanding Shelby's brigade, singled out Thrailkill and his "sharpshooters" for special recognition during one phase of the failed invasion, Thrailkill's recruiting efforts proved even more fruitless than the overall mission. "Having no facilities for recruiting," Thrailkill said tersely, "we met with no success."[5]

In early May 1863, Marmaduke ordered Thrailkill to return to Little Rock. From there he was summoned to the Confederate Trans-Mississippi headquarters at Shreveport, and part of his detail was sent back east of the Mississippi. In late May, Thrailkill again returned to Little Rock and shortly afterwards proceeded into Missouri, by way of Jacksonport, Arkansas, with the remaining members of his recruiting corps[6]

On July 18, as Thrailkill was riding alone through Clinton County dressed in full Confederate uniform bearing the insignia of his rank, he was stopped by three members of the local Enrolled Missouri Militia, including a lieutenant, who were dressed in civilian attire. The Union men confiscated two navy revolvers from Thrailkill, who informed them that he was a soldier in Price's army. In an attempt to extract information, they responded that they were Southern men. Thrailkill, thinking they were "pirates of the brush," offered to enlist them in the Confederate Army and showed them his orders signed by General Price and other high-ranking Confederate officers. He said, however, that he was opposed to bushwhacking and wished to conduct the war on honorable principles. When asked if he knew anything of Joe Hart, Thrailkill replied that he was not acquainted with Hart but that he'd like to meet him. (Unknown to Thrailkill or the militiamen, Hart had been killed five days earlier.) Thrailkill also added that he planned to enlist into the Southern army the recruits of George Calvert, a cohort of Hart who had been taken prisoner.[7]

The militiamen then revealed their true identities and told Thrailkill he was their prisoner. Thrailkill bowed politely, invoked his claim to be treated as a prisoner of war, and cited his fair treatment of Union soldiers who had come into his hands at various times during the war. The lieutenant said he was satisfied Thrailkill was not a bushwhacker and that the fair treatment he claimed to have shown Union soldiers would be reciprocated. Thrailkill was accordingly delivered to St. Joseph the next day and turned over to the provost marshal general of the district.[8]

In early September, Thrailkill was sent to Gratiot Street Military Prison in St. Louis. After languishing there for several months, he was tried by military commission in January 1864 on a charge of "transgression of the laws of war." The specification read as follows:

> In this, that he, John Thrailkill, a rebel enemy of the United States, and belonging to and serving as a Captain in the army of the so-called Confederate States of America, did, about the month of July, A. D., 1863, enter and come within the lines of the regularly authorized and organized military forces of the United States, and within the State of Missouri, with the purpose, object and intent of raising and obtaining within said State of Mo. recruits for service in the army of the so-called Confederate States, and for the accomplishment of said purpose and intent, continued to travel about within said state of Mo. until arrested, on or about the 18th day of July, A. D., 1863, at the county of Clinton and State of Missouri.[9]

Thrailkill pled guilty to the specification but not guilty to the charge, essentially admitting that he had done what Union officials said he had done but denying that his actions were illegal. The prosecution offered no evidence other than the orders Thrailkill was carrying on him when captured, and Thrailkill's only defense was a brief statement explaining his reasons for coming into Missouri and citing his Confederate authority to do so. The judge advocate conceded that Thrailkill's orders were genuine, but the defendant was nonetheless found guilty of both the specification and the charge.[10]

Thrailkill was sentenced to be confined at Alton, Illinois, at hard labor for the duration of the war. Major-General Rosecrans, commanding the Department of the Missouri, confirmed the sentence in February, and Thrailkill was transferred to Alton Military Prison on May 4, and put to work in a stone quarry. In June he escaped by walking away from the quarry. After reporting to Confederate authorities at Atlanta, he was promptly sent back into Missouri on recruiting duty.[11]

Shortly after arriving in northern Missouri, Thrailkill fell in with Confederate recruiting officer Colonel John C. Calhoun "Coon" Thornton. Also operating with Thornton at the time was the guerrilla band of former Quantrill lieutenant Fletch Taylor, whose men included Frank and Jesse James. After parleying with members of the

Enrolled Missouri Militia stationed at Platte City on July 9, Thornton determined that the "Paw Paws" would not fight his men. ("Paw Paw" was a derisive term applied to the Enrolled Militia, especially those suspected of harboring Southern sympathies.) So, he and Taylor marched into Platte City the next day with about a hundred men and took possession of the town, taking down the U. S. flag and hoisting a Confederate banner in its place. On July 11, Thrailkill rode into town with another fifty to seventy-five men. Many of the militia switched sides and joined the guerrillas, with some donning Confederate uniforms. By the time the rebels rode out of Platte City on the twelfth, their combined force had swelled to at least 250.[12]

Leaving Platte City, the guerrillas rode north and skirmished with a detachment of the Second Colorado Cavalry near Camden Point on July 13. With the Federals in pursuit, the rebels then retreated south into Ray County and split into two groups. Thrailkill and Taylor lingered in the Ray County area with a force of about 200 men while Thornton moved northeast with about the same number of men. On July 17, the force under Thrailkill skirmished with forty-seven soldiers of the Second Colorado under Captain Thomas Moses, Jr. at Fredericksburg near the Clay County line. After a sharp exchange, the Federals scattered to the brush with a loss of six men killed, four wounded, and two missing but not before inflicting, according to Union accounts, even heavier casualties on the rebels. A local historian, writing several years after the war, reported only that the Federals were "badly routed" in the affray.[13]

After the skirmish, Thrailkill marched east toward Richmond but bypassed the county seat and turned north toward Caldwell County. The rebels plundered stores and committed other depredations as they went, but Taylor's men and not Thrailkill's did most of the pillaging. Near Knoxville, in northern Ray County, Taylor's guerrillas killed three men of the Enrolled Missouri Militia. In southeast Caldwell County, a squad that was said to be commanded by Frank James seized two more Enrolled Militia from their homes early on the morning of July 19, took them down the road, and shot them. Near Black Oak later the same morning, a detachment of twenty-six Enrolled Militia belonging to Captain William D. Fortune's company spotted Thrailkill and Taylor approaching, and some of them mistook the rebels for their own men. "Look! There comes Fortune," one of them is reported to have said. Quickly realizing the true identity of the guerrillas, a second Union man replied, "It looks like damned bad fortune for us."[14]

In what ironically turned out to be their good fortune, the militia were captured by Thrailkill and not Taylor after the latter left the main road in a flanking movement. By the time he rejoined Thrailkill, the militia had already surrendered, and Thrailkill protected them from Taylor's men, who tossed threats around and groused because they hadn't gotten to the Union men first. Thrailkill assured the frightened captives that he was a Confederate officer and that he did not kill prisoners. Accordingly Thrailkill confiscated the horses and serviceable weapons of the Union men, required them to sign paroles stating that they would not again take up arms against the South until exchanged, and then turned them loose. Shortly before noon, Thrailkill left Black Oak and headed southeast into Carroll County. He doubled back later in the day when he realized he would not be able to get south of the Missouri River, and the rebels once again spent the night near Black Oak.[15]

The next morning, July 20, Thrailkill rode west toward Kingston and reached the town in mid-afternoon. The raiders pulled up in front of the courthouse, where they promptly took down the Union flag. They removed another American flag from a grocery and consumed a large quantity of whiskey stolen from the store. "The guerrillas…were thirsty as Sahara camels," according to one report, "and thought the beverage all the better because it came from an establishment that had a Union flag over it."[16]

The raiders then plundered the rest of the businesses and robbed many citizens on the streets. One store was unmolested because Thrailkill thought it belonged to a Southern sympathizer, and private residences were also undisturbed. In addition, Thrailkill reportedly overrode Taylor's desire to burn the courthouse. Anticipating General Price's planned invasion of Missouri and his recapture of the state for the Confederacy, Thrailkill remarked that the rebels would need the courthouse to hold court in themselves. In all, the guerrillas took about $6,000 in money and other loot before marching west out of Kingston in the late afternoon.[17]

Late the same night, July 20, the rebels rode into Mirabile in southwestern Caldwell County and resumed their pillaging. The guerrillas robbed stores and private citizens and took several Union men prisoner. While in town, Thrailkill learned that two of his recent recruits who had left his command to return home had been killed the night before by local militia because of their temporary disloyalty. Many of Thrailkill's men, especially Taylor's guerrillas, clamored that the prisoners should be killed in revenge. Thrailkill himself angrily announced that just the previous morning he had captured and paroled twenty-six Caldwell County militia and now soldiers from the same organization had killed two of his men. He was reportedly on the verge of allowing Taylor to carry through with the executions when one of the prisoners gave the sign of freemasonry. After a brief, private consultation with the man, Thrailkill ordered that all the prisoners be released. Amidst much grumbling over their leader's command, the guerrillas then mounted up and rode out of town sometime after midnight on the Plattsburg road. Denied their lust for blood, the rebels took with them another $6,000 in booty as a consolation.[18]

After daylight on July 21, near the Clinton County line, Taylor's guerrillas redressed their disappointment in Mirabile by gunning down a local militiamen in his front yard. Around eight or nine in the morning, the rebels approached Plattsburg, and about ten o'clock Thrailkill sent a courier into town under a flag of truce demanding a surrender of the place. The message read as follows: "Commanding Officer at Plattsburg: I hereby demand an immediate surrender of the town. We are not bushwhackers, but Confederate soldiers. Your men will be treated as prisoners of war. John Thrailkill, Major, Commanding Confederate Forces."[19]

Captain Benjamin F. Poe, commanding one hundred Enrolled Missouri Militia at Plattsburg, determined to try to hold the town. He had previously sent out a scout of twenty-six men under Captain John W. Turney to ascertain the location of the guerrillas, and he now dispatched a messenger with the following reply to Thrailkill's demand: "Major John Thrailkill: Sir, we are not here for the purpose of surrendering, but to defend the flag of our country. B. F. Poe, Captain, Commanding Post."[20]

At about the same time the messenger started out, the guerrillas got into a skirmish with Turney's squad and fired on the messenger as well. Turney himself was killed in the brief clash. The rest of the Federals scattered and then retreated to Plattsburg to help defend the post. Poe also rallied a number of citizens as additional reinforcements. Meanwhile, a militia force under Major Samuel P. Cox, sent out from Livingston and surrounding counties in pursuit of the guerrillas, was bearing down from the northeast, prompting Thrailkill to retire in a southerly direction toward Clay County.[21]

In Clay County, Taylor and his party of about fifty guerrillas left Thrailkill and continued south to link up with Bloody Bill Anderson. Thrailkill, meanwhile, turned northwest, cut across the southwest corner of Clinton County, and went into Platte County. On July 23, the pursuing militia finally caught up and skirmished with Thrailkill north of Camden Point. Major Cox reported one man killed and several wounded during the fracas, and Thrailkill suffered a similar loss. One eyewitness claimed that Thrailkill "handled his men with great skill, and was cool and courageous," during the brief engagement.[22]

Unable to get his recruits across the river with Federals pressing him from several directions, Coon Thornton disbanded his men sometime in late July. Many of them returned to their homes, while some of the more belligerent denounced their leader as a coward and went over to Thrailkill. A St. Joseph newspaperman, in reporting the story, said Thrailkill was "endowed with considerable ability as a partisan leader, much more we think than Thornton, who is a huge lubber with but little brains." The reporter added, however, that Thrailkill was "a desperado of the worst class."[23]

During late July and early August, Thrailkill lingered in the area of northwestern Clay County. Robbing and harassing Union citizens, his men roamed from the vicinity of Ridgely just across the county line in northeastern Platte to the Fishing River bottoms of central Clay, where Taylor was making his headquarters. On August 4, Thrailkill, with eighty to a hundred men, attacked a detachment of twenty-two militiamen about eight miles south of Plattsburg near the Clinton-Clay county line. The Federals promptly fell back to their post at Plattsburg with one man wounded.[24]

After the skirmish, Thrailkill and Taylor rode south to cross the Missouri River with a small squad of men. Taylor had turned his guerrillas over to the newly-arrived Bill Anderson, and most of Thrailkill's men also lingered in Clay County. After crossing the river on the evening of August 4 near Missouri City with their horses swimming behind them, Thrailkill and Taylor went into camp near the Jackson-Lafayette county line with George Todd and other partisan leaders. The total number of guerrillas in camp was approximately three hundred.[25]

On the night of August 8, Taylor and Thrailkill's squad started back to re-cross the river when they were attacked by a party of Jackson County militia about four miles from Independence. Taylor was shot in the left arm, and the bone shattered just above the elbow. His horse was mortally wounded but galloped on for about fifty feet before falling. With the assistance of one of his men, Taylor mounted behind Thrailkill just as Thrailkill was shot in the back of the neck. Despite their wounds, the two made their escape. Three days later, Taylor had his arm amputated by a doctor at Wellington, while Thrailkill made it across the river despite his injury. On the evening of August 12, he stopped near Liberty to have his wound dressed by a Union woman.[26]

Thrailkill then proceeded to the guerrilla camp in Platte County, where he reunited with his recruits. A week and a half later, on August 23, he crossed back to the south side of the Missouri River in command of at least 150 men. Around the middle of September, he re-crossed to the north side, made a juncture with guerrilla leader Silas Gordon, and began gathering recruits again in the Clay County area.[27]

About the same time, Todd's guerrillas also crossed to the north side of the river, and on September 17 the combined force, under Thrailkill's command, attacked a detachment of Federal militia in Ray County between Richmond and Lexington. The rebels killed six, wounded several, and took two prisoners, with no reported casualties of their own. The guerrillas continued in a northwesterly direction into the eastern edge of Clay County before turning east for a march across the state.[28]

On the morning of September 20, Thrailkill sent a flag of truce into Keytesville in Chariton County demanding the town's surrender. The messenger stated that Thrailkill had about 250 men and that he would burn the town and kill all the soldiers at the post if the demand was not met within fifteen minutes. Lieutenant Anthony Pleyer, commanding the local militia, had thirty-five men stationed at the courthouse, twenty-five of whom were considered fit to bear arms.

Even some of these twenty-five, however, were dubious warriors who had expressed reluctance to fight Confederate soldiers. They said they would fight bushwhackers, but they considered Thrailkill a regular Confederate officer. After consulting with Chariton County Sheriff Robert Carman, Pleyer marched his men out of the courthouse and surrendered (an action for which he was later strongly reprimanded).[29]

Thrailkill, who in reality had only about sixty-five men, rode in and took possession of the town. According to Pleyer, Thrailkill told him, as he was drawing up a parole for the militiamen, that he could not have prevented his men from burning the town and killing every last man if Pleyer had not surrendered. To underscore the point, Thrailkill pointed out George Todd, who remarked to Pleyer that the Federals need not consider him a Confederate officer. Todd said he was a bushwhacker and that he "intended to follow bushwhacking as long as he lived."[30]

The parole that Thrailkill handed to the militiamen read as follows: "Chariton County, Missouri, September 20, 1864. This is to certify that Lieutenant Pleyer and a detachment of Captain Owen's company was captured by me, and put on parole of honor not to be broken on the penalty of death. By order of John Thrailkill, Major, Commanding Recruits."[31]

After the surrender, the U. S. flag was taken down from the courthouse, and Thrailkill made a speech to the militia exalting the Confederacy and its flag. The address was greeted by applause and hurrahs, and at least seven of the Federals went over to the Confederate side.[32]

The work of plunder then began. The courthouse was set on fire, and Sheriff Carman, a staunch Union man, was shot and killed after he tried to protect some of the county records. William Young, reportedly the only other actively loyal citizen in the town, was marched outside Keytesville and shot as well. The rebels also took horses, weapons, and money from the town's other citizens. Thrailkill, however, ordered the money returned, and most of it was. After the raid, the rebels continued east on the Glasgow Road, aiming for the Perche Hills along the Boone-Howard county line and a rendezvous with Bill Anderson and other guerrilla leaders. This area had been a haven for bushwhackers throughout the war, and Anderson had recently made Rocheport in western Boone County his unofficial headquarters.[33]

On September 23, shortly after their arrival in the area, Thrailkill and Todd rode down on a Federal wagon train ten miles northeast of Rocheport and killed twelve men of the Third Cavalry Missouri State Militia. The rest of the Federals scattered in disarray, and the guerrillas set the wagons on fire. Some of the bodies of the dead soldiers were thrown into the blaze.[34]

That night, Thrailkill and Todd went into camp south of Fayette in Howard County. The next morning Bill Anderson, Quantrill, and other guerrilla leaders rode in, and the entire guerrilla force started north. After being repulsed at Fayette, the rebels continued north and threatened Huntsville, then turned east. During the September 27 slaughter of Major Johnston's troops southeast of Centralia, the attacking guerrillas were divided into three companies under Thrailkill, Todd, and Anderson. However, Thrailkill, like Holtzclaw, did not participate in Anderson's massacre of unarmed soldiers in Centralia earlier in the day.[35]

After Centralia, little else is known with certainty about Thrailkill's movements during 1864. In early October he was reported in the Mussel Fork area of eastern Chariton County (Holtzclaw's old stomping grounds) with three hundred men, and on October 10, he and Thornton were supposedly spotted in Clay and Platte counties. An apparently conflicting report from about the same time suggested that he crossed the Missouri River to rendezvous with Price's army near Boonville. Then, as Price started eastward along the south side of the river, a party of guerrillas, thought to be under Thrailkill, Todd, and Dave Pool, killed thirty Union men at a German settlement in Lafayette County on October 13. Later in the month, Thrailkill with about 150 men was reported in the Montevallo area of southeastern Vernon County in advance of Price's retreat.[36]

Thrailkill went south and spent the winter with Price's army, but the following spring, he was reported back in Missouri. He and Silas Gordon were supposedly spotted in Clay County with about 150 men near the first of April. If Thrailkill, in fact, returned to Missouri in 1865, his latest sojourn in the state proved brief, as he soon reunited with Price's army and after the war accompanied Shelby on his expedition to Mexico. Unlike many of the expatriate Missourians,

Thrailkill remained in Mexico, where he associated himself with General Porfirio Diaz's government and became successful in the mining, cattle, and railroad business. He died in 1895 at Mexico City.[37]

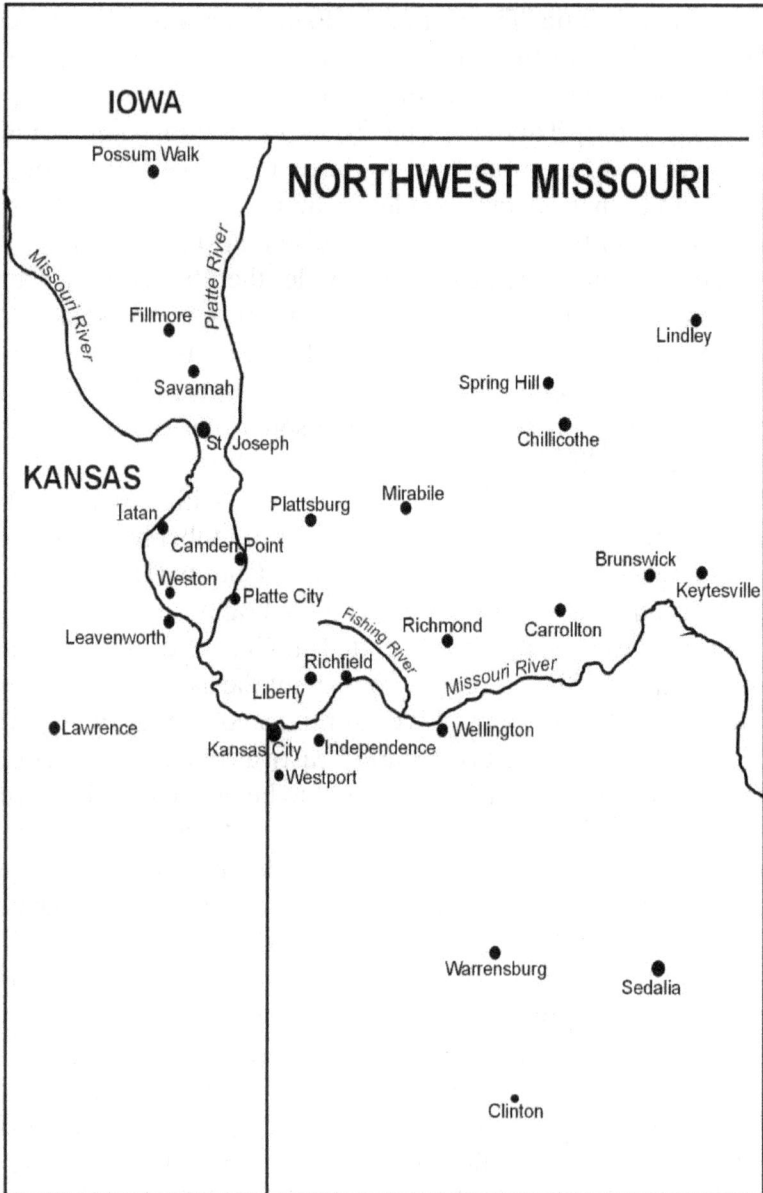

IOWA

Possum Walk

NORTHWEST MISSOURI

Missouri River

Platte River

Fillmore

Lindley

Savannah

Spring Hill

St Joseph

Chillicothe

KANSAS

Iatan

Plattsburg

Mirabile

Camden Point

Brunswick

Weston

Keytesville

Platte City

Fishing River

Richmond

Carrollton

Leavenworth

Richfield

Liberty

Missouri River

Lawrence

Wellington

Kansas City Independence

Westport

Warrensburg

Sedalia

Clinton

Map of northwest Missouri, showing haunts of Hart, Thrailkill, and Gordon.

13
Silas Gordon: The Only Whacker of Any Prominence

An occasional ally of Thrailkill, Silas M. Gordon was the youngest son of William Gordon and Lucretia Muir, who married in Clark County, Kentucky, on March 10, 1814. Silas was born about 1835, and the family moved to Platte County, Missouri, around 1840. William Gordon died prior to 1850, and at the time of the 1850 census, fifteen-year-old Silas was living with his mother in Platte County with no other members of the family in the household.[1]

Growing up, Si Gordon attended school in the Weston vicinity, and he was apparently an upstanding student who did little to call attention. In 1864, a former schoolmate expressed surprise that he had become a notorious guerrilla: "Little did we think when attending school with him a few years ago that he would turn out the man he has."[2]

A staunch Union newspaperman in Gordon's hometown, however, told a different story. Without offering specifics, he claimed that Gordon, "by his villainy in youth,...broke a devoted mother's heart;" later murdered a man; and, during the time leading up to the war, was a fugitive from the law, "sheltering himself from justice in the wilds of Kansas."[3]

When the Civil War broke out, Gordon joined the Missouri State Guard as a private in Major "Coon" Thornton's battalion of Brigadier General Alexander E. Steen's Fifth Division and was engaged at Carthage, Wilson's Creek, and Dry Wood Creek. When Price's army moved north after the action at Dry Wood on September 2, Gordon crossed the river into his northwest Missouri haunts with a commission to raise his own company in the Platte County area. On September 16, 1861, at Platte City, he and his recruits skirmished with the advance guard of Colonel Robert F. Smith's Sixteenth Illinois, killing the Federal guide. The next day Gordon's budding command re-crossed the river with other troops of the Fifth Division in time to reinforce General Price at the Siege of Lexington.[4]

Shortly afterwards, Gordon, now a captain in the State Guard, went back to the north side of the river and resumed his recruiting and marauding in the Platte County area. In response to the rebel activity, Major Peter A. Josephs marched from St. Joseph to Platte County in late October with a militia force of about 150 men. Recently called out by Missouri Provisional Governor Hamilton R. Gamble, (although not yet authorized by the U. S. War Department), the "six months' men" swept into Platte City on October 30 and surrounded the place with pickets. Major Josephs had learned during his approach to the town that Gordon was present, and he hoped to trap the rebel leader inside the city limits. Gordon was, indeed, at Platte City at the time, but he avoided detection by hiding beneath a church house. After nightfall, he managed to escape and began organizing his men to resist the Union occupation of Platte City.[5]

The next day, Josephs sent out scouts on the roads leading into Platte City, and at least one of the scouting parties met and skirmished with the guerrillas. A Union account immediately following the action reported that the camp of "the rebel desperado Si Gordon" was overrun and that five horses, several wagons, and twelve guns were confiscated. The compiler of the 1885 *History of Clay and Platte Counties*, on the other hand, claimed that all of the Union scouts were driven back into Platte City "at a break neck speed."[6]

During or shortly after the skirmish, several of the Union pickets who had been left to guard the town were also attacked in a separate action, and at least one was mortally wounded. When the Union scouting parties returned to town, Major Josephs positioned two cannons "in the direction of the supposed enemy" and fired five shots, but it was "not known that any of the rebels were killed."[7]

Two days later, on November 2, 1861, Major Josephs and his command marched out of Platte City on the Weston road. Gordon and his men lay in ambush at Bee Creek a few miles west of Platte City, and when the Union troops approached, the guerrillas opened fire, driving Josephs's advance guard back into the main body. The major formed his men and opened with his artillery. Many of the raw Southern recruits scattered at the first fire of the heavy guns, but the skirmish continued sporadically for about an hour before a lack of ammunition compelled the rest of the guerrillas to retreat. A Union correspondent claimed that as many as thirty rebels were killed and a large number captured, including Gordon himself, and that the Federal side had none killed and only a handful wounded. Again the county historian of 1885 begged to differ. He said the Union lost four killed and seven wounded, while the Southern side had only two wounded, one of whom later died.[8]

On November 6, Gordon accosted and disarmed a Federal lieutenant named Hollister when the officer crossed the Missouri River from Kansas on the Weston ferry. Upon learning the news, Union officials at Leavenworth immediately dispatched two companies of troops and one piece of artillery to Weston, but Gordon and his guerrillas were nowhere to be found.[9]

Also on November 6, Gordon issued a proclamation from his Platte County headquarters, and a Leavenworth newspaper printed it two days later:

> TO WHOM IT MAY CONCERN: I adopt this course, that I may not longer be misrepresented.
>
> I am charged with being a Bandit and Robber. Such is not my position. I am acting in defense of the certain and legitimate rights of myself and neighbors against wrongdoers, coming from whatever quarter they may. As far as I am able I will punish thieves and robbers. I do not propose interfering with the movement of Federal troops, legitimately made; but I will oppose armed force passing through, or being quartered in our County, for the purpose of molesting our citizens, or taking their property. These duties belong to the civil authorities. Let them discharge them. All others are left to our regular armies now in the field. Honorable men will let the test of war settle it. I am certain the good people of Platte will support me in this course.
>
> Si Gordon, Captain[10]

Around the middle of November, Gordon and his band roamed east toward Chariton County. At Plattsburg, in Clinton County, he captured James H. Burch, an "uncompromising Union man" and member of the Missouri State Convention. During the trip he also took one or two other prominent Union men prisoner, and he delivered all of the captives to Price's headquarters south of the river.[11]

On November 25 at Platte City, Gordon captured two Union men from Weston who had traveled to the county seat to attend court.

Gordon and his band started off toward Liberty with the prisoners. A detachment of home guards from Weston set out in pursuit but turned back when they neared Platte City after learning that "the secessionists had gathered in great force at that place and were determined to give battle...."[12]

On November 27, the home guards left Weston, and the following day Gordon rode in and took possession of the town with about thirty men. The gang robbed several stores belonging to Union men. Then, when a northbound train on the Kansas City to St. Joseph Railroad pulled into town for its scheduled stop, the guerrillas immediately surrounded it. Among the passengers were Captain Thomas Moonlight and Captain John W. Rabb, artillerists in the Kansas Brigade, along with two other Federal officers, a Captain Harrison and a Lieutenant White. Gordon took all four officers prisoner, and sent the train back to Leavenworth, where its unexpected return created "considerable excitement."[13]

Although Captain Harrison quickly escaped, Gordon held the other three officers captive. He and Moonlight immediately entered into negotiations for an exchange of prisoners, with two residents of Platte County, Jesse Morin and Lee Oldham, acting as intermediaries. Captain Rabb and Lieutenant White were left in the charge of Mr. Oldham, while Moonlight was allowed to continue to St. Joseph, in the company of Mr. Morin, to try to effect the exchange—himself and the other two Federal officers for a similar number of rebel prisoners that were then being held at St. Joseph. Oldham agreed to protect the Federal captives in exchange for Moonlight's pledge to return.[14]

Almost as soon as Moonlight had left, however, Gordon took the two officers from Oldham and whisked them away to Liberty via Platte City. From Liberty, the captives were sent south to Price's army or, in Moonlight's words, "to God knows where." (They were exchanged or released on parole a few days later.) Gordon also dispatched a party of men to pursue Moonlight and bring him back, but they didn't catch him, because he had taken a different road. After learning what had happened, Moonlight sent a letter to Oldham from St. Joseph on November 30 stating that Gordon's treachery had absolved him of any obligation to return to Platte County.[15]

The day after Moonlight's capture, "Gordon and his freebooters" waylaid another train at Weston, "took possession of the mails and express goods, and made off with them." Then the following night the guerrillas burned the railroad bridge near Iatan, north of Weston.[16]

By late November of 1861, many loyal citizens had been driven from Platte County by "the scoundrels under Si Gordon" and were "constantly flocking" to St. Joseph and other Union-held towns. "It is unsafe for any Union man to travel in Platte County," a newspaper correspondent said, "as Gordon's band...is sure to arrest and hold in durance vile every man suspected of loyalty.[17]

So, when Major-General David Hunter was installed as commander of the Union's newly formed Department of Kansas with headquarters at Leavenworth, one observer greeted the appointment with enthusiasm. Suggesting that Colonel Smith, who had previously occupied Platte County and had had a dubious skirmish with Gordon in September, was "an idiotic dotard of cowardly proclivities," the editor of the *Leavenworth Conservative* crowed that "General Hunter is ready and willing to take care of Platte County."[18]

True to the newspaperman's prediction, Hunter soon turned his attention to the trouble across the river. On December 2, 1861, from Leavenworth, he issued a manifesto to the "trustees of Platte City, Platte County, Missouri," which read as follows:

> Gentlemen: Having received reliable information of depredation and outrages of every kind committed by a man named "Si Gordon," a leader of rebel marauding bands, I give you notice that unless you seize and deliver the said Gordon to me at these Head Quarters within ten days from this date, or drive him out of the county, I shall send a force to your city with orders to *reduce it to ashes, and to burn the house of every Secessionist in your county, and to carry away every negro.*
>
> Col. Jennison's regiment will be entrusted with the execution of this order.
>
> The following named persons are particularly directed to this notice: David Hunt, Clinton Cockerill, James Merryman, Robert Cain, John Murray, H. T. Freeland, Wm. Paxton, W. C. Remington, Andrew Tribble, R. P. S. Ely, Jackson Miller, Robert Clark, W. Tutman, H. M. Cochrane, Samuel M. Hayes, Joseph Todd and Jonas Burkhart.

D. Hunter,
Maj. Gen. Commanding[19]

Some of the named individuals were, no doubt, friends or relatives of Gordon, while others were simply prominent men who were known to nurse Southern sympathies. Clinton Cockerill, for example, was Gordon's next-door neighbor at the time of the 1850 Platte County census, and during the war he became a member of the Order of American Knights, a secret Confederate organization that was particularly active in border states like Missouri.[20]

On the evening of December 6, four days after Hunter's proclamation, Gordon and some of his band visited the home of a man named William Zabriskye in Platte County just across the river from Leavenworth and "took off every horse and saddle on the farm."[21]

Prompted, according to the compiler of the 1885 Platte County history, by his desire to save the property of Southern citizens, Gordon left the county shortly after Hunter's proclamation. However, the Union's growing impatience with him, if a report that reached eastern Missouri is to be believed, may have had as much to do with Gordon's departure as his concern for the citizens of the county. In early December, a man arrived at Hannibal by train from western Missouri and claimed that "Sy Gordon, the notorious chief of Northwest Missouri," had been shot at a hotel in Platte County and was not expected to live. Two Union citizens supposedly had ridden up and shot him on sight for having bragged about his role in burning the Platte River bridge.[22]

If, indeed, Gordon was shot in early December, he wasn't hurt as seriously as the report suggested, because he rode south at about the same time he was supposed to be on his deathbed. Neither his concern for the property of his Southern-sympathizing neighbors nor the Union's determination to exterminate him likely had much to do with the decision, as he was probably already making plans to leave at the time of Hunter's order. At any rate, his company and five other companies of recruits from Platte and neighboring counties marched south to join the Confederate Army almost immediately after the guerrillas' visit to the Zabriskye farm. Indeed, Gordon probably took Zabriskye's horses in anticipation of the trip.[23]

A rumor reached Leavenworth on December 13 that Gordon had been captured or killed by Federal soldiers near Liberty, "but, as it turned out, he was not among those taken, having proceeded by another road to Lexington, where, when last heard from, he was relating his experiences to a gaping crowd of ragged Secessia."[24]

From Lexington, Gordon continued his trip to southwest Missouri and arrived near the middle of the month. He was enrolled into Confederate service at Springfield on December 16, 1861, by Major Robert R. Lawther and assigned to Colonel Elijah Gates's First Missouri Cavalry regiment of the First Missouri Brigade (the same unit John Thrailkill joined a week later). On December 31, Gordon was elected captain of Company I. Marching south from Springfield with the First Cavalry, Gordon participated in the actions at Sugar Creek and Bentonville, Arkansas, in mid-February 1862 and the Battle of Pea Ridge in early March.[25]

From Arkansas, the Missourians marched east and took part in the engagement at Farmington, Mississippi in early May 1862. Not long afterwards, Gordon was re-elected captain during a re-organization of Confederate forces, and his unit was re-assigned to Brigadier General John S. Bowen's Brigade of Major General Mansfield Lovell's Division, Army of the Mississippi. Gordon fought with Bowen's brigade at the engagement at Iuka (Mississippi) in mid-September and at the Battle of Corinth in early October. In mid-October, Bowen was transferred to Price's Army of the West and made commander of a division. Gordon's unit was assigned to Brigadier General Martin Green's brigade of Bowen's division as dismounted cavalry. Gordon was wounded around mid-December in some unknown action and was listed as "unable for service—gunshot wound."[26]

In late February 1863, Gordon was reported absent without leave, and the First Missouri Cavalry muster roll for March and April listed him as having deserted on February 23 on the Big Black River, Mississippi. In mid-September 1863, he was dropped from the roll. However, other evidence suggests that Gordon was captured and later paroled and sent west of the Mississippi on recruiting duty. If he was captured unbeknown to his own unit, it could explain why he was listed as a deserter. Another report suggests that, during the time in question, Gordon, like Quantrill, made a trip to Richmond seeking a colonel's commission and authority to raise a regiment under the Partisan Ranger Act.[27]

At any rate, not long after Gordon was listed as a deserter, he was back in the Missouri-Kansas border area, either as a recruiter or a fugitive. He was first rumored to be in the area in mid-May 1863, when "satisfactory proof" reached Leavenworth that he was back home in Platte County. A detachment of soldiers from the fort crossed the river and, upon being refused admittance to the house where Gordon was rumored to be staying, promptly set it ablaze. A man came to the window carrying a double-barreled gun, and the soldiers opened fire, killing him instantly. The soldiers supposed their victim to be Gordon, but he turned out to be a man named McBratney.[28]

Gordon himself was apparently in Douglas County, Kansas, when McBratney was shot. Near the time of the incident in Platte County, a man reported to be one of Gordon's guerrillas was killed near Lawrence. In a separate incident at about the same time, another guerrilla was seriously wounded and taken prisoner in a brief skirmish with soldiers west of Lawrence. Brought to Leavenworth, the injured man said that Gordon had been with him during the skirmish and that he (Gordon) had also been wounded. Just a few days later, another guerrilla was arrested in Leavenworth and accused of being a "friend and aid of Cy Gordon," and four days after this incident, yet another Gordon man was arrested and put in the guard house as the round-up of Si's confederates continued.[29]

On June 20, 1863, a rumor surfaced in Wyandotte, Kansas, that "the veritable Cy. Gordon" had taken breakfast in town four days earlier. "We do not vouch for the truth of the story," the editor of the local newspaper allowed, "but it easily *may* be true." The editor expressed little doubt that Gordon and Quantrill "keep themselves perfectly posted in regard to our means of defense, either by their own observation or through such spies as they choose to send among us."[30]

However, nothing more was heard from Gordon until he turned up in southern Kansas shortly before the October 6, 1863, action at Baxter Springs. According to one post-war account of the action, Gordon had been in the area at least a couple of weeks prior to Quantrill's attack. A band of guerrillas led by Gordon supposedly waylaid and robbed two civilian mailmen between Fort Scott and Fort

Gibson in late September and let it be known that Quantrill meant to pay a visit to Baxter Springs in the near future.[31]

In the days following the Baxter Springs massacre, reports suggested that Si Gordon was one of the guerrilla leaders, along with Quantrill, who led the attack. Although it was erroneously reported that Colonel John T. Coffee was also one of the rebel leaders at Baxter Springs, it seems likely that Gordon did participate in the attack. An account written immediately after the action said General Blunt's chief scout, William Tough, although he was dressed in bushwhacker attire, was recognized by Gordon as the scout was making his way back through guerrilla lines to the general's side after riding forward with Major Henning to investigate the action that was taking place at the fort. Gordon, who knew Tough, alerted his comrades, and he and his small party of guerrillas exchanged a volley of fire with the scout as the latter made his escape.[32]

After the action at Baxter Springs, however, Gordon did not accompany the Quantrill command south but instead lingered in the area of the southern Kansas border as he had been doing for some time prior to the action. Less than a week after Quantrill's attack, Gordon led a raid on the Osage Mission (at present-day St. Paul) in southern Kansas. After roaming in the vicinity for several days, Gordon and about twenty-five guerrillas took possession of the mission on Sunday, October 11, during religious services, timing their raid "to obtain the most plunder." The rebels stole a number of horses, guns, and clothing, and they also captured two soldiers of the Ninth Kansas Cavalry but later paroled them. A party of Osage Indians were normally stationed at the mission in the service of the Federal army, but they had gone to Baxter Springs after learning of Quantrill's attack. These were the same Indians who, the previous May, had annihilated a party of Confederates that were on their way to Colorado and New Mexico to organize guerrilla bands there, and Gordon's attack may have been carried out partially in retaliation for the previous incident.[33]

On October 28, 1863, a party of fifteen guerrillas came up to within thirteen miles of Humboldt, plundered several homes, and "killed one half-breed." The rebel band immediately left for the South after this raid. Very possibly this was Gordon's gang, because he was known to have been in the same general area two weeks earlier. Also, in late November a Union citizen living at Humboldt wrote a letter reporting that Gordon had been roaming along the border separating Kansas and Indian Territory several weeks earlier disguised as a Federal captain.[34]

The following spring Gordon, with twenty men, turned up again in Indian Territory, northeast of Tahlequah near the Arkansas border, where he fell in briefly with Colonel William P. Adair of Stand Watie's Indian brigade. Around April 15, 1864, Adair sent Gordon on a scout after Federal Indians of the Kansas tribe. Quantrill, on his journey north after wintering in Texas, also made a juncture with Adair in mid-April, and it's possible that Gordon continued north with Quantrill's guerrilla command.[35]

In May 1864, a guerrilla lieutenant named Willard Hadley, who had been with Gordon in northern Missouri during 1861, was hanged at Warrensburg. However, Gordon himself was not specifically heard from again until August of 1864, when he showed up in his home territory of Platte County. Gordon's reappearance alarmed the Union citizens of Platte and stirred the soldiers stationed at Weston to action.[36]

On the morning of August 18, a detachment of the Seventeenth Illinois Cavalry found Gordon at the home of a "*good loyal citizen*" in a local, rural neighborhood and surrounded the residence. Gordon made a break for the brush amid a hail of bullets and managed to escape, minus his horse, saddle, and boots.[37]

The next day, Gordon went to Platte City with a body guard of six men, visited old acquaintances, and made a speech in which he said he had been fighting for the Southern cause for three years and it was now time for his friends to fight, too. Before leaving, he furnished himself "at the expense of the citizens" with a new pair of boots, saddle, and other gear to replace what he had lost the morning before.[38]

On August 20, a detachment of the Ninth Missouri State Militia came upon Gordon and three bushwhackers near Platte City and chased them for several miles, capturing their commissary supplies, which consisted of "a side of old bacon and some corn bread." Another report about the same time suggested that Gordon, with band of eight men, was "running through the county" and picking up recruits.[39]

On August 21, after three days in the saddle, the weary Weston troops finally called off their chase after Gordon. The next day, August 22, they resumed their "wolf hunt" and had a running fight with Gordon near Farley. Once again, Gordon narrowly escaped, and two of his men were killed. The fighting was at such close quarters that one of Gordon's men beat one of the soldiers about the head with his rifle, and the Federals also had one man badly injured in a fall from his horse. When General Fisk learned of the skirmish, he wired Major Hiram Hilliard, commander at Weston, urging him to "make an end of Cy Gordon."[40]

Around the first of September 1864, Gordon, who, according to Major Hilliard, was "the only whacker of any prominence now left" in northwest Missouri, was spotted going north toward the Iowa line. By the middle of the month, however, he was back in the Clay County area, where he made a juncture with John Thrailkill, his fellow officer from the First Missouri Cavalry. One Union observer predicted that General Fisk would soon make the district "too hot for Cy Gordon's land pirates," but the threat didn't prevent Gordon and Thrailkill from "stealing horses and picking up recruits."[41]

A few days after the juncture between Gordon and Thrailkill, they were joined by George Todd. The entire command then rode east, raided Keytesville on September 20, and took part in the fight with Major Johnston's troops at Centralia on September 27.[42]

In early October, Gordon was said to have crossed the Missouri River with Thrailkill near Portland in Calloway County. Gordon was presumably still with Thrailkill when the latter reportedly re-crossed the river around October 10 and made a junction in Clay County with Coon Thornton, Gordon's old State Guard commander.[43]

Gordon spent the winter of 1864-65 in Texas, and the next spring he and Thrailkill reappeared together in Clay County near the end of March in command of 150 bushwhackers. In mid-May, Gordon was again reported in Clay, having recently crossed the river from Jackson County with a few men. Little, however, was heard from Gordon after this. After the war, he lived in Texas near Sherman, the old guerrilla wintering spot, and, according to at least one report, the small community of Gordonville was named after him.[44]

14
Rucker, Pulliam, and Company

John F. Rucker was born around 1830 in Virginia, and the family moved to Missouri during his youth. At the time of the 1850 census, Rucker was living in Howard County with the Adam Hendrix family, and he was still living in Howard County when he married Jane Cowden in Boone County on June 2, 1853. At the time of the 1860 census, the couple was living in Rocheport, where Rucker was a merchant.[1]

When the Civil War started, Rucker joined Brigadier General John B. Clark's Third Division of the Missouri State Guard. He was sworn into service on May 15, 1861, in Cooper County by Major John B. Clark, Jr., the general's son. On June 14 Rucker was commissioned as a second lieutenant in Company D of the younger Clark's First Regiment, and he was later engaged at Carthage, Wilson's Creek, and Lexington. Sometime during the summer of 1861, Rucker took command of Company D. Then on November 5, 1861, he was promoted to major and served as an aide-de-camp in the Third Division.[2]

Prior to the Battle of Pea Ridge in early March of 1862, Major Rucker took command of the skeletal First Regiment, as the younger Clark had been promoted to colonel and given command of the division. According to Colonel Clark's after-battle report, Rucker "behaved with great gallantry" at Pea Ridge and was seriously wounded. Although the injury proved less severe than Clark thought, Rucker was captured and taken to Springfield. On July 7, 1862, he was transferred to Gratiot Street Prison in St. Louis.[3]

James Drury Pulliam, a man with whom Rucker would be associated later in the war, was also from Howard County. The son of Benjamin G. Pulliam and Sarah Margaret Head (and the grandson of Drury Pulliam who died in Saline County in 1849), J. Drury was born in Howard around 1840. The family moved to Caldwell County, Texas, about 1852, but when the Civil War began, young Pulliam, who listed his occupation as lawyer, came back to his native state to join the Missouri State Guard. He served on the staff of Colonel Edwin Price, son of Sterling Price and commander of the Third Regiment of Brigadier General John B. Clark's Third Division, the same division Rucker was in. During his service with the state forces, Pulliam saw action at the Battle of Elkhorn (Pea Ridge) in March of 1862.[4]

Pulliam went east with General Price's army in the spring of 1862, and he was enlisted into Confederate service on May 7 at Corinth by Rucker's old commander, Colonel John B. Clark, Jr. On May 15, 1862, Pulliam was made a sergeant in Captain John M. Hickey's company of Colonel Eugene Erwin's Sixth Missouri Infantry. On August 27 Pulliam was sent back to the Trans-Mississippi Department on recruiting duty with Colonel Waldo P. Johnson. From Little Rock, during the second week of September, Johnson sent Pulliam and about thirty other recruiting officers into Missouri "for the purpose of enlisting and swearing into the service of the C. S. Army all the able-bodied men they could meet with."[5]

Meanwhile, shortly after his arrival in St. Louis during the summer of 1862, Rucker escaped from Gratiot Street Prison and returned to his home territory around Rocheport. On August 1, he and about forty "brigands" under his command took possession of the town. The next day, Rucker boarded a steam boat at the Rocheport landing and demanded all the government horses and supplies that were on board, but he left empty-handed after becoming convinced that the only horses and provisions on board were privately owned. Then, after a couple of months of recruiting in the area, he crossed the river and started south in early October in company with Colonel Caleb Dorsey, who was on his way to link up with Confederate forces who had retired to northwest Arkansas after the engagement at Newtonia in late September. On October 20, the rebel party, which numbered about 300, skirmished with Federal troops near Marshfield in Webster County with a loss of four killed, twenty-seven captured, and "a good many" wounded, according to a Union officer, while the Federals reportedly lost only one man killed and one wounded.[6]

According to his own testimony, Rucker started back north from Arkansas about the middle of December 1862 with his brother Horace "Harvey" Rucker and "Old Man Flanigan." Around January 6, 1863, in Camden County, Missouri, the party was arrested by some Union militia and taken to nearby Linn Creek. Rucker was wearing a gray uniform with major's buttons when captured. Also, a letter that a Confederate officer had written to his wife from Pocahontas,

Arkansas, and that Rucker was apparently planning to deliver was found on Rucker's person. Besides the private communications of husband to wife, the letter contained the following statement: "Major Rucker leaves today for Boone County, Missouri, to bring out his men."[7]

Accompanied this time by his brother, Rucker was sent back to Gratiot Street Prison, from where Major Rucker gave a statement in early February and asked to be released on parole. Despite the uniform he was wearing when captured, he claimed he was not in Confederate service when taken prisoner because he had resigned his commission the previous October. Despite the contents of the confiscated letter, he also maintained that he was not on a recruiting expedition and that the officer who had written to his wife was mistaken. Rucker admitted that he had considered such a mission but had decided, instead, to go home and "if the Confederate Army came in and got possession of Missouri in the spring, then I thought I might go out again." Federal authorities, however, remained unconvinced by Rucker's dubious vow of innocence, and his request for parole was denied.[8]

Meanwhile, Pulliam had allied himself with Sidney D. Jackman shortly after arriving in the Missouri-Arkansas area on recruiting duty in the late summer of 1862. Although Jackman was living in Bates County at the outbreak of the Civil War, he, like Pulliam and Rucker, was originally from the Howard County area, and his mother still lived there. Jackman had recently recruited a regiment and been commissioned a colonel in the Confederate Army, but in early November of 1862, he resigned command of his regiment in order to go back into Missouri on further recruiting duty. Jackman made Pulliam his junior assistant adjutant general with the rank of captain, and the recruiting party started north from the Huntsville, Arkansas, area around the middle of November.[9]

Jackman's command reached the familiar territory of Howard County around the first of the year, and a few days later, on the night of January 11, 1863, a group of about fifteen guerrillas under Pulliam rode into Columbia to try to break some rebels, who had been incarcerated on civil charges, out of jail. They fired into the jail and exchanged a few lively shots with a handful of guards lodged in the

Map of Northeast and North Central Missouri showing the principal haunts of Rucker, Pulliam, Holtzclaw, Jackson, and Jim Anderson.

nearby courthouse, but the only damage they did was to accidentally shoot and mortally wound one of their own men. Before he expired, the dying man identified several of his confederates, including Pulliam. Jackman later blamed the failure of the mission on Pulliam's dissipation, as he claimed that Pulliam was "pretty well fired up" with whiskey at the time.[10]

Late on the night of March 14, Pulliam and Jackman called at the Rocheport home of a local militia captain, Robert G. Lyell, with the intention of kidnapping him and hanging him from a bridge. Fearful that he would be recognized, Jackman sent Pulliam to the door and only made his appearance after Pulliam was admitted. Once inside, however, the two rebels decided against killing the man, because of the supplications of his wife. Instead, they contented themselves with merely stealing the captain's pistol and horse.[11]

With his request for parole having been turned down, Rucker soon resorted to a wilier plan for securing his freedom. Around the middle of March 1863, he and several other prisoners at Gratiot Street donned Federal uniforms that had been smuggled in by Southern sympathizers living in St. Louis. One of the group feigned smallpox, and the others, pretending to be his doctors and nurses, carried him out of the prison, supposedly to the hospital. As soon as the party reached the street, however, "the patient got suddenly well," and the whole group made their escape.[12]

Having gained his freedom again, Rucker, as he was wont to do, returned to his home territory, where he quickly hooked up with Jackman and Pulliam. In the wee hours of the morning of April 23, 1863, Rucker called at the Glasgow home of Brigadier-General Thomas J. Bartholow, commanding the Enrolled Missouri Militia in the district. When an insistent rapping awoke the general from his sleep, he struck a light, went to the door, and demanded to know who the man was and what he wanted. Rucker said he had a message from Colonel Odon Guitar, whose headquarters were at Columbia. After some reluctance, Bartholow admitted the mysterious caller and had a brief interview with him. As Rucker was leaving, Bartholow followed him toward the door. Several of Rucker's allies lurked just outside the entrance, and when Bartholow reached the doorway, one of them forced his way in and helped his leader overpower the general. The mysterious caller then announced himself as Major Rucker of Jackman's command and told the general that he was Jackman's prisoner.[13]

Rucker and his confederates gave Bartholow time to dress and then escorted him through the night to Jackman's camp about twelve miles southeast of Glasgow. The next day Bartholow met with Jackman and negotiated his own exchange. In consideration of his release, he offered a pardon to a man named Maxwell who had been accused of harboring some of Jackman's men but whom Bartholow already believed to be innocent. It wasn't much of a concession, but Jackman accepted the offer and released the general unharmed. (Some accounts of this affair suggest that taking Bartholow hostage had been pre-arranged between Jackman and Maxwell as a means of obtaining amnesty for Maxwell and that Bartholow was relieved of his command as a result of the debacle.)[14]

Shortly after this incident, Jackman sent Pulliam east into Pike and Lincoln counties on recruiting duty, while Jackman lingered in the Howard County area. Pulliam landed in northern Lincoln County around the last of April with a band of about twenty-five men and immediately started causing "disturbances." The guerrillas stole a number of horses in the Auburn area, and on April 30 a party of Lincoln County militia tracked the thieves into southern Pike County. The rebels, however, lay in wait and opened fire on the Federals from the bushes, wounding five. The militia "not knowing the strength of the guerrillas thought prudent to retire to the prairie near by."[15]

When word of the guerrilla attack reached Hannibal, another party of Lincoln militia who had been detached to Hannibal, came down into their home county in search of the bushwhackers. Near Louisville on May 2, they captured P. J. Davis, who had "been an active rebel since the beginning of the rebellion" and was suspected of having participated in the attack on the militia two days earlier. Davis was taken out and shot, "three balls entering his breast, killing him instantly." The militia then went to the house of a man named James Wren, burned his house, and took him prisoner, because he had supposedly "openly boasted of being a guerrilla."[16]

Two days later, on the evening of May 4, the guerrillas went on a robbery spree in the Paynesville area of southeast Pike County. They stole two horses from one Union man, two horses and two saddles from another, two horses and two saddles from a third, two guns and a revolver from a fourth, and another revolver from a fifth. They also reportedly committed "other depredations not enumerated."[17]

Near the same time and in the same general area, Pulliam, with his command now swollen to almost fifty guerrillas, called at the home of W. S. Schooler and "tried to get him to swear to support the

Southern Confederacy." When Schooler refused, the gang promptly robbed him of a revolver, ammunition, and some clothes. They also tried to steal his horses, but the animals were out in the fields and could not be corralled.[18]

On the night of May 11, 1863, Pulliam and gang, looking for more weapons and horses, visited the house of a prominent citizen named H. V. P. Block. The man had no guns, and his horses "did not suit them." So they took only a heavy blanket. The rebels informed Block that they were "not horse thieves and murderers but 'Partisan Rangers' commissioned to recruit for the rebel service." Pulliam told Block that he would hold him and another citizen from Lincoln County personally responsible if there were any more house burnings by Federal militia. He also handed Block a letter with a request that it be forwarded to a local militia colonel. In the letter, Pulliam suggested that if certain parties now being held prisoner by the Federals, including James Wren, were released, he would withdraw from Lincoln and Pike counties and no longer molest the citizens of the area. Otherwise, Pulliam said, he would remain in the counties and "retaliate to the fullest extent."[19]

Pulliam suggested to Block that the colonel's reply could be published in a local newspaper of which the guerrilla chief was a regular reader. The editor, however, commented that he didn't know how Pulliam came by the paper because "we are sure he is not a subscriber." The editor, who had been privy to Pulliam's letter, also remarked that "we have rarely met with a cooler piece of impudence."[20]

Two nights later, on May 13, some of Pulliam's gang raided the area of New Harmony in southwest Pike County. Calling at the home of a man and his wife, the rebels asked to be allowed to search the house, and, according to the lady's own account, "we complied with all their *polite* requests with the same grace that a well-bred dog starts of his own accord to leave a room when he sees preparations on foot to kick him out." Ransacking the house, the guerrillas stole three guns from the woman's chamber and carried off from the rest of the house "everything of any use they could."[21]

One of the gang cursed the woman's aged father and threatened to "blow his brains out," and several of them announced their intent to kill every militia member they came across. The rebels then compelled the woman's husband at the point of a bayonet to guide them to his barn, where they stole two horses and "every saddle, bridle and halter on the place."[22]

From the woman's house, the guerrillas took the road toward New Harmony, "robbing every Union house they passed." In town they stole the property of nearly everyone "except the open or concealed rebel sympathizers," taking several thousand dollars' worth of goods within a few hours. The lady, however, concluded her story by admitting that, "perhaps for rebels they were tolerably civil."[23]

Pulliam landed back in the Howard County area during the latter part of May, and on the morning of June 1, 1863, a detachment of fifteen Enrolled Missouri Militia from Glasgow under Captain Samuel W. Steinmetz went out looking for Jackman, not realizing that he had been reinforced by Pulliam's return from Pike County. The Federals accidentally came upon the rebels, numbering approximately fifty, entrenched in a ravine about two miles north of Rocheport, and the soldiers were under attack before they knew what was happening. Two militiamen were killed in the melee, one wounded, and another taken prisoner. Four others struck out in various directions, while the main body hightailed it toward Fayette with the rebels in pursuit. During the chase, a Howard County citizen was killed while on his way to the county court at Fayette. Union officials suggested that the guerrillas killed him intentionally, while, according to the Southern side of the story, the man accidentally got caught in a crossfire between the fleeing militia and a squad under Pulliam.[24]

When the militiamen reached Fayette with word of the attack, Captain Reeves Leonard of that post took fifty men of the Missouri State Militia Cavalry and went back out in search of "Jackman, Rucker, Pulliam, and company," as Leonard's superior officer, Lieutenant-Colonel John F. Williams, dubbed the rebel force. Leonard found the guerrillas that afternoon northeast of Rocheport where the morning skirmish had occurred. Leonard promptly attacked the rebels and, after a fight of about twenty minutes, "drove them flying before him." The guerrillas lost two killed and six wounded, while the Federals reported five men wounded, including Leonard himself. Jackman claimed the odds against him in this fight were seventy-five Federals compared to only ten or twelve in his "little squad," and he said both Rucker and Pulliam "behaved splendidly...against such great odds."[25]

On the night of June 5, some of Jackman's men went to Hallsville in northern Boone County, took a quantity of horseshoes from the blacksmith shop, and paid for them in Confederate money. They then took eight plugs of tobacco from a local merchant and paid him with a promissory note from the Confederate States of America. It was signed "John H. Brown, Acting Quartermaster, Jackman's Regiment." On their way out of town, the gang impressed two horses from a man living on the outskirts of Hallsville.[26]

On June 10, a squad of rebels under Rucker and Pulliam stopped a stage near Concord in Callaway County and took Lieutenant Thaddeus J. Stauber, provost marshal of the county, off the stage. After rifling through the baggage and finding nothing of interest, they took a horse from the team that was pulling the stage and mounted Stauber on it. Then they allowed the stage to go on its way as they rode off with their prisoner. Stauber had recently confiscated all the property of a rebel sympathizer in Callaway County and sold it at auction. So perhaps Rucker and Pulliam had special plans for the captive, but two days later he made his escape before the rebels were able to carry out their design. Stauber said afterwards that "during his stay with the bushwhackers they treated him kindly."[27]

On the morning of June 18, forty soldiers from Colonel Guitar's Ninth Missouri State Militia Cavalry came upon about a hundred rebels under "Jackman, Rucker, and company" camped near the Missouri River a mile and a half upstream from Rocheport on the farm of a Southern sympathizer. A sharp skirmish ensued during which both sides lost at least a couple of men either killed or wounded. Among the wounded was Jackman himself, who was treated in the brush by two doctors from Rocheport.[28]

The Union report was mistaken in identifying the rebels as "Jackman, Rucker, and company," because, at least according to Jackman, Rucker not only was absent but was also to blame for bringing about the skirmish. Against Jackman's instructions, Rucker had taken a prospective recruit into his trust and given out the location of Jackman's camp. The man turned out to be a Union spy, and rather than alerting Jackman to what he had done, Rucker simply went home to nearby Rocheport. At first Jackman chalked the blunder up to whiskey, because "Rucker had got to drinking." However, when Rucker refused to take over command of the guerrillas while Jackman was laid up with his wound, Jackman began to suspect Rucker of treachery, and he was finally convinced of it when Rucker lied to him about having made arrangements for the command to cross the Missouri River.[29] This, of course, is Jackman's version of events and should, therefore, be taken with a grain of salt, because Jackman tended to be generous with his criticism of almost everyone except himself.

On the evening of July 1, Congressman James S. Rollins and several other delegates to the State Convention at Jefferson City were returning to the Columbia area via steamboat. Around ten o'clock the boat landed at Providence, where the passengers disembarked. Shortly afterwards Drury Pulliam rode into town with a gang of about twenty men, all of whom were reportedly dressed in Confederate uniform. Pulling up in front of a general store, the group demanded to know the whereabouts of Rollins, and he soon presented himself at the doorway. Pulliam dismounted, placed the congressman under arrest, and turned him over to two of his men with orders to keep the prisoner under close guard. The rest of the gang then proceeded to plunder the store, taking "from the most valuable down to the smallest article which they could lay their hands on."[30]

One of the band, a "great desperado" named William Hunter, denounced the congressman as a "damned old abolitionist and Lincolnite." Hunter said he had been after Rollins for a long time and that he meant to "kill him and send him to hell." After the guerrillas had plundered the store of everything they wanted, Rollins managed a short conversation with Pulliam, who "was altogether civil in his language." About the same time several ladies who were present also intervened on behalf of the congressman, and he was promptly released. Around midnight the band mounted up and rode out of town, "each man packing off as much as he could carry."[31]

(This was not Congressman Rollins's first brush with bushwhackers, as William Hunter had plundered his farm a year and a half earlier. It also would not be his last encounter with guerrillas. In the fall of 1864, on the day of the Centralia Massacre, Rollins was briefly held prisoner at that place by some of Bill Anderson's gang, and in the spring of 1865, as related in a previous chapter, the congressman was waylaid on the road between Centralia and Columbia by Jim Jackson.)

On July 4, 1863, three days after the pillaging at Providence, a detachment of the Ninth Missouri State Militia Cavalry under Major Daniel M. Draper routed a band of guerrillas under Pulliam in the Blackfoot Hills. The Federals took about twenty prisoners and confiscated a good deal of equipment.[32]

Although Jackman accused Rucker of skulking and hiding in the woods during the late summer of 1863, it's quite possible that he was, as he claimed, trying to make arrangements for the command to go south. On the night of September 7, 1863, Brigadier-General Egbert B. Brown, commanding the District of Central Missouri at Jefferson City, got word that "the notorious Captain Rucker, associate of Jackman," had been seen on a skiff on the Missouri River in Callaway County near St. Aubert with five fishermen, although the general suspected that the angling gear was merely a "cloak to other movements."[33]

Brown detailed fifty soldiers to the landing across the river from St. Aubert. Early the next morning a party of twenty crossed to the village and marched to the home of a man named Bagby three or four miles from town, where Rucker was reported to be staying. Arriving at daylight, the troops found Rucker at the house just as he arose and was emerging through the front door to "perform his morning ablutions." Upon seeing the soldiers, Rucker turned and bolted through the house to the rear exit but was met with a volley of shots as he tried to escape to the brush. One shattered his left wrist, and the other passed through his hip and abdomen. Brown said later the same day that Rucker had been severely wounded and left in the hands of a doctor. In another report the next day Brown reportedly erroneously that "the notorious Manner Rucker" had been mortally wounded. Instead, he was once again taken prisoner and confined at Jefferson City.[34]

A month later, in the mid afternoon of October 2, 1863, Pulliam charged into Rocheport with about thirty rebels, including John Brown, Russ Palmer and a man named Purcell, all of whom had been riding with the guerrilla leader throughout the year. (John Brown had been with Pulliam during the attempted jail break in January, and he was, of course, the man who had signed himself as Jackman's acting quartermaster when the gang had impressed supplies at Hallsville in early June. Purcell had been with Pulliam and Rucker when they kidnapped the Calloway County provost marshal later in June, and Russ Palmer was identified as one of the guerrillas who had dashed into Providence with Pulliam on July 1 and arrested Congressman Rollins. A man named Palmer was also one of the rebels taken prisoner on the Fourth of July when Major Draper had routed Pulliam's band in the Blackfoot Hills, although it's not clear whether it was Russ Palmer.) After taking possession of Rocheport, the guerrillas "proceeded to robbing stores on a grand scale." They took about $600 worth of clothing and saddles and also stole a horse from a local citizen. They departed town about eight o'clock that evening "well loaded down."[35]

Later the same night the gang called at the home of a citizen living near Rocheport and robbed him of ten dollars, which was all the money he had. They also robbed a "party of poor emigrants," who were camped nearby, of all the money they had and two horses that the travelers were using to pull their wagon. At last report, the gang was thought to have crossed the Missouri River and gone south.[36]

In the summer of 1864, preparatory to Price's invasion of Missouri, Pulliam was sent into the state to recruit a company, but, according to Jackman's later report, he was "captured and brutally murdered" before he was able to complete the task. "I had been intimately associated with him for two years," Jackman said, "and had watched him when his character was tested by every conceivable danger in the sternest degree, and the result of my observation was that I had never known a young man of more daring or chivalry."[37]

Meanwhile, Rucker was bouncing back and forth between a jail cell and freedom's open air. Shortly after his latest capture in the fall of 1863, he again mounted a campaign to get himself paroled as he had during his stay at Gratiot earlier the same year. This time, though, instead of resorting to escapade, he relied on his influence and political connections. Shortly before Christmas of 1863, he wrote a letter to General Brown suggesting that, because of his feeble health (presumably as a result of the wounds he received when captured), he could not stand to be confined until his hearing, which would not be scheduled until at least a couple of months later. Rucker asked to be paroled to his home in Boone County and promised to report at a time designated by the general. The prisoner also called the general's attention to the medical opinion of surgeon Robert P. Richardson of Brown's staff, who forwarded a note suggesting that Rucker needed open air and the use of a buggy. General Brown referred the matter to Lieutenant-Colonel Theodore A. Switzler, his assistant provost marshal, with instructions that Rucker be released on parole within the limits of Cole County.[38]

However, the actual granting of the parole was delayed for some unknown reason; so a little over a month later, while still languishing in jail, Rucker enlisted the aid of influential men throughout the state to plead his case. In early February of 1864, Major-General Rosecrans, Commanding the Department of the Missouri at St. Louis, received a letter from several members of the Missouri Senate and House of Representatives. The lawmakers claimed Rucker was on his way home determined to accept a presidential amnesty when he had been "shot down and disabled for service" the previous fall. They said Rucker only wanted to return home and be a loyal citizen the rest of his life and that he was willing to give a bond and to take an oath of allegiance to the United States. Rucker, though, balked at the last condition, which was perhaps why the parole had not been immediately granted back in December. He said he understood and accepted the obligation inherent in such an oath, but he requested that he be exempted from actually taking the oath. Rosecrans yielded to the political pressure and ordered that the prisoner be released on parole, even without the oath of allegiance, and Rucker was allowed to return home.[39]

Apparently, though, he did something to violate the agreement or cause suspicion, because in early May, Rosecrans sent orders to Colonel Switzler at Jefferson City to notify Rucker "to appear forthwith in St. Louis at headquarters" and report to Colonel John P. Sanderson, provost marshal general of the department. Rucker arrived in St. Louis around the first of June, his parole was revoked by Colonel Sanderson on June 3, 1864, and he was arrested the next day and taken to Gratiot.[40]

Still in feeble health, Rucker was sent to the prison hospital not long after his arrest. It may be that he thought he was dying, because on August 3, 1864, he forwarded a request to General Rosecrans from the hospital asking that the general "be so kind as to permit me to accompany Father Willoughby to church in order that he may baptize me properly. I give you my word as a gentleman that I will not abuse your confidence." He signed the note "Respectfully yours, J. F. Rucker," and added a postscript reminding the general that he had been on parole for several months prior to his arrest. Rosecrans forwarded the matter to Colonel Sanderson with a notation that he had no objection to granting the request, and presumably Rucker was allowed to undergo the religious ceremony he sought.[41]

In September, after a review of his case by Colonel William Hoffman, commissary general of all prisoners west of the Mississippi, Rucker was transferred from Gratiot to Alton Military Prison across the river in Illinois. In November he came down with a case of bronchitis and spent a few days in the prison hospital at Alton. At the close of the war, in June of 1865, he was sent back to Gratiot and was paroled to distribute supplies to Confederate prisoners and then to return home.[42]

Rucker's war-time wounds (or the amount of time he spent in prison) may have led indirectly to an early demise, but he lived until April of 1867, two years after the war's close and almost four years after he had been "mortally" wounded. He is buried at Rocheport.[43]

15
How Many Bolins Are There?

Around 1825, John Bolin and his wife, Nancy, migrated to southeast Missouri from Tennessee and settled near the present-day Stoddard-Cape Girardeau county line.[1] The couple had nine children, including five sons. By 1860, the four oldest sons; thirty-four-year-old William, twenty-nine-year-old John F., twenty-five-year-old Nathan, and twenty-three-year-old Thomas; were married and living on their own. Only the youngest, twenty-year-old Jesse, remained at home.[2]

When the Civil War broke out, at least two of the brothers joined the Missouri State Guard. In August of 1861, Nathan and Jesse Bolin joined Captain Griffith's Company D, Fifth Regiment Infantry, of Brigadier General M. Jeff Thompson's First Division. They were discharged on December 27, 1861, after four months' service.[3]

On February 1, 1862, a little over a month after Nathan and Jesse Bolin were discharged from the State Guard, John F., Nathan, and Thomas Bolin were enrolled in Confederate service at Clarkton, Missouri, by Captain Solomon G. Kitchen. The recruits rode to Memphis, where Kitchen's company was assigned to the Second Missouri Cavalry as Company B. After a few months of regular Confederate service, however, at least one Bolin apparently tired of the grind. On October 28, 1862, at Salem, Mississippi, Thomas deserted and returned to Missouri.[4]

Thomas Bolin was evidently able to explain his absence to the satisfaction of military authorities, because he later re-entered Confederate service, although the exact date of his return is unknown. So, it's not clear whether he took part during the summer of 1863 in the Bolins' most notorious and daring deed of the war, the affair at Round Pond.

On the evening of August 1, a Union wagon train, bearing sanitary and commissary supplies, stopped overnight on the road between Cape Girardeau and Bloomfield, Missouri, in a swampy area near the Castor River, not far from where the Bolins grew up. A party of about ten rebels, including at least two of the Bolin brothers (John and Nathan), lurked nearby. During the night, the bushwhackers, using handspikes as well as revolvers for weapons, charged out of the swamp into the sleepy camp, killing ten men outright and mortally wounding two others before the groggy Federals could react. Of the six soldiers and six teamsters killed, some were reportedly shot at point-blank range while still asleep. Fleeing at first alarm, a few Federals managed to escape, but several others were taken prisoner.[5]

The guerrillas announced themselves as the Bolin gang and compelled the prisoners to set fire to the wagons. As the train went up in flames, the rebel leader alluded to the fact that Union soldiers had burned his home. "This is the way *I* burn houses," he remarked sarcastically.[6]

In all, twenty-six wagons of the thirty-wagon train were virtually consumed by fire, and a few mules also burned to death. Before starting off, the bushwhackers chopped down a nearby telegraph pole and cut the wires. They captured about twenty Federal horses and scattered the rest. Then they rode off into the night, taking with them the prisoners, whom they released about two miles away.[7]

In the wee hours of the morning of December 28, 1863, John F. Bolin and another Bolin (probably Nathan) led a raid by a party of twelve guerrillas on the Bollinger County seat at Dallas (now Marble Hill). They killed county treasurer James A. Stevens and robbed him of money and bed quilts. Next, they shot a young man named William Crites and took thirty dollars from his pockets as he lay dying. They stole twenty-five dollars from John Lutes and took many articles from his home. When Sheriff James M. Fraser and a justice of the peace appeared on the scene, the guerrillas wounded the sheriff and fired several errant shots at the justice of the peace. The bushwhackers then stole two horses from a man named Eaker and forced him to guide them as they galloped off into the night. Afterwards, the sheriff complained to Union authorities that the raid was but one of many that had taken place in the Dallas vicinity, and he requested that militia be sent to the area for the protection of citizens.[8]

Sheriff Fraser was apparently not the only one up in arms over the activities of the Bolin gang. In early January of 1864, four citizens in neighboring Dunklin County fought with and killed two of the gang. Colonel John B. Rogers, commander of the Union post at Cape Girardeau, reported the incident with some glee. "Loyal citizens are anxious to kill guerrillas in Dunklin," Rogers chortled.[9]

On February 3, 1864, a band of bushwhackers under John F. Bolin were foraging on Halcomb Island a few miles below Cape Girardeau when they were attacked by Captain Shibley of Rogers's Second Missouri State Militia Cavalry. The Federals routed the guerrillas, killing seven of them and capturing eight, including Bolin himself, without any loss on the Union side. The militia captured thirteen horses and also confiscated fifteen wagons of corn that the guerrillas had taken from area farms.[10]

After the prisoners were brought to Bloomfield on February 4, Brigadier General Clinton B. Fisk, Commander of the St. Louis District, wired his congratulations to Colonel Rogers on Bolin's capture but tempered his praise with concern that there might be other Bolins still at large. Fisk had previously been stationed in southeast Missouri himself and was no doubt familiar with the seemingly ubiquitous Bolins. "How many Bolins are there in Southeast Missouri?" he demanded of Colonel Rogers.[11]

Rogers replied that there were three Bolins. (In truth, there were at least four Bolin brothers who had served in the Missouri State Guard and/or the Confederacy, but there may have been only three who were active at this time.) The colonel, well aware of the normal Union policy of taking no prisoners when it came to dealing with notorious guerrillas, assured General Fisk that the capture of Bolin had been an error. "No one knew the fiend until he was brought in and recognized by citizens," Rogers explained. "We are ready to rectify all such mistakes."[12]

When he learned that Bolin was on the road to Cape Girardeau under guard, the colonel wired Fisk again asking for specific instructions on how best to carry out the rectification once the prisoner arrived. "Shall I shoot him without trial or try him by drum-head court and muster him out?"[13]

Fisk's response that Bolin might be forwarded to St. Louis or some other Union headquarters for trial did not set well with Rogers. When Bolin arrived in irons the next day, February 5, the colonel sent another wire to Fisk pressing his argument that Bolin should be tried locally. Bolin, he reminded the general, "commanded at the Round Pond massacre; is guilty of many cold-blooded murders of citizens.... The feeling here is intense against his being sent away from here for trial."[14]

While at Cape Girardeau, Bolin reportedly gave a confession, citing his participation in the Round Pond affair and the raid on Dallas. He said he had killed six or seven men in total, including one of his own cousins, who had refused to stop when ordered to do so.[15]

On the same day the prisoners arrived, Colonel Rogers wired General Fisk yet again asking for advice on how to handle the men captured with Bolin, all of whom claimed to be regular Confederate soldiers. Fisk answered that they should be tried by the same commission that tried Bolin. "If they are regular soldiers of the rebel army," he added, "they will be able to show it. They are undoubtedly guerrillas."[16]

Late the night of February 5, before Colonel Rogers had a chance to convene his drumhead court, a large mob of soldiers and citizens came up with a plan of rectification of their own. They took Bolin from the guard and hanged him without the formality of the trial that Rogers had belatedly sought. The following day, the colonel anxiously assured General Fisk that most of the officers had tried to prevent the lynching. They were unwilling, however, to use force against their own men, he explained, and nearly all the soldiers of the post took part in the act.[17]

"It will hardly be necessary to give Bolin a trial (now)," Fisk replied wryly.[18]

Fearful that Fisk's sardonic message would be seen as tacit approval of the lynching and would encourage more violence among the soldiers at Cape Girardeau, Rogers telegraphed the general requesting a reprimand for failing to prevent the hanging. Although the colonel left no doubt that he felt the killing of Bolin justified, he thought a reproof from the general would put him in better position to restrain his men from future unruliness.[19]

General Fisk promptly complied with the request. After expressing his regret that Rogers failed to prevent the unlawful hanging of Bolin, Fisk instructed the colonel to take decisive steps to prevent similar violence toward the other captured guerrillas. "I would prefer that no such villains be taken prisoner," the general added by way of clarification, "but after they have been captured and imprisoned within our lines, law and order and the well-being of the community imperatively demand that they receive a proper trial...."[20]

John F. Bolin was dead, but Federal authorities had not heard the last of the Bolin brothers. In early March, 1864, Nathan Bolin, as part of Kitchen's command, was leading a small band in the area of Crowley's Ridge, a chain of hills extending from northeast Arkansas into northern Dunklin County. Around May 10, he crossed the St. Francis River with fifty men and headed east toward the Charleston area. Colonel Rogers notified the commanding officer at Charleston and also sent out scouting parties from Bloomfield in a fruitless search for Bolin. Then on the 16th, Rogers learned some of Bolin's men had been at Sikeston. He immediately dispatched a company of 150 soldiers to the vicinity from Cape Girardeau, ordered another eighty from Bloomfield to try to get below the guerrillas to cut off a southern retreat, and sent instructions to Charleston that all available men from that post should aid in the hunt for the bushwhackers. The network of Federal scouts, however, failed to turn up any sign of Bolin and his men. Claiming the search had been very thorough, Rogers blamed its failure on "the dense foliage of the swamps and the high water in them."[21]

As soon as the Federals called off the search, Bolin came out of hiding and rode into the small village of Hamburg just three hours after some of the Union soldiers had passed through. The guerrillas burned a Catholic church, set fire to some other buildings, and pillaged the community. Afterwards, they immediately returned to the swamp and again eluded the search parties sent back out in pursuit of them.[22]

In late May, 1864, Nathan Bolin, with twenty guerrillas, was spotted on Horse Island near the Missouri-Arkansas line. Forty soldiers were sent out in futile pursuit of the bushwhackers.[23]

During the late summer of 1864, the Confederate Army began a concentration of forces in northern Arkansas in anticipation of General Price's invasion of Missouri, and most of the Confederate forces in southern Missouri, including guerrillas, answered the call. Nathan Bolin and his band joined the army at Jacksonport, Arkansas, in mid-August. A month later, he was sent back into Missouri as an advance scout for the invasion. He was spotted seventeen miles north of Bloomfield with nineteen men on September 18, one day before the main Confederate Army under Price left Pocahontas, Arkansas, and pushed into Missouri.[24]

Price's invasion, of course, ended in disaster for the Confederate cause in Missouri, but the boot heel area of the state had not quite heard the last of Nathan Bolin. Like most of the guerrilla leaders, he was determined to hold out to the bitter end. In early January of 1865, Bolin was still in northern Arkansas with Price's army, but he was soon back in southeast Missouri, where he and his gang skirmished with a detachment of Federal soldiers from Bloomfield in early March. The guerrillas lost two men killed and several wounded.[25]

Like a wounded animal returning to its lair, Bolin sought the familiarity of his old stomping grounds. On March 26, he and his band of about thirty men robbed a wagon on the road between Bloomfield and Cape Girardeau near "the old Bolin farm" and took one man prisoner. In mid-April, Bolin surfaced in the same vicinity on Hickory Ridge with about thirty or forty men, and a Federal scout went out looking for him.[26]

With the war winding down, Bolin started south to link up with other Confederate forces. In late April, he was reported north of Kennett with about a hundred men, plundering and laying in supplies.[27]

The supplies would not be needed. The Bolin brothers were among the soldiers surrendered by Brigadier General M. Jeff Thompson to Major General Greenville M. Dodge, Commander of the Union Department of the Missouri, near Jonesboro, Arkansas, on May 11, 1865. Nathan Bolin was listed as captain of Company H, Ninth Regiment, Missouri Cavalry. One brother, Thomas J. Bolin, was a first lieutenant and another brother, Jesse Bolin, was a private in the same company. The Bolin brothers ranged in height from five feet, nine inches to six feet tall, and all were described as having blue eyes, dark hair, and dark complexions. They were paroled at Wittsburg, Arkansas, on May 25, 1865.[28]

SOUTHEAST MISSOURI

DeSoto

Big River

Big River
Mills

Potosi

Boone Terre

ILLINOIS

Pilot Knob

Farmington

Ironton

Fredericktown

Mississippi River

St. Francis River

Castor River

Dallas
(Marble Hill)

Patterson

Cape Girardeau

Ohio River

Bloomfield

Charleston

Sikeston

KENTUCKY

ARKANSAS

Clarkton

TENNESSEE

Crowley's Ridge

Map of southeast Missouri showing principals haunts of Hildebrand and the Bolins.

16
Sam Hildebrand and His Gang[1]

The Bolins' infamy among Union soldiers and citizens in southeast Missouri during the Civil War was rivaled only by that of Samuel S. Hildebrand. (Today, Hildebrand is probably more renowned than the Bolins, but much of his notoriety is because of post-war books that were published about him.)

Hildebrand's great-grandfather, John Hildebrand, was the very first American to settle away from the early French villages in what later became Missouri. In 1774, he settled on Saline Creek south of St. Louis in the area that became Jefferson County near where the creek flows into the Meramec River. Around 1800, Sam's grandfather moved up the Big River, another tributary of the Meramec River, and settled in what became St. Francois County. Still later, Sam's father, George Hildebrand, settled farther down the Big River near Bonne Terre.[2]

Sam Hildebrand was born on January 6, 1836, and he was fourteen at the time of the 1850 census. The family was living in St. Francois County at the time, and Sam was listed as the third of five sons. George Hildebrand and his wife, Rebecca McKee, also had three daughters. Later in 1850, Sam's father died, and in 1854 Sam married Margaret Hampton and soon started a family of his own.[3]

According to Sam's version of his life story, his first major grievance against the Federal government came in November of 1861 when a Union vigilante committee hanged his nineteen-year-old younger brother, James Franklin "Frank" Hildebrand, on a trumped-up charge of horse stealing. Up until this time Sam had supposedly maintained a strict position of neutrality, taking no part in the war, and another brother, William, had even joined the Union Army at the start of the conflict. Only after Frank's death did Sam declare himself a rebel, get himself commissioned as a roving major by Missouri State Guard brigadier-general Jeff Thompson, and take to the bush to avenge his brother's murder. Then the following July, the Union added insult to injury by killing Sam's older brother, George Washington Hildebrand. Wash was supposedly working in the nearby lead mines, minding his own business, and taking no part in the war when a company of cavalry rode up and opened fire on him and another man without provocation. Later the same month, Federal troops showed up at Rebecca Hildebrand's home, burned the house, and killed Sam's youngest brother Henry, who was only thirteen at the time, for not moving promptly when ordered to do so.[4]

The major occurrences in this story doubtlessly did happen, but the scant, primary documentation that exists suggests that members of the Hildebrand family may not have been as blameless as Sam portrayed them in his autobiography. For instance, the official records show that "one Hildebrand" and another man were already considered "notorious leaders of the rebels" in the Jefferson County area as early as September 1, 1861. This, of course, might not have been a reference to Sam Hildebrand or even to one of his brothers, but, if not, it almost certainly referred to a cousin or other relative.[5]

Later in September of 1861, at Pilot Knob, just across the Francois County line in Iron County, William Hildebrand was found "guilty of treason against the United States Government" and sentenced to "hard labor during the existing war between the United States and the revolting States." The specific terms of William Hildebrand's punishment called for him to work on the fort at Ironton under guard. While it is not definitely known that this William Hildebrand was Sam's brother, there is nothing to suggest otherwise, and it is easy to see how Sam, in relating his life story, might have construed his brother's being sentenced to work on the fort at Ironton as his having joined the Union service at the start of the war. Perhaps his brother did join regular Federal service later in the war, but the evidence seems to suggest that, at least early in the war, his service was a good deal less than voluntary.[6]

As for George Washington Hildebrand, Union records suggest that he was already considered a notorious "rebel outlaw" when he was killed in the summer of 1862. On July 10, his uncle, John S. Roan (or Rowan), who himself was described as a "noted outlaw" and "the supposed head of a gang of murderers and horse thieves in St. Francois County," was killed when he reportedly made a break for freedom after he had been taken prisoner at his home and was being escorted away. The next day, according to the Federal side of the story, a scouting party opened fire on Wash and another man when they were spotted near Roan's house, fled at the sight of the soldiers, and refused to stop when ordered to do so.[7]

Also, census records indicate that Sam's youngest brother, Henry, had to be older than thirteen in the summer of 1862, since he had been listed as three years old twelve years earlier. If his brother's death happened the way Sam said it did, it was, of course, an appalling violation of justice, regardless of how old Henry was, but one can imagine that a fifteen-year-old boy might have been more physically mature and more defiant of Federal troops than a thirteen-year-old.[8]

Although Sam Hildebrand was undoubtedly active throughout 1862 and early 1863 as his autobiography suggests, the only version of his activities during this time from the Union side is a sketchy account by Captain F. Kellermann, the provost marshal at Potosi, written in the late spring of 1863. In a letter to Captain Charles C. Allen, assistant provost marshal at St. Louis, Kellermann mentioned several episodes from 1862 that Hildebrand later related in his autobiography, but Kellermann predictably cast the incidents in a different light than Hildebrand did in his life story. Hildebrand, for example, portrayed his killing of Firman McIlvaine as a righteous act of revenge, because McIlvaine, as head of a corrupt and partisan vigilante committee, had supposedly ordered the hanging of Sam's brother Frank and then boasted of the deed. Kellermann, on the other hand, said simply that during the summer of 1862 Hildebrand had killed "in the harvest field the only son of Mr. McIlvaine and killed many other Union men." The provost marshal also, of course, portrayed the vigilante committee as a legitimate group, organized at the beginning of the war for the protection of Union men and their property, which had gradually evolved into a local militia unit.[9]

One of the earliest raids carried out by Hildebrand's gang that can be confirmed by contemporaneous records is a foray Sam and six of his men made into St. Francois County in late May of 1863. Hildebrand had previously removed his family to Arkansas, but now he was back in his home territory harassing Union citizens and exacting revenge on his old enemies. On the evening of May 28, he stopped in the community of Big River Mills at the home of John Highley, who had been a member of the vigilante group against whom Hildebrand had sworn vengeance. Hildebrand called Highley from his house and "set a double-barrel shotgun upon his breast, ordering him to open his store." At the same time, he told Highley he meant to kill a number of Union men in the area, including Joe McGahan, another member of the vigilante committee, who was now a lieutenant in the local militia.[10]

After not finding enough supplies, particularly powder and lead, at Highley's store to satisfy their needs, the rebels mounted up and rode six miles to Flat River, where they robbed the store of John Bean, another member of the "vigilante mob." Later the same night and still in the same neighborhood, the guerrillas shot two Union men, one of whom was named Davis. When word of the raid reached the local militia, Captain James Craig, yet another former vigilante and sworn enemy of Hildebrand, set out in pursuit of the rebels but failed to overtake them as they escaped to the south.[11]

Craig, according to Provost Marshal Kellermann, had "spent the whole of last summer...trying to get ahold of" Hildebrand. A member of the Fifth Missouri Militia at the time, Craig and his men had "shot Roan (Hildebrand's uncle), two brothers of Hildebrand, and six or eight others of his gang but never could get this Samuel Hildebrand, although they chased him twice pretty closely and wounded him once." Craig now sought authority, along with Lieutenant McGahan, to track down the guerrillas and "bring the scalp of Hildebrand to St. Louis."[12]

Kellermann wrote Captain Allen at St. Louis that many of the Union men in the St. Francois County area had left the previous summer out of fear of Hildebrand. He said they had only recently returned and that they were "now again frightened and will abandon their crops and everything, because they know that Hildebrand declared that he will never stop until he had everyone's life. He is one of the most bloodthirsty rebels in the country." Kellermann recommended Craig as the best man to track down Hildebrand because of the captain's familiarity with the woods and swamps in the area. "If Hildebrand is killed," the provost marshal concluded, "Saint Francois County is safe."[13]

Craig apparently had no better success in accomplishing his special mission than he had in catching up with Hildebrand immediately after the raid on Big River Mills and Flat River, because Hildebrand was not mentioned again in government records until the fall of 1863 when Union officials began receiving reports from citizens complaining of the Federal inability to do anything about the robbery and pillaging of guerrillas in southeast Missouri. Responding to the criticism, General Fisk, commanding the District of Southeast Missouri headquartered at Pilot Knob, wired Captain Hiram A. Rice, stationed at Fredericktown, admonishing him to be more vigilant. "Do you hear anything more from Hildebrandt (sic)?" the general demanded. "I will give any of your boys eighty acres of land that will bring in his head either on or off his shoulders."[14]

Captain Rice promptly sent his "boys" on a scout after Hildebrand south of Fredericktown. The gang, however, eluded capture by dividing into two groups, "six with Hildebrandt (sic) and seven with neighbors," and heading into the swamp. Rice explained that his men "could not get up in time to head them off."[15]

Union officials continued to receive complaints about "the disturbed state of affairs in Saint Francois and Washington Counties." General John M. Schofield, commanding the Department of the Missouri at St. Louis, inquired of General Fisk about the matter, and Fisk replied on October 29 that he was doing everything he could to restore law and order. He assured Schofield that he had "been after the Hildebrandts (sic) unceasingly; have killed one of them and four others of the same gang."[16] The one Hildebrand killed is surely a reference to one of Sam's deceased brothers (Frank, Wash, or Henry); however, all three of them had been killed before Fisk took over in southeast Missouri.

Less than a month later, Hildebrand passed Fredericktown in Madison County going north. He and about twenty men, part of them dressed in Federal uniform, reached Farmington in St. Francois County on November 25, 1863, and plundered the town. General Fisk complained of lack of civilian cooperation in alerting Union officials to Hildebrand's presence and helping to prevent the pillaging. In an order directing Captain Rice to go out after Hildebrand, Fisk observed, "The people must have known he was in the country. Press every man, horse, and gun you can find, and let the hunt, pursuit, and extermination be sure and swift." In a second dispatch, Fisk added, "Don't stop until you kill these rascals. Go at once. Kill them as you find them."[17]

Like Rice's previous hunt, this one proved fruitless. On December 1, however, Captain William T. Leeper wired Fisk from Patterson crowing that a party of Union citizens on Cedar Creek in

Wayne County had skirmished with the Hildebrand gang, killing one guerrilla, wounding another, and taking two prisoners.[18]

Toward the end of December, Hildebrand was wounded in a skirmish with a detachment of the First Missouri Cavalry near Bloomfield, and two weeks later he was reported as having died. "He is sure enough dead," Colonel John B. Rogers, commanding at Cape Girardeau, told General Fisk in early January 1864.[19]

As was frequently the case where the bushwhackers were concerned, the Federal celebration of the news of Hildebrand's demise was premature. Instead of dying as he was supposed to have done, Hildebrand merely retired to the Illinois side of the Mississippi River to nurse his wounds. When a Union scouting party crossed the river in search of guerrillas in early April of 1864, one of the men they arrested was a Hildebrand follower named Landon Green.[20]

By mid-July, Hildebrand and his gang were back in their old stomping grounds around Big River Mills in St. Francois County, having come from Illinois, and their presence was again causing "great alarm and disquiet" among the Union people in the vicinity. On July 18, Brigadier-General Thomas Ewing, Jr., commanding the St. Louis District, ordered Colonel John F. Tyler at Pilot Knob to "go out to find and kill them, whether found in Illinois or in this state." Tyler replied the next day that a scout had just come in from chasing after guerrillas and that the soldiers had killed two men thought to belong to Hildebrand's gang and run three others out of Saint Francois County. In addition, the Federals confiscated a horse and three guns.[21]

Sometime in the fall of 1864, Hildebrand made a juncture with Dick Berryman, a Confederate captain and recruiting officer who carried on a guerrilla-like campaign in southeast Missouri in conjunction with Price's invasion of the state. On the evening of October 6, a detachment of 200 men of the Sixth Cavalry Missouri Volunteers under Major Samuel Montgomery came upon about 300 men under Berryman and "the notorious Sam Hilderbrand" (sic) on Big River near Bonne Terre, where the guerrillas had pressed a mill into service. When the Federals attacked, the guerrillas scattered in all directions, according to Montgomery, with a loss of twenty-one men killed and a number of others wounded. In addition, the Federals took one prisoner, while the major claimed that the only loss on his side was one man severely wounded. Despite the reported rebel loss,

Berryman and Hildebrand still had about 300 men with more recruits coming in when they were spotted a week later on the St. Francis River west of Farmington.[22]

Little else was heard from Berryman after Price's failed invasion, but Hildebrand became even more active than before, if the frequency with which his name is mentioned in the official records is any indication. The South's forlorn situation during the winter and spring of 1864-1865 cooled the fervor of many Missouri guerrillas, while the increasing realization that their cause was hopeless spurred others, like Hildebrand, into a desperate frenzy of activity. (Another explanation for the frequent mention of men like Hildebrand in Union reports during this time period is that, after repelling the threat represented by Price, Federals in Missouri had more time to devote to chasing after bushwhackers, even when they were involved in relatively minor mischief.)

Around March 1, 1865, "Hildebrand and neighbors" were holed up in the swamp land south of St. Francois County. The provost-marshal of the district complained, "These bands rob and murder the people, scouring the country in small squads, and have even attacked the pickets at Ironton." A week later, a Federal scout went out from Bloomfield to try to intercept Hildebrand at Indian Ford, but they found some of Bolin's gang instead.[23]

Around the middle of March, Colonel John L. Beveridge, commanding at Pilot Knob, sent out several scouting parties in search of Hildebrand and his gang in the Farmington area, but the scouts met "no success." Beveridge reported the futile mission to district headquarters, and General Ewing replied, suggesting that a force be concentrated on Big River around Tyler's Mills instead of at Farmington, because the former area was where Hildebrand's family lived. "See if you can't devise some plan to catch Hilderbrand (sic) and his confederates," Ewing urged, and he then went on to suggest his own plan. "By sending men in citizens' clothes to watch for him, he could be caught."[24]

On April 2, Captain John Noyes of the Seventh Kansas Cavalry, stationed at Farmington, got word that Hildebrand and seven of his men had taken breakfast near Big River Mills. Noyes sent out two scouting parties, and one of them came upon Hildebrand's trail on the Farmington to Potosi road. Realizing they were being pursued, the guerrillas struck out through "thick woods and by-paths" and doubled back toward Farmington. About two miles from town, they took a black man prisoner and carried him with them to a spot seven miles from Farmington, where they killed him. The guerrillas were leading about fourteen horses during their flight, and they stole another six from teams on the Pilot Knob road when they crossed it five miles from Farmington.[25]

The next day, April 3, the rebels added to their herd of horses when Hildebrand and about fifty men showed up at Doe Run, four miles south of Farmington, and started robbing teams. A detachment of 115 soldiers went out from Pilot Knob in pursuit of the guerrillas, and messengers were sent to other outposts to try to head the gang off on their flight south. Neither the pursuing party nor the soldiers stationed at the outposts south of Pilot Knob had much luck, though. A scout sent out from Patterson to Indian Ford came back with a report that they "could not find Hildebrand or hear anything of him."[26]

On April 24, Hildebrand reappeared four miles east of Big River Mills. Captain Kellermann, now stationed at DeSoto, wrote to Major Harrison Hannahs at district headquarters offering to send a party of ten Federals to Cadet in eastern Washington County to watch out for Hildebrand. "It is a new moon again, and he is getting ready for another raid," Kellermann predicted.[27]

Hannahs referred the matter to Brevet Brigadier-General John L. Beveridge, commanding the sub-district at Cape Girardeau, and Beveridge promised to "look after Hildebrand" as soon as the more pressing concern of a rumored invasion by Confederate brigadier-general Jeff Thompson was taken care of.[28]

On April 28, Union officials at Potosi were also advised to "look out for Hildebrand." The Federal vigilance may have driven the guerrillas into hiding, because nothing else was heard from Hildebrand until three weeks later when he turned up in St. Francois County "robbing citizens," and a company of the Seventh Kansas Cavalry was sent out in pursuit of the gang. The next day, May 18, Hildebrand was reported in the Farmington neighborhood with citizens and militia in pursuit.[29]

On the morning of May 22, 1865, Hildebrand and four other men were robbing a store at Valles Mines in southern Jefferson County when they were surprised and attacked by a party of soldiers who were on a scout from Big River Mills. One of the guerrillas was killed, and Hildebrand himself was "supposed to be wounded in the leg, as he had great difficulty in getting on his horse." Once mounted, though, Hildebrand and the other rebels made their getaway in a southerly direction.[30]

Although the legendary version of this incident suggests that it happened in late April, the official records clearly show it happened on May 22. As might be expected, the legend explains Hildebrand's pillaging of the store as an act of vengeance toward the store owner, who had supposedly cheated Sam and his family out of their homestead at the beginning of the war.[31]

After the war, Hildebrand, like Jesse James and several other former guerrillas, had trouble adjusting to civilian life. He had become so used to pillaging and bushwhacking that he knew no other way of life, and there is probably also some truth to the legend that Federal authorities and Union citizens would not *let* Hildebrand simply retire to a peaceful existence. At any rate, as the title of the first book written about him in 1869 suggests, Hildebrand the guerrilla became *Hildebrand the Outlaw, the Terror of Missouri*. He was finally killed on March 21, 1872, by town constables in Pinckneyville, Illinois, where he had recently taken up residence under an assumed name.[32]

17
The Missouri Guerrillas: Who Were They?

Much has been written about the Civil War guerrillas in Missouri, and the story of their escapades seems to hold an enduring fascination for many readers. It is my own fascination with the guerrillas that has resulted in this book, and the primary purpose of the work has been merely to examine the Civil War careers of certain guerrillas who are lesser known than Quantrill but whose stories are nonetheless intriguing. However, a few critical observations about the guerrillas, as suggested by the lives chronicled here, are inescapable. We might start by briefly examining what has previously been written about the guerrillas.

During the war, newspapers in Missouri contained almost daily accounts of bushwhacking exploits of one sort or another, and many of the official reports written by Federal officers in the region centered around engagements with guerrillas or scouting expeditions for the purpose of tracking down guerrillas. Since the Southern press in the state was largely suppressed, most of the newspaper accounts had a pro-Union slant, and the reports written by Federal officers were obviously pro-Union as well. So, the portrait of the Missouri guerrilla during the Civil War that emerges from extant, contemporaneous writings is predominantly one of a brigand.

On March 13, 1862, Major General Henry Halleck, commanding the Department of the Mississippi, issued Special Order Number 2 from his St. Louis headquarters setting forth the Union's official policy toward guerrilla bands. "...Every man who enlists in such an organization forfeits his life and becomes an outlaw," the order declared. "All persons are hereby warned that if they join any guerrilla band they will not, if captured, be treated as ordinary prisoners of war, but will be hung as robbers and murderers."[1] So, from almost the beginning of the war, guerrillas were, in the official Union view, nothing but outlaws, and the Northern press merely reflected this view. Meanwhile, the guerrilla side of the conflict was not widely told at the time, at least not in print.

In 1877, twelve years after the war's end, John N. Edwards, a newspaperman and General Joseph Shelby's former adjutant and chief

Re-enactment photos depicting guerrilla warfare. (Jasper County Records Center)

of staff, published *Noted Guerrillas,* the first significant account of the guerrillas' activities from a Southern perspective. (Two books about Sam Hildebrand had already been published by this time, but *Noted Guerrillas* was the first that purported to tell the general story of the Missouri partisans and did not focus entirely on one man.) To say that Edwards was sympathetic toward the guerrillas is an understatement. Concentrating on the exploits of William Quantrill and his followers, Edwards portrayed the guerrillas as larger-than-life, avenging heroes, and he routinely sacrificed the facts in the process.

Confederate historians accepted Edwards's version of events without reservation. John C. Moore, in his 1899 *Confederate Military History of Missouri*, claimed that the guerrilla warfare in Missouri was "strictly a war of retaliation" for Federal atrocities.[2] Former guerrillas also adopted the Edwards myth in relating their war-time deeds. For instance, John McCorkle's *Three Years with Quantrill*, published in 1914 and perhaps the best-known of the guerrilla memoirs, related many of the same incidents contained in the Edwards book and even used similar wording in some instances. Dime novels about Quantrill and his associates, published in the late 1800s and early 1900s, continued to exaggerate the exploits of the guerrillas and perpetuate the heroic myth first fabricated by Edwards.

In 1910 William Connelley published *Quantrill and the Border Wars,* the first important critical biography of Quantrill. Connelley, of course, had access to the official records and other documents. In addition, he interviewed numerous surviving guerrillas and other living persons who could shed light on Quantrill's story. The result was a very thorough work that remains a valuable source of information even today. However, *Border Wars* is seriously flawed because the author was just as biased against Quantrill as Edwards was in favor of him. Indeed, one of Connelley's specific objectives was to refute the Edwards myth and show that the guerrillas, far from being heroes, were depraved villains. To Connelley, for instance, Bill Anderson was "more savage than a mad wolf," and Quantrill's soul was a "hideous, monstrous, misshapen thing."[3]

B movies of the early to mid-1900s perpetuated the caricature of madness drawn by Connelley. Productions like 1950's *Kansas Raiders* and 1958's *Quantrill's Raiders* tended to portray the guerrilla chieftain and his followers as ruthless killers who terrorized women and children as well as men, when, in truth, the unwritten guerrilla code especially prohibited molesting women and children. Meanwhile, apologists for the guerrillas continued to churn out books patterned after the Edwards model, depicting the guerrillas as quixotic heroes. Carl Breihan's *Quantrill and His Civil War Guerrillas,* published in 1959, is an example.

Not until the mid-1950s did modern scholars begin to look at the Missouri guerrillas with a semblance of balance. Jay Monaghan's 1955 work, *Civil War on the Western Border*, was one of the first books approaching an objective study of the guerrillas. Other authoritative works soon followed. Richard Brownlee's *Gray Ghosts of the Confederacy* published in 1958 and Albert Castel's *William Clarke Quantrill: His Life and Times* published in 1962 are among the more notable examples. More recent scholars like Michael Fellman (*Inside War*—1989), Thomas Goodrich (*Black Flag*—1995), and Edward Leslie (*The Devil Knows How to Ride*—1996) have provided additional insight and perspective.

However, many popular misconceptions persist concerning the Missouri guerrillas. Who exactly were they? Where did they come from? Why were they fighting? (Donald L. Gilmore's *Civil War on the Missouri-Kansas Border* counters many of the same misconceptions that I discuss below, but the author's defense of the guerrillas strikes me as a bit overzealous.)

One widespread idea about the guerrillas is that they were relatively few in number. This concept has resulted, at least in part, from the fact that almost all of the literature on the guerrillas since the war, starting with *Noted Guerrillas*, has tended to focus on Quantrill and his associates. As Fellman has pointed out, the popularity of the Edwards myth influenced even the compilers of the official records, causing them to include a disproportionate number of reports and letters dealing with Quantrill.[4] Nevertheless, one need look no farther than the official records to realize that the idea of the guerrillas as a small group is a false notion. While Quantrill was certainly the most noted Missouri guerrilla of the war, he was far from the only one. Guerrillas, in bands small and large, swarmed throughout the entire state, although their concentration was heavier in some areas than it was in others.

Another common misconception is the idea that the guerrilla bands were a conglomeration of adventurous men from all parts of the country who often had already gained reputations as notorious, disreputable characters even before the Civil War began and who simply used the conflict as an opportunity to indulge an already well-developed appetite for robbery and plunder. This idea was first promulgated by Union observers like the editor of the *Leavenworth*

Daily Conservative, who suggested early in the war that Quantrill's guerrillas were all hardened desperados from far and wide.[5]

Connelly's biography of Quantrill further shaped the idea, because the author went to great lengths to show a pattern of crime and cruelty established early on by Quantrill and some of his lieutenants, such as Bill Anderson. Connelley claimed, for instance, that Quantrill, as a child, took great delight in inflicting pain on animals and that he had already committed a cold-blooded murder in Illinois before migrating to Kansas in the mid-1850s. However, no solid evidence exists to support either charge. Also, Connelley's characterization of Anderson as "one of the most desperate guerrillas and horse-thieves on the border" as early as 1861 is an exaggeration.[6]

Even modern scholars have not altogether refuted this notion of the guerrillas as a gathering of desperate characters from the far-flung reaches of the country. For example, respected historian Herman Hattaway, while pointing out that most of the Missouri guerrillas at the start of the war were "tough, young farm boys," says in his commentary accompanying the 1992 edition of *Three Years with Quantrill* that others "came from among the hundreds of restless young men who had flocked to the region to engage, in one manner or another, in the perilous and profitable overland trade to New Mexico."[7] While this statement is indisputably true, the implication that it applied to a significant minority of the guerrillas is not. It may have applied to Quantrill, but it applied to very few of his men. The number of Quantrill's bushwhackers who, before the war, were footloose young men drawn to the Kansas-Missouri border area by the booming trade along the Santa Fe trail in search of riches and adventure was quite small. Moreover, the exclusive focus on Quantrill's band obscures the fact that most of the Missouri guerrillas, scattered throughout the state, lived nowhere near the Santa Fe trail.

Unlike the editor of the *Leavenworth Daily Conservative*, even most Union observers during the war recognized the reality—that the bushwhackers tended to operate in their own backyards. At the outset of the war, they were mostly boys who lived with their parents or young men who were already married and settled; and after they became guerrillas, they usually took to the bush in the areas where they had grown up or, in the case of the married men, where they and their families had been living at the time the war commenced. A study of the 1860 Jackson County census, for example, clearly shows that most of Quantrill's early recruits came from the immediate Jackson County area and that, at the time of the census, most were mere lads still living in their parents' homes or else young farmers or farmhands. See, for example, my article entitled "We Rode With Quantrill" in the November 1996 issue of *America's Civil War*.

A related fallacy about the guerrillas is that the war turned all of them into bloodthirsty monsters. If they were not already hardened criminals, so the reasoning goes, they became ruthless men because of the degenerating effects of the war. There is, of course, some truth to this idea. After all, Quantrill's gang did produce savage war-time figures like Bill Anderson and Arch Clement, and it spawned post-war outlaws like the James brothers. However, the caricature of the guerrillas as inhuman fiends is a one-sided depiction. Partly because of the desperate situation in which they found themselves, especially late in the war, the Confederate guerrillas committed more than their share of atrocities, but the Union side committed many of its own. See, for example, Castel's *A Frontier State at War* (1958), Goodrich's *Black Flag* (1995), and "Better Off in Hell" by Matt Matthews and Kip Lindberg in the May 2002 issue of *North & South* for accounts of some of the atrocities by Kansas jayhawkers like Jennison and Hoyt.

The common conception of the guerrillas as savages also often fails to differentiate among them. The deeds of a few have tended to color them all as vicious men. Recall, for example, Colonel Blair's statement near the end of the war (related in Chapter Two) that William Marchbanks was "as bad as Quantrill." This was a gross exaggeration, but lumping all the guerrillas together as heartless monsters was not an unusual proclivity among Union observers. In truth, the number of bloodthirsty killers among the guerrillas was relatively small. Many, if not most, maintained their humanity and returned to relatively normal lives after the war, if they survived it. This is true of several of the subjects of this book, including, of course, Marchbanks.

Another misconception, related to the idea that the guerrillas were all ruthless men, is the notion that they were indiscriminate in their pillaging and preyed on Southern and Northern citizens alike. The facts, however, suggest that even the fierce killers like Bill Anderson and Jim Jackson tended to target Radical Union men. Thus

the editor of the *St. Louis Missouri Democrat* opined in the fall of
1864 (see Chapter 8) that Jackson killed Union men everywhere he
found them—"that is, *radical* Union men." Sometimes those singled
out were current or former members of the Union militia. Just as often,
the victims were targeted for revenge because of a particular deed to
which the guerrillas took offense. Recall, for example, Holtzclaw's
attempt to kill Clark Green in the summer of 1864 (related in Chapter
9) specifically because he had been a recruiting officer who had
enlisted black troops into the Federal army. There were, of course,
occasional instances of indiscriminate pillaging, but the common idea
that the bushwhackers went about the countryside constantly
harassing citizens of all political persuasions tends not to be true.

Still another erroneous conclusion that many people have
drawn about the guerrillas is that they totally lacked military
legitimacy. The Missouri partisans certainly fit the concept of what
we normally think of as guerrillas in the sense that they operated in
small bands and usually either wore civilian clothes or donned the
uniform of the enemy. Because of this, Union observers during the
war viewed the guerrillas with disdain and considered them totally
illegitimate. This, of course, is why General Halleck issued an order
outlawing such partisan bands.

The perception that the guerrillas were nothing but outlaws
persists even in the modern literature. For example, although
Fellman's *Inside War* offers a penetrating study of the psychology of
the guerrilla warfare in Missouri, the author based some of his insights
and conclusions about how the guerrillas saw themselves on the
incorrect assumption that none of them held regular Confederate
commissions.[8] Thus, the author characterized Thrailkill's claim to be
a Confederate officer when he was captured in the summer of 1863 as
an example of "guerrilla double-mindedness." According to Fellman,
the guerrillas were proud of their "near-outlaw" status, but at the same
time they sometimes insisted on being treated as legitimate soldiers.[9]

In fact, Thrailkill was wearing a full Confederate uniform
with the insignia of his rank at the time he was captured in 1863, and
he stated to his captors, who were dressed as civilians and claimed at
first to be Confederate sympathizers, that he was opposed to
bushwhacking. Thrailkill was not ambivalent, as Fellman suggests, on
the issue of how he saw himself. He was, at least in the eyes of the

Confederacy, always a legitimate military officer, and he always saw himself as such. While the same statement does not apply unequivocally to all of the guerrilla leaders, many of them had at least some official sanction. (Even Union officials recognized Thrailkill's status as a Confederate officer at his court martial in early 1864. They nevertheless found him guilty of "transgression of the laws of war" because they saw any claim the Confederacy might stake on Missouri as illegitimate and indeed because they saw the "so-called Confederate States" themselves as illegitimate.)

Many of the rank-and-file members of the partisan bands, of course, were "guerrillas" not only in the popular sense of the word, because they wore civilian clothes, but also in the stricter sense that they were not members of an organized army at the time of their bushwhacking exploits. However, with few exceptions, their leaders, like Thrailkill, were officers in the Missouri State Guard or the Confederacy. When men like Thrailkill and Joe Hart were carrying on their bushwhacking exploits, they were also serving, at least ostensibly, as recruiting officers and had been commissioned as such. Even Quantrill, whom many observers might argue was among the more unlawful of the guerrillas, probably had more military legitimacy than he is usually given credit for. He was, according to Connelley, given a Confederate commission after the Battle of Independence in August of 1862, and some evidence suggests that prior to this time he might have been acting as a nominal officer in Upton Hays's Missouri State Guard regiment.[10]

Even the rank and file guerrillas had a certain level of legitimacy from the Confederate standpoint. In June of 1862, Major-General Thomas C. Hindman, commanding the Trans-Mississippi District, issued an order authorizing citizens to form partisan bands "for the effectual annoyance of the enemy...in that part of the district to which they belong." Such bands were authorized to organize and elect a captain any time as many as ten men came together for such a purpose. They were expected to outfit themselves as best they could and "report to these headquarters from time to time."[11]

If the guerrillas were not ruthless outlaws from far and wide, who were they? A more accurate characterization would be to say that they were ordinary young men from Missouri who became caught up in the extraordinary circumstances of a civil war within their state.

They tended to come from, if not well-to-do families, at least well-established families. Their parents often were among the very early settlers of Missouri. Cole Younger, for example, came from a prominent family in the Jackson-Cass County area. Clifton D. Holtzclaw's father, James, while not a leading citizen, was among the very early settlers of Howard County and was apparently respected in the community. Far from considering themselves outlaws, when the guerrillas first took to the bush, as Fellman has pointed out, they felt that they were the ones who were upholding traditional values. In the minds of the guerrillas and their families, Radical Union men who defended the stealing of property (i.e. slaves) in the name of emancipation and Kansas jayhawkers like Doc Jennison who raided across the border into Missouri were the infidels and lawbreakers.[12]

The guerrillas also considered the presence of the Federal army in their state an unwanted, foreign occupation. Although some of them (e.g. George Todd) came to embrace their outlaw status, most of them felt in the beginning, at least, that they were simply protecting their homes and families from an oppressive Federal government the same way the first patriots had opposed British rule.

One last characteristic of the guerrillas, which so far has been merely hinted at, needs to be discussed in some detail. The guerrillas tended to be most prevalent and most active in the river counties on either side of the Missouri (in an area that, even today, is sometimes called "little Dixie"), in the southeast part of the state along the west bank of the Mississippi, and in the western part of the state along the Kansas border. Not coincidentally, these were also, with the exception of the latter region, the areas of the state where plantation-like farms had created a demand for slave labor and where the concentration of blacks was the greatest. (The intense guerrilla warfare in counties like Bates and Vernon mainly resulted from their proximity to Kansas and tended to be a carry-over from the earlier border conflict over the question of whether "Bleeding Kansas" would be admitted to the Union as a free or slave state.)

Only some of the guerrillas came from slave-holding families. The percentage was no doubt greater than the percentage of the state's citizens as a whole who held slaves (only about one family in eight), but the ratio was still fairly small. However, nearly all of the guerrillas had Southern roots. If the guerrillas themselves had not been born in

Kentucky, Tennessee, or one of the other Southern border states, their parents usually had been. Almost without exception, the guerrillas identified with Southern culture, accepted the inferior status of blacks as a given, and opposed abolition.

While it is true, as authors like Leslie have argued, that slavery was not an overriding issue for many of the guerrillas and most had other, more immediate reasons for fighting such as parental expectations and bonds of friendship, the issue of race and slavery imbued the political discussion surrounding the Civil War in the Missouri region (as elsewhere) at every turn. Thus in May of 1861, at the very outset of the war, Waldo P. Johnson, the recruiting colonel who accompanied Drury Pulliam to the Trans-Mississippi, proclaimed in a speech at Stockton, Missouri, "Not to be a secessionist is to be a disgraceful advocate of Negro equality." Johnson, who lived at Osceola and had been a U. S. Senator before the war, went on to suggest that a Unionist was "a man with a white skin but a nigger's heart."[13]

In contrast, in April 1863, at the mid-point of the war, D. W. Wilder, editor of the misnamed *Leavenworth Daily Conservative*, aggressively asserted, "Slavery is a crime and every apologist for it is a criminal. The man who defends slavery must be made infamous, and he will be, when this war is ended, and when the manly and Democratic Puritan takes the place of the haughty and aristocratic cavalier."[14]

Admittedly, these uncompromising positions were exceptions, and Editor Wilder's sentiment would have been even rarer at the beginning of the war. By the spring of 1863, the emerging ascendancy of Radicalism had no doubt emboldened Wilder, but there was never a time in the Civil War when slavery was a non-issue for people like D. W. Wilder and Waldo Johnson.

And whether the guerrillas would have admitted it even to themselves, there was never a time that slavery was not an implicit issue for them, too. Although the guerrillas hardly fit the mold of the "haughty and aristocratic cavalier," it was ultimately the world of the Southern gentleman that they were fighting for, because their immediate reasons for fighting, like parental expectations, were intertwined with Southern culture and Southern culture was intertwined with slavery. This became more evident toward the end of the war when the guerrillas saw their world disintegrating. Upholding slavery, or rather expressing their outrage over the fact that the institution was crumbling before their eyes, was why men like Jim Jackson terrorized and killed blacks during the latter part of the war. Upholding slavery is also why guerrillas hated Radical Union men, carried out raids against their property, and often killed them, because Radicals were almost always abolitionists. In fact, the two terms were virtually synonymous. Thus, C. D. Holtzclaw told the citizens of Laclede in June of 1864 that he had nothing against Union men as long as they weren't abolitionists. The abolitionists, though, ought to be killed.

Those of us fascinated by the story of the Missouri guerrillas cannot claim the moral high ground on both the issue of traditional values and the issue of human rights. We can't say, on the one hand, that the guerrillas were ordinary young men upholding traditional values and try to suggest, on the other hand, that slavery was not one of the traditional values they were upholding. It was. The Confederacy and the Missouri guerrillas were on the wrong side of history.

The guerrillas, almost from the moment they took to the bush, were fighting a losing battle. Although many of them had private reasons for fighting that seemingly had little to do with slavery and some even had legitimate grievances against the Federal government, they were also ultimately fighting for a cause that history has proved unjust. Does this make them bad men? I don't think so, and that's why I still find their story fascinating.

End Notes

Works frequented cited are identified by the following abbreviations:

CMS   *Columbia Missouri Statesman*
CSR   Compiled Service Records of Confederate
Soldiers Who Served in Organizations from the
State of Missouri, Record Group 109, Micro-
film copies at National Archives, Kansas City
Branch.
HVC   *History of Vernon County, Missouri* (1887;
reprint, Clinton, Mo.: The Printery, 1974).
Individual Citizens   Union Provost Marshals' File of Papers
Relating to Individual Citizens, Record Group
109, microfilm copies of National Archives
records, Missouri State Archives, Jefferson
City. (Fold3 cited if accessed digitally.)
KCDJC   *Kansas City Daily Journal of Commerce*
KCWWJC   *Kansas City Weekly Western Journal of
Commerce*
LDC   *Leavenworth Daily Conservative*
LDT   *Leavenworth Daily Times*
OR   *War of the Rebellion: A Compilation of Official
Records of the Union and Confederate Armies*
(1880-1902; reprint, Oakman, Alabama: H-Bar
Enterprises, CD-ROM, 1996). All citations are
to Series 1 unless otherwise stated.
SJWH   *St. Joseph Weekly Herald*
SLTWMR   *St. Louis Tri-Weekly Missouri Republican*

Chapter One
THE RISE OF GUERRILLA WARFARE IN MISSOURI

1. Eugene Morrow Violette, *A History of Missouri* (1918; reprint, Cape Girardeau, Mo.: Ramfre Press, 1960), 325. This history; *Switzler's Illustrated History of Missouri*; and Adamson's *Rebellion in Missouri, 1861: Nathaniel Lyon and His Army of the West*, in addition to the sources specifically cited in subsequent notes, provided background for this chapter.

2. *SLTWMR*, 18 April 1861.
3. *OR*, vol. 3, 4-9, for reports on the Camp Jackson affair.
4. See, for example, Michael Fellman, *Inside War: The Guerrilla Conflict in Missouri During the American Civil War* (New York: Oxford University Press, 1989), 10.
5. *OR*, vol. 3, 374-381.
6. Thomas L. Snead, *The Fight for Missouri* (1886; reprint, Independence, Mo.: Two Trails Publishing, 1997) 200.
7. Violette, 375.
8. *OR*, vol. 13, 835.

Chapter Two
WILLIAM MARCHBANKS: AS BAD AS QUANTRILL

Note: Most of the titles of chapters two through fifteen are quotes from Union correspondence.

1. HVC, 334; 1850 Vernon County census; and 1840 Overton County census.
2. *HVC*, 206-212, for the story of the Denton-Hardwick feud.
3. *Ibid.*, 263.
4. CSR, M322, Reel #186, military service file of William Marchbanks, and Records of United Daughters of the Confederacy, Lamar Chapter No. 258, 1898-1996, Paris, Texas, statement of soldier's wife. The Vernon County history says Marchbanks's commission dated from April 10, two days prior to the firing on Fort Sumter, but there appears to be no other written record of this. If the date is accurate, it probably reflected the approximate date that he began his recruiting activities.
5. Diary of Joseph Harrington Trego, microfilm #MS 1008.01, Kansas State Historical Society, Topeka.
6. CSR, M322, #186, military service file of Robert Marchbanks; *OR*, v. 3, 27.
7. Military service file of Robert Marchbanks; *OR* vol. 3, 27-28.
8. *HVC*, 280, 390; military service file of Robert Marchbanks.
9. Special Orders Number 16, Brigadier General James S. Rains, 31 January 1862, copy in possession of the author, courtesy of Susan Hejka; *HVC*, 296 and 334. The Vernon County history suggests that

Marchbanks was recruiting his company with the intention of taking the men south to join the Confederacy, and Marchbanks's wife gave her husband's date of entry into the Confederate Army as 10 November 1861, coinciding with the expiration of his initial six-month enlistment in the State Guard; however, the only official documentation shows that Marchbanks was still a member of the State Guard in early 1862.

10. Military service files of William and Robert Marchbanks; Richard L. Norton, comp. and ed., *Behind Enemy Lines: the Memoirs and Writings of Brigadier General Sidney Drake Jackman* (Springfield, Missouri: Oak Hills Publishing, 1997), 39-40.

11. Military service file of William Marchbanks; *HVC*, 334; Norton, *Behind Enemy Lines*, 145.

12. *HVC*, 334; *OR*, Series 2, v. 5, 503; military service file of Benjamin F. Parker, microfilm copy, M322, #193.

13. *OR*, v. 22, 318; *Kansas City Daily Western Journal of Commerce*, 19 May 1863, quoting the *LDC*.

14. *HVC*, 312-316.

15. *Ibid.*

16. *Ibid.*

17. *Ibid.*, 314 and 335.

18. *OR*, v. 22, 544.

19. *Ibid.*, 454.

20. *HVC*, 335.

21. *OR*, v.22, 621.

22. *Ibid.*, 625, 680, and 732.

23. *OR*, v 34, pt. 3, 420; v. 34, pt. 1, 954; v. 41, pt. 2, 63 and 165; *Mound City (Ks.) Border Sentinel*, 15 July 1864 and 19 August 1864.

24. *OR*, v. 41, pt. 1, 188.

25. *LDC*, 30 August 1864, citing the *Paola (Kans.) Herald*; *OR*, v. 41, pt. 2, 924.

26. *HVC*, 335; *OR*, v. 41, pt. 1, 642, 678.

27. *OR*, v. 48, pt. 1, 1143; *HVC*, 413.

28. *HVC*, 335; e-mail correspondence with Susan Hejka, January 2002.

Chapter Three
HENRY TAYLOR, COMMANDING BUSHWHACKERS IN
SOUTHWEST MISSOURI

1. 1860 Vernon County census; *LDC*, 8 July 1862; *HVC*, 248-250 and 873-874. The 1860 census lists the birthplace of Henry Taylor as Missouri, but the county history says he was born in Kentucky and came to Missouri at a very early age.

2. *HVC*, 330; CSR, M322, #190; and Peterson et al., *Price's Lieutenants*, 266.

3. *LDC*, 22 April 1862.

4. CSR, M322, #190; Individual Citizens, Reel #F1402.

5. *HVC*, 331; *LDC*, 22 April 1862; Individual Citizens, Reel #F1402.

6. *HVC*, 331; Individual Citizens, Reel F1402.

7. CSR, M322, #190; *HVC*, 331. The *HVC* says Taylor's capture of the Kansas soldiers near the state line occurred after his men were sworn into service by Coffee, but the available firsthand evidence suggests otherwise.

8. Individual Citizens, Reel #F1402.

9. *HVC*, 331; *OR*, vol. 8, 355; *Richmond Northwest Conservator*, 11 September 1862, citing the *Springfield Journal*; Individual Citizens, Reel F1463. The newspaper report identifies the colonel who led the raid at Humansville as Polk Frazier, while the Individual Citizens' file gives his name as James M. Frazier.

10. *HVC*, 300, 331, and 874; *Fort Scott Western Volunteer*, 3 May 1862; *LDC*, 22 April 1862.

11. *HVC*, 300, 304; *OR*, vol. 13, 54 and 56.

12. *LDC*, 22 April 1862.

13. Diary of Joseph Harrington Trego, Microfilm #MS 1008.01, Kansas State Historical Society.

14. *LDC*, July 8, 1862; Individual Citizens, Reel #F1402.

15. *OR*, Series 2, vol. 4, 667; *HVC*, 331.

16. *HVC*, 317. There are many accounts of men being saved during the Civil War in Missouri by their membership in the Masonic Lodge. Some of these tales, no doubt, have been invented or exaggerated, but their sheer prevalence suggests that many are probably true.

17. *HVC*, 331.

18. *LDC*, 10 July 1863. See also the *HVC*, 331, and the Trego diary. Although the county history says Taylor was exchanged in September of 1863 and afterwards joined Marchbanks, the *LDC* report shows that the incident at the Beale home occurred in late June. So Taylor's release from parole probably occurred at least a couple of months earlier than the county history says.

19. *LDC*, 10 July 1863; *HVC*, 331.

20. *Ibid.*

21. *OR*, vol. 22, pt. 1, 442-443.

22. *HVC*, 332; *Fort Scott Union Monitor*, 15 October 1863.

23. *OR*, vol. 34, pt. 1, 936; *HVC*, 322. The county history says Taylor raided the Ury home on May 20, but the official records clearly show that the incident occurred several days prior to this.

24. *OR*, vol. 34, pt. 1, 936; *HVC*, 322-323.

25. *OR*, vol. 34, pt. 1, 936-937; *HVC*, 323.

26. *OR*, vol. 34, pt. 1, 954, pt. 4, 144; *HVC*, 332. I have used the phrase "according to Taylor" in the foregoing account, because, although the compiler of the county history does not quote Taylor directly, he makes it clear that Taylor was his main source for events in which Taylor was directly involved.

27. *OR*, vol. 41, pt. 2, 63; *HVC*, 332-333.

28. *HVC*, 333; *OR*, vol. 41, pt. 3, 547-548; *St. Joseph Weekly Herald and Tribune*, 27 October 1864; *KCWWJC*, 29 October 1864. The Union report of the sacking of the railroad identifies the guerrilla leader only as "Taylor," but this was very likely Henry Taylor, since Fletch Taylor is supposed to have given up bushwhacking after having his arm amputated.

29. *HVC*, 333; *OR*, vol. 48, pt. 2, 337 and 373.

30. *OR*, vol. 48, pt. 2, 513, 523-524, 528, and 550; *HVC*, 334; *Fort Scott Union Monitor*, 25 May 1865.

31. *HVC*, 334 and 873-874.

Chapter Four
TOM LIVINGSTON: THE CHIEF OF BUSHWHACKERS

(This is a similar version of a chapter that originally appeared in the author's *The Civil War on the Lower Kansas-Missouri Border*.)

1. Ward L. Schrantz, *Jasper County in the Civil War*, (1923; reprint, Carthage, Mo.: Kiwanis Club, 1988), 104, and 1860 Jasper County census. Schrantz called Livingston a bachelor, probably because, at the time of the 1860 census, he was living with William Parkinson and Parkinson's wife, Sarah, with no children in the household. However, Joel Livingston stated in his 1911 *History of Jasper County* that Tom Livingston had been married and that his wife had died after giving birth to two children. This is confirmed by later evidence, including a the author's e-mail correspondence (27 January 2002) with John Livingston, a descendant of Tom Livingston. (Livingston's children had been sent to live with relatives after his wife's death.)

2. Peterson et al. *Sterling Price's Lieutenants*, 276. Although Livingston was associated with Talbott during the early stages of the war, some evidence suggests that he may have commanded an "independent company" that was only loosely affiliated with Talbott's Eleventh Cavalry. See, for example, the *SLTWMR*, 23 December 1861. Also, Britton (*The Civil War on the Border*, 1898) characterizes Livingston's command in the summer of 1861 as a guerrilla band.

3. *LDC*, 21 September 1861; *Humboldt (Kans.) Civil War Days News*, 2003

4. William G. Cutler, *History of the State of Kansas*, vol. 1, (Chicago: A. T. Andreas, 1883), 669; *OR*, Series 2, v. 1, 135; *LDC*, 26 October 1861.

5. Cutler, *History of the State of Kansas*, 669; *OR*, Series 2, v. 1, 135.

6. Joel T. Livingston, *History of Jasper County*, vol. 1 (Chicago: The Lewis Publishing Company, 1912), 54.

7. *Ibid.*

8. Peterson et. al., 276; *Confederate Organizations, Officers, and Posts 1861-1865: Missouri Units* (Springfield, Mo.: Ozarks Genealogical Society, Inc., 1988), 1. See also *OR*, vol. 22, pt. 1, 321-322, for evidence of Livingston's Confederate authority. Two articles in the *Carthage Evening Press* (July 11, 1938 and July 11, 1953) suggest that Livingston received a commission under the Partisan Ranger Act in the spring of 1862.

9. Schrantz, p. 105.

10. Marvin L. Van Gilder, *Jasper County: The First Two Hundred Years* (The Jasper County Commission, 1995), 88. See also the *Carthage Weekly Press*, 19 October 1911.

11. *OR*, vol. 8, 749.

12. *History of Newton, Lawrence, Barry, and McDonald Counties, Pt. 1* (Chicago: Goodspeed Publishing Co., 1888) 477.

13. *Carthage Evening Press*, July 11, 1938.

14. *Fort Scott Western Volunteer*, 3 May 1862.

15. *OR*, vol. 8, 94-95.

16. *OR*, vol. 13, 858; Peter Wellington Alexander papers (microfilm copy), University of Arkansas Library, Fayetteville, letter from Colonel Emmett MacDonald to General Hindman, 11 October 1862.

17. *OR*, vol. 13, 552.

18. Livingston's *History of Jasper County* says this incident occurred in mid-June of 1862, but Shelby's report of 27 October 1862 (*OR*, vol. 13, 979) says that he camped on Coon Creek in August and skirmished there with Cloud.

19. *OR*, vol. 13, 277-278 and 661.

20. *OR*, vol. 13, 277; *LDT*, 24 September and 30 September 1862; *SJWH*, 25 September 1862.

21. Livingston, *History of Jasper County*, 57.

22. *OR*, vol. 13, 672.

23. *Ibid.*, 744.

24. *OR*, Series 2, vol. 4, 667.

25. *OR*, 13:353; *LDC*, 16 November 1862 and 20 November 1862.

26. *OR*, vol. 13, 353.

27. *Ibid.*

28. Schrantz, p. 104.

29. *LDT*, 16 December 1862, quoting the *Bourbon County Monitor*.

30. *OR*, vol. 22, pt. 1, 874.

31. *OR*, vol. 22, pt. 2, 33.

32. *OR*, vol. 22, pt. 1, 219.

33. *OR*, vol. 22, pt. 2, 48.

34. *Ibid.*, 109.

35. *LDC*, 6 March 1863.

36. *OR*, vol. 22, pt. 1, 233.

37. "Returns from Military Posts: Fort Scott, Kansas, 1859-1866" (Microfilm M617, #1137, National Archives and Records Administration, Central Plains Region, Kansas City); *OR*, vol. 22, pt. 1, 233. The returns from Fort Scott also shows a skirmish between Livingston and a detachment from the fort on January 11 below

Carthage during which the guerrillas had several men taken prisoner but also took several of their own. Livingston himself was not in the Carthage area at this time, but some of his men may well have skirmished with the Fort Scott troops.

38. *OR*, vol. 22, pt. 1, 233-234.

39. *Ibid.*, 234.

40. *Ibid.*, 236.

41. *Ibid.*, 238.

42. *Ibid.*

43. *OR*, vol. 22, pt. 1, 238; Livingston, *History of Jasper County*, 59.

44. CSR, M322, #193, Livingston's military service file.

45. *LDC*, 25 November 1862; F. A. North, *History of Jasper County, Missouri, Pt. 2* (Des Moines: Mills and Co., 1883), 393; *Carthage Evening Press*, 11 July 1938.

46. CSR, M322, #193.

47. *Ibid.* Following is the list of soldiers Livingston claimed to have paroled without an exchange: "Thos. Houghton, Gilbert Schooling, Silvenius Keller, Isaac N. Spencer, M. C. Wilbanks, John W. Henry, Caswell Humbard belonging to Major Allen's company at Bower's Mill. Sergeant T. H. Raymore, Wm. Kinross, Thos. Cauthen, B. F. Fugate, Eli Cates, C. J. Drummond, F. M. Southard, Samuel Jones, Wm. T. Hart belonging to Major Eno's command at Newtonia. W. H. Alberty, Hugh Watkins, Oliver Hunt, Coleman Simmons, Allen Hurt, Robert E. Nealy (of) Major Eno's command. John Cook (of) Col. Phillips' command at Greenfield. Samuel Hicks (of) Capt. Henning (at) Neosho. Samuel Pearcy, Major Eno's command. Samuel Hill (of) Major Allen, Bower's Mill."

48. *OR*, vol. 22, pt. 2, 193.

49. *Lexington Weekly Union*, 6 June 1863.

50. OR (Supplement), vol. 53, 457.

51. *OR*, vol. 22, pt. 1, 320; *LDC,* 16 May 1863.

52. *OR*, vol. 22, pt. 1, 321.

53. *OR*, vol. 22, pt. 2, 282; *SJWH*, 28 May 1863.

54. *OR*, Series 2, vol. 5, 503; *LDC*, 14 May 1863; *OR*, vol. 22, pt. 1, 330.

55. *OR*, vol. 22, pt. 1, 330.

56. *Ibid.*

57. *Ibid.*

58. *Ibid.*, 330-331.

59. *Ibid.*, 331.

60. *OR*, vol. 22, pt. 1, 329; *Lexington Weekly Union*, 6 June 1863.

61. *OR*, vol. 22, pt. 1, 321.

62. *LDC*, 23 May 1863, 31 May 1863; *OR*, vol. 22, pt. 1, 322. See also Hugh L. Thompson, "Baxter Springs as a Military Post, 1862-1863," written in 1895 and reprinted in the Baxter Springs News, 1 October 1931, and Dolph Shaner, "Sherwood—The Ghost Town," in the *Joplin Globe,* 11 February 1934.

63. OR, vol. 22, pt. *1, 322.*

64. OR, vol. 22, pt. 1, 322; *LDC*, 23 May 1863.

65. *OR*, vol. 22, pt. 1, 322.

66. *Ibid.*

67. The Union officer's letter is quoted in William N. Pearson, *Sherwood: The Forgotten Village*, (the author, 1978), 9-10.

68. Regimental Letter Book, 1st Kansas Colored Infantry (Microfilm M858, roll 5, frame 4176), National Archives and Records Administration—Central Plains Region, Kansas City.

69. *Ibid.*, frames 4177-4178, and Thompson in *Baxter Springs News,* 1 October 1931.

70. Regimental Letter Book, M858, roll 5, frame 4179.

71. *Ibid.*, frames 4181-4182.

72. *Ibid.*, frame 4182.

73. *Ibid.* See also Thompson in *Baxter Springs News*, 1 October 1931; *OR*, vol. 22, pt. 1, 322; and Dudley T. Cornish, *The Sable Arm: Black Troops in the Union Army 1861-1865* (1956; reprint, Lawrence: University Press of Kansas, 1987), 145-146.

74. *OR*, vol. 22, pt. 1, 342.

75. Thompson in *Baxter Springs News*, 1 October 1931; OR, vol. 22, pt. 1, 322; *LDC*, 23 June 1863.

76. *OR*, vol. 22, pt. 2, 330.

77. *OR*, vol. 22, pt. 1, 445; *History of Hickory, Polk, Cedar, Dade, and Barton Counties, Missouri* (Chicago: Goodspeed Publishing Co., 1889), 423.

78. *Carthage (Weekly) Press*, 19 October 1911.

79. *Ibid.*

80. *OR*, vol. 22, pt. 1, 445; *Carthage Evening Press*, 11 July 11 1938; *KCDJC*, 18 July 1863.

81. *OR*, vol. 22, pt. 2, 393; *KCWWJC*, 26 September 1863; *Fort Scott Union Monitor*, 15 October 1863; Van Gilder, 89

82. Interview with Steve Weldon, Jasper County Archivist, 29 June 1999.

Chapter Five
THE NOTORIOUS SHERIFF CLEM

1. 1860 Bates County census; CSR, M322, #180; Norton, *Behind Enemy Lines,* 20-21.

2. *OR*, vol. 3, 455; *HVC*, 390-391; Norton, 26.

3. Norton, 28-29.

4. CSR, #180; *LDC*, 5 November 1861, quoting the *Osawatomie Herald.*

5. *LDC*, 5 November 1861, quoting the *Osawatomie Herald*; Cutler, *History of the State of Kansas*, vol. 2, 1106.

6. *Ibid.*

7. CSR, M322, #180; *LDC*, 16 November 1861.

8. *LDC*, 20 and 21 December 1861; Cutler, 1106-1107.

9. *LDC*, 20 December 1861; Cutler, 1107.

10. *LDC*, 20 December 1861; *History of Cass and Bates County, Missouri* (St. Joseph: National Historical Company, 1883), 858.

11. *OR*, 22, pt. 1, 204; CSR, M322, #37; Norton, *Behind Enemy Lines*, 26.

Chapter Six
THE SO-STYLED COLONEL PARKER

1. *LDT*, 27 February 1862.

2. *Liberty (Mo.) Tribune*, 21 March 1862.

3. *OR*, Series 2, vol. 1, 271.

4. *OR*, vol. 8, 357. See also the *SJWH*, 10 April 1862.

5. *Des Moines Daily State Register*, 11 April 1862.

6. *Ibid.* and *OR*, vol. 8, 357.

7. *OR*, vol. 8, 360-361.

8. CSR, M322, #193, military service file of Benjamin F. Parker.

9. *Ibid.*

10. *OR*, Series 2, vol. 5, 503; *OR*, Series 1, v. 22, pt. 2, 265.

11. *SJWH*, 21 May 1863; *KCWWJC*, 18 July 1863.

12. *OR*, Series 2, vol. 5, 549-550; *SJWH* 21 May 1863.

13. *OR*, Series 2, vol. 5, 551.

14. *SJWH*, 21 May 1863.

15. *KCWWJC*, 18 July 1863.

16. *Ibid.*

17. *OR*, vol. 22, pt. 1, 332; *Kansas City Daily Western Journal of Commerce* 17 May 1863.

18. *OR*, vol. 22, pt.1, 332.

19. *OR*, vol. 22, pt. 1, 334.

20. *SJWH*, 23 July 1863.

21. *LDC*, 22 May 1863. See also *SJWH*, 28 May 1863.

22. *KCDJC*, 26 May 1863 and 29 May 1863.

23. *KCWWJC*, 27 June 1863. Parker's claim to have killed a Union major was discredited in the Kansas City paper.

24. *OR*, vol. 22, pt. 1, 372; *KCWWJC*, 20 June 1863.

25. *KCDJC*, 1 July 1863 and 2 July 1863. See also Edwards, *Noted Guerrillas.*

26. *Ibid.*

27. *Ibid.*

28. *OR*, vol. 22, pt. 2, 378.

29. *KCDJC*, 23 June 1863; *SJWH*, 2 July 1863, 16 July 1863, and 23 July 1863. A report emerged after the Lawrence massacre that Bennet Wood was one of the sub-chiefs who participated in it, but the man who participated in the Lawrence raid was apparently named Benton Wood.

30. *KCWWJC*, 1 August 1863.

Chapter Seven
THE DESPERATE REBEL JOE HART

1. 1840 and 1850 censuses of Nelson County, Kentucky; *Marriage Records, Southern States*, vol. 1, CD 229, (Automated Archives, Inc., 1994); 1860 census of Andrew County; *SJWH*, 16 July 1863.

2. Individual Citizens, fold3.com, Joseph L. Hart, Image #286846044; 1860 Andrew County census.

3. Individual Citizens, fold3.com, Joseph L. Hart, Image #286846044; Unfiled Papers Belonging in Confederate Records, National Archives Microfilm Publication M-347, Roll 335, online at www.fold3.com,

J.L. Hart, #259295926, Joseph L. Hart, #259296630 (hereafter cited as Unfiled Papers, followed by the person's name and the image number).
4. Richard C. Peterson et al. *Sterling Price's Lieutenants: A Guide to the Officers and Organization of the Missouri State Guard 1861-1865* (Shawnee Mission, Kansas: Two Trails Publishing, 1995) 297; John N. Edwards, *Noted Guerillas* (St. Louis: Bryan, Brand & Company, 1877), 261-262. Although Edwards is generally unreliable, many of the key events he mentions did occur. It's just that he was given to great exaggeration in describing the details. For example, Hart may well have been captured near Corinth at some point, but Edwards' glowing account of his arrest and escape is almost surely embellished.
5. *SJWH*, 23 July 1863.
6. "A Guerrilla's Diary," *Harper's Weekly*, vol. 9, no. 468 (December 16, 1865): 790. Another early entry in the diary was a love poem inscribed by twenty-one-year-old Martha Lou Claybrook of Missouri City, Clay County, to a man named Frank, presumably Frank James, who had been a near neighbor of Miss Claybrook's and was now a member of Hart's band of guerrillas. See the 1860 Clay County census.
7. *Noted Guerrillas*, 263-264; *Liberty Tribune*, 6 March 1863; *SJWH*, 19 March 63. Edwards says that Hart served as a private in Todd's command, an assertion that is demonstrably untrue.
8. *Noted Guerrillas*, 264-266; *Harper's Weekly* (16 December 1865), 791.
9. *Harper's Weekly* (16 December 1865), 791; 1860 Andrew County census.
10. *Harper's Weekly* (16 December 1865), 791.
11. *Ibid.*
12. *Ibid.*
13. *Ibid.*
14. *Harper's Weekly* (16 December 1865), 791; *OR*, 22:1, 335-336; *Kansas City Daily Western Journal of Commerce*, 22 May 1863; *SLTWMR*, 22 May 1863. According to Hart's diary, he rendezvoused with the gang that included Frank James in time to participate in the Missouri City raid, but all Union sources say Hart was not present.
15. *CMS*, 5 June 1863, quoting the *St. Louis Union; Harper's Weekly* (16 December 1865), 791.

16. *Harper's Weekly* (16 December 1865), 791; *Liberty Tribune, 29 May 1863; LDC*, 30 May 1863.

17. *Harper's Weekly* (16 December 1865), 791.

18. *SJWH*, 23 July 1863.

19. *Ibid.*

20. *SJWH*, 11 June 1863; *Harper's Weekly* (16 December 1865), 791.

21. *Harper's Weekly* (16 December 1865), 791; *STJWH*, 23 July 1863.

22. *SJWH*, 18 June 1863.

23. *SJWH*, 23 July 1863; Individual Citizens, Reel F1274.

24. *SJWH*, 23 July 1863.

25. *SLTWMR*, 14 July 1863, quoting the *St. Joseph News*, 10 July 1863.

26. *SLTWMR*, 14 July 1863, quoting *St. Joseph News*, 10 July 1863; *SJWH*, 16 July 1863.

27. *SJWH*, 16 July 1863; *SLTWMR*, 14 July 1863, quoting *St. Joseph News*, 10 July 1863.

28. *SJWH*, 16 July 1863.

29. *Ibid.*

30. *Ibid.*

31. *SJWH*, 23 July 1863.

32. *Ibid.*

33. *Ibid.*

34. *Ibid.*

35. *Ibid.*

36. *SJWH*, 16 July 1863.

37. *SJWH*, 23 July 1863; *History of Caldwell and Livingston Counties, Missouri* (National Historical Company: St. Louis, 1886), 797.

38. *SJWH*, 23 July 1863; *History of Caldwell and Livingston Counties, Missouri*, 796.

39. *SJWH*, 23 July 1863.

40. *OR*, vol. 41, pt. 1, 434; Individual Citizens, Reel F1145.

Chapter Eight
THE ELUSIVE JIM RIDER

1. Jim Rider's full name is given in *General Orders of the War Department, Embracing the Years 1861, 1862 & 1863, vol. 2* (New

York: Derby & Miller, 1864), 336.

2. Joseph M. Beilein, Jr., *"The Presence of These Families Is the Cause of the Presence There of the Guerrillas": The Influence of Little Dixie Households on the Civil War in Missouri*, Master's Thesis, University of Missouri, Columbia, 2006; Soldiers' Records: War of 1812-World War I, Missouri State Archives, Jefferson City, Missouri, www.sos.mo.gov/archives/soldiers/; 1850 U.S. Census, Saline County, Missouri, microfilm copy at Joplin (Mo.) Public Library. Mart Rider's parents were John Rider and Nancy Morris, who married in Sumner County, Tennessee, in 1821. About 1839, Nancy, now a widow, moved to Missouri and settled in the Cass County area, but Jim Rider apparently had no close connection to this family. Mart Rider's father, John, was a brother of the George Rider who settled in Jackson County, Missouri, and it's possible that George Rider of Saline County was their cousin, since his family, like theirs, came to Missouri from Tennessee in the late 1830s, but no definite connection has been proved.

3. Missouri Marriage Records, 1805-2002, www.ancestry.com, accessed March 18, 2014 (hereafter cited as Missouri Marriage Records); Unfiled Papers, Jas. W. Rider, Image #256635481, accessed 13 October 2014.

4. Individual Citizens, fold3.com, Talitha Alice Rider, #291601893, accessed 13 October 2014; Unfiled Papers, James W. Rider, #256635103.

5. Missouri Marriage Records; Unfiled Papers, James W. Rider, #256635200, #256635272.

6. Unfiled Papers, James W. Rider, #256635260, #256635282, #256635297.

7. Williams, Walter, ed., *A History of Northwest Missouri* (Chicago: The Lewis Publishing Company, 1915), 563; *History of Livingston County* (St. Louis: National Historical Company, 1886), 1045; Unfiled Papers, James Rider, #256634943.

8. *General Orders of the War Department, Embracing the Years 1861, 1862 & 1863, vol. 2* (New York: Derby & Miller, 1864), 332-337; Union Provost Marshals' File of Papers Relating to Two or More Civilians, Missouri State Archives, Jefferson City, Missouri, www.sos.mo.gov/archives/provost/provostPDF.asp,   Microfilm F1659, #22017, accessed 19 March 2014 (hereafter cited as Two or

More followed by the roll number and file number). Thomas Joseph Ballew's name is alternately given as Joseph Thomas Ballew.
9. Two or More, F1586, #1570, #1711, #1739.
10. Unfiled Papers, James W. Rider, #256635103.
11. Unfiled Papers, James Rider, #256634909.
12. *Ibid.*, #256634885.
13. *Ibid.*, #256634889.
14. *Ibid.*, #256634856.
15. *Ibid.*, #256634968.
16. *Ibid.*, #256634841, #256634943.
17. Unfiled Papers, Jas. Rider, #256635428.
18. Unfiled Papers, James W. Rider, #256635103, #256635125.
19. *History of Carroll County, Missouri* (St. Louis: Missouri Historical Company, 1881), 326-327; *History of Caldwell and Livingston Counties, Missouri* (St. Louis: National Historical Co, 1886), 998.
20. *Jefferson City Missouri State Times*, 31 January 1863.
21. *Ibid.*
22. Unfiled Papers, James W. Rider, #256635169.
23. Unfiled Papers, James Rider, #256634961..
24. Unfiled Papers, James W. Rider, #256635178.
25. *Ibid.*, #256635103, #256635125; Unfiled Papers, James Rider, #256635011.
26. Unfiled Papers, James W. Rider, #256635103, #256635125.
27. Ibid., #256635367; Unfiled Papers, James Rider, #256634995, #256635011.
28. Unfiled Papers, James W. Rider, #256635086, #256635250.
29. Individual Citizens, fold3.com, George Rider, #291601809-291601810, #291601820, #291601822.
30. *St. Louis Daily Missouri Democrat*, 24 July 1863; *St. Louis Daily Union*, 24 July 1863.
31. *History of Carroll County*, 334.
32. Individual Citizens, fold3.com, George Rider, #291601824, #291601826; Two or More, F1602, #6595.
33. *The History of Linn County, Missouri* (Kansas City, Missouri: Birdsall and Dean, 1882), 352, 393.
34. *St. Joseph Weekly Herald*, 19 November 1863, quoting the *Carroll County Democrat.*

35. U.S. Civil War Draft Registration Records, www.Ancestry.com, accessed 18 March 2014. A "J.W. Rider" also registered for Federal service in Jackson County in November of 1863, but this was likely John W. Rider of Jackson, who was a cousin of Mart Rider. This John W. Rider might also have been the man whose name (i.e. J.W. Rider) appeared, along with the name "George Rider," on a July 1862 roster of William Quantrill's company, although John W. Rider of Cass County, who had a brother named George, is perhaps a more likely candidate to be the Quantrill man.

36. *Ibid.*

37. *History of Carroll County*, 340.

38. Individual Citizens, fold3.com, Talitha Alice Rider, #291601893-291601894. According to Robert Shannon's later statement, Tabitha Rider's stay at his house occurred near the first of August, and this date is corroborated by the statement of another witness. However, given the fact that Tabitha was arrested in January of 1865, her recollection of the amount of time she spent at the various residences during the summer and fall of 1864 does not compute with the August 1 date. Either she spent less time at some of the places than she later recalled, or else some of the stopovers that she remembered as having occurred after her visit to Shannon's house actually predated that visit.

39. Ibid., #291601894.

40. *OR*, vol. 41, pt. 1, 530, and pt. 4, 89-90.

41. *OR*, vol. 41, pt. 4, 139, 188.

42. *Ibid.*, 566. The Jackson whom Fisk mentioned in connection with Rider was notorious guerrilla leader Jim Jackson, another confederate of Holtzclaw.

43. *Ibid.*, 607.

44. *History of Linn County*, 644; Individual Citizens, fold3.com, Talitha Alice Rider, #291601901.

45. Individual Citizens, fold3.com, Talitha Alice Rider, #291601894.

46. *History of Linn County*, 394-395.

47. *Ibid.*, 395.

48. *Ibid.*, 395-396.

49. Individual Citizens, fold3.com, Talitha Alice Rider, #291601894.

50. *Lexington Union*, 4 February 1865, quoting the *Carrollton Democrat*.

51. Two or More, F1629, #14018 and F1633, #15158; Individual

Citizens, fold3.com, Talitha Alice Rider, #291601894-291601895; Individual Citizens, fold3.com, _____ Riders, #291601785.
52. OR, v. 48, pt. 1, 290.
53. *Ibid.*, 297.
54. Missouri Marriage Records; 1880 U.S. Census, Daviess County, Missouri, Heritage Quest online, http://www.heritagequestonline. com/hqoweb/library/do/index, accessed 22 October 2014.

Chapter Nine
JIM JACKSON AND HIS INFERNAL CLAN

1. Bill Jackson, son of former Missouri Governor Claiborne Jackson, also had a guerrilla band during the latter part of the war and was sometimes confused with Jim Jackson. However, Bill Jackson, who operated mainly in the Saline County area, was not nearly as active nor as notorious as Jim Jackson, who mainly operated north of the Missouri River.
2. *CMS*, 16 June 1865 and 30 June 1865.
3. *OR*, vol. 41, pt. 1, 178.
4. *Ibid.*, 178-179.
5. *CMS*, 2 September 1864.
6. *Ibid.*
7. *Ibid.*
8. *SLTWMR*, 21 September 1864. See also *OR*, vol. 41, pt. 3, 233. Upon entering Callao, the rebels reportedly announced themselves as Quantrill men, but they were thought by citizens to be part of Anderson's band. Since Jim Anderson and Jim Jackson led the only sizeable guerrilla force known to be in the general area at the time Callao was sacked, the raid on the town can be attributed to them with some confidence.
9. *SLTWMR*, 21 September 1864; *St. Louis Daily Union*, 21 September 1864.
10. *OR*, vol. 41, pt. 3, 276. The rebels who entered St. Catharine were, like those at Callao, thought to be part of Anderson's gang. Circumstances suggest that the only guerrilla leader among the rebels at St. Catharine who was named Anderson was probably Jim Anderson.

11. *OR*, vol. 41, pt. 4, 24; *History of Lewis, Clark, Knox and Scotland Counties, Missouri* (St. Louis & Chicago: Goodspeed Publishing Company, 1887), 707. The Goodspeed history says Jim Jackson's raid through the northern counties of Missouri took place in September, but it was probably early October, as the Iowa portion of the raid is known to have occurred in mid-October.

12. *St. Louis Daily Union*, 19 October 1864, quoting both the *Ottumwa (Ia.) Courier*, 13 October 1864, and the *Burlington (Ia.) Hawkeye*, 14 October 1864. The newspaper accounts report the killing of only three men, but the Goodspeed history says a total of seven Iowa men were killed during the raid.

13. *OR*, vol. 41, pt. 4, 566; *KCDJC*, 11 November 1864.

14. *KCDJC*, 11 November 1864.

15. *OR*, vol. 41, pt. 1, 923.

16. Individual Citizens, Reel #1306.

17. *OR*, vol. 41, pt. 4, 930, 931, 937, and 938.

18. *OR*, vol. 48, pt. 1, 424 and 451.

19. *Ibid.*, 485.

20. *Ibid.*, 31.

21. *OR*, vol. 48, pt. 1, 31; *St. Joseph Morning Herald and Tribune*, 24 January 1865, citing the *Huntsville Randolph Citizen*; *Lexington Weekly Union*, 21 January 1865. Both the *Citizen* and the *Union* reported that Jackson and Brown were riding a sleigh when they were overtaken and attacked by Denny, and the *Union* said a violin and a set of crutches were found in the abandoned sleigh.

22. *OR*, vol. 48, pt. 1, 32.

23. *Ibid.*, 32-33.

24. *Ibid.*, 33.

25. *CMS*, 24 February 1865.

26. *Ibid.* Rumans's father had been killed by Federal troops the previous summer for sheltering his son Abe and two other bushwhackers.

27. *Ibid.*

28. *CMS*, 24 February 1865, and *OR*, vol. 48, pt. 1, 949.

29. *OR*, vol. 48, pt. 1, 949.

30. *OR*, vol. 48, pt. 1, 125 and 970; *CMS*, 10 March 1865, quoting the *Huntsville Randolph Citizen*.

31. *OR*, vol. 48, pt. 1, 979 and 999; *CMS*, 10 March 1865, quoting the *Huntsville Randolph Citizen*.

32. *OR*, vol. 48, pt. 1, 128 and 999; *CMS* 10 March 1865, quoting the *Huntsville Randolph Citizen*; *History of Boone County, Missouri* (St. Louis: Western Historical Co., 1882), 546.

33. *OR*, vol. 48, pt. 1, 1089-1090.

34. *Ibid.*, 1096.

35. *Ibid.*, 132-135 and 1103.

36. *Ibid.*, 1163.

37. Letter of A. H. Lancaster to the Provost Marshal at Hannibal, dated March 16, 1865, at New London, Letters Received file 2593, Record Group 393, National Archives, Washington, D.C., quoted in Fellman, *Inside War*, 70.

38. *CMS*, 24 March 1865.

39. *CMS*, 31 March 1865.

40. *CMS*, 24 March 1865.

41. *OR*, vol. 48, pt. 1, 1257.

42. *Ibid.*, 1223.

43. *Ibid.*, 1231 and 1239.

44. *CMS*, 14 April 1865, quoting the *Fulton Telegraph*.

45. *CMS*, 5 May 1865. See also the *History of Boone County*'s account of the Centralia Massacre.

46. *CMS*, 5 May 1865.

47. *Ibid.*

48. *Ibid.*

49. *CMS*, 12 May 1865.

50. *OR*, vol. 48, pt. 1, 290-291.

51. *Ibid.*, 296.

52. *OR*, vol. 48, pt. 2, 872.

53. *CMS*, 16 June 1865.

54. *CMS*, 30 June 1865, quoting the 23 June 1865 *Paris (Mo.) Mercury*.

55. *CMS*, 30 June 1865, quoting the 23 June 1865 *Paris Mercury*; *Louisiana (Mo.) Journal*, 1 July 1865.

56. *CMS*, 30 June 1865, quoting the 23 June 1865 *Paris Mercury*.

57. *Ibid.*

58. *Ibid.*

59. *Ibid.*

Chapter Ten
CLIFTON D. HOLTZCLAW: A FIEND IN HUMAN FORM

1. The title is from a reference General Fisk made to Holtzclaw and Caleb Perkins as "fiends in human form" (*OR*, vol. 41, pt. 2, 719).
2. *Howard County Advertiser*, 3 September 1863; 1840 and 1860 censuses of Howard County, Missouri.
3. CSR, M322, #135 and #184; Missouri Adjutant General's Office Confederate Cards, Missouri Soldiers, 1861-65, War Between the States (Microfilm reel #6), Missouri State Archives, Jefferson City, Missouri. See also the Confederate Service pension application of James P. Holtzclaw, microfilm copy at the State Archives.
4. CSR, M322, #135; Missouri AGO Confederate Card files for Clifton Holtzclaw and his brothers (Reel #6).
5. *OR*, vol. 34, pt. 3, 97, pt. 4, 225; *St. Joseph Morning Herald*, 10 September 1864.
6. Individual Citizens, Reel #F1291.
7. *Ibid.*
8. *St. Joseph Morning Herald*, 10 September 1864.
9. *OR*, vol. 22, pt. 1, 446. Some reports (e.g. *St. Louis Daily Union*, 15 July 1863) suggest that the leader of the attack at the Watson home was Bill Holtzclaw, but it was almost certainly Clifton Holtzclaw, since he was known to be in the area at the time and since Bill had been killed several months earlier.
10. *Howard County Advertiser*, 3 September 1863; Individual Citizens, Reel F1476. The soldier of the Ninth Missouri State Militia Cavalry whom Holtzclaw captured may be the man named Bullock of whom Jackman spoke in his memoirs. Jackman said that, in the summer of 1863, he sent Holtzclaw to arrest Bullock for being a Union spy and that the prisoner was shot and his body thrown into the river. See Norton, *Behind Enemy Lines*, 175-176.
11. *OR*, vol. 34, pt. 3, 576.
12. *Liberty Tribune*, 17 June 1864, quoting the *Brunswick (Mo.) Brunswicker*. See also *CMS*, 17 June 1864 and 24 June 1864.
13. *Ibid.*
14. *Ibid.*

15. Transcript of J. W. Terman trial by military commission at St. Joseph, July and August, 1864, National Archives, Washington, D. C.; *CMS*, 24 June 1864.

16. *History of Linn County, Missouri* (Kansas City, Mo.: Birdsall and Dean, 1882), 593; *OR*, vol. 34, pt. 1, 1028. See also *History of Caldwell and Livingston Counties, Missouri*, 966-967. Several Union men were killed by bushwhackers in Chariton County in mid-June in retaliation for the Terman raid, but it's not definitely known that Holtzclaw was responsible for the killings.

17. *OR*, vol. 34, pt. 1, 1028; *History of Linn County*, 593.

18. *OR*, v. 34, pt. 1, 1031; *Caldwell County Banner of Liberty*, 24 June 1864, quoting *St. Joseph Tribune*; *Saint Louis Daily Union*, 23 June 1864, quoting *St. Joseph Herald*.

19. *History of Linn County*, 593; *OR*, vol. 34, pt. 1, 1031-1032.

20. *History of Linn County*, 593; *OR*, vol. 34, pt. 1, 1028 and 1031.

21. *OR*, vol. 34, pt. 1, 1028 and 1031.

22. *OR*, vol. 34, 1028; *History of Linn County*, 593.

23. *OR*, vol. 41, pt. 1, 10.

24. *Howard County Advertiser*, 15 July 1864.

25. *Ibid.*

26. *Ibid.*

27. *Ibid.* See also *OR*, vol. 41, pt. 2, 109.

28. *OR*, vol. 41, pt.1, 71-72 and pt. 2, 668-669.

29. *OR*, vol. 41, pt. 2, 252 and 272.

30. *OR*, vol. 41, pt. 2, 424.

31. *St. Louis Daily Union*, 29 July 1864.

32. *OR*, vol. 41, pt. 1, 178.

33. *OR*, vol. 41, pt. 2, 894-895.

34. *OR*, vol. 41, pt. 2, 564, and pt. 1, 178.

35. *OR*, vol. 41, pt. 1, 178-179.

36. *OR*, vol. 41, pt. 1, 200, and pt. 2, 640.

37. *OR*, vol. 41, pt. 2, 657.

38. *Ibid.*, 704-705.

39. *OR*, vol. 41, pt. 1, 259, pt. 2, 808; *CMS*, 19 August 1864.

40. *Ibid.*

41. *CMS*, 26 August 1864.

42. *OR*, vol. 41, pt. 2, 808 and 895.

43. *OR*, vol. 41, pt. 1, 300; *CMS*, 2 September 1864.

44. *St. Joseph Morning Herald*, 10 September 1864.

45. *OR*, vol. 41, pt. 1, 760. It is not known whether the "Hackley" farm mentioned by Fisk is the same place Jim Jackson visited in the fall of 1864, since several families named Hackley lived in the vicinity of Holtzclaw's mother.

46. *St. Joseph Morning Herald*, 19 September 1864 and 20 September 1864.

47. *St. Joseph Morning Herald*, 19 September 1864, and 24 September 1864. At least one report identified Griffith as a member of Bill Stephens's guerrilla band rather than Holtzclaw's. Stephens sometimes operated in conjunction with Holtzclaw and may have been a lieutenant in his command.

48. *OR*, vol. 41, pt. 1, 415-416. A report reached St. Joseph in late September that Holtzclaw had dashed into Fayette and robbed the bank of $14,000, but there appears to be no corroborating evidence of the raid. The report was probably a faulty account of the unsuccessful attack at Fayette on September 24.

49. The Centralia Massacre is chronicled in numerous sources, but see especially the *History of Boone County* for a good, early account.

50. *OR*, vol., 41, pt. 1, 424.

51. *OR*, vol. 41, pt. 1, 443-445, and pt. 4, 90.

52. *OR*, vol. 48, pt. 1, 452.

53. *OR*, vol. 48, pt. 1, 1096, and pt. 2, 25.

54. Individual Citizens, Reel F1476; R. S. Bevier, *History of the First and Second Missouri Confederate Brigades 1861-1865*, appendix, (St. Louis: Bryan, Brand and Company, 1879); Missouri Office of the Adjutant General, Confederate Cards (Microfilm Reel #6); 1880 Linn County, Kansas census.

Chapter Eleven
THE OTHER ANDERSON: BLOODY BILL'S BROTHER JIM

Note: A similar version of this chapter originally appeared as an article in the January 2003 issue of the *Missouri Historical Review*, and the author extends his appreciation to the State Historical Society of Missouri for permission to reprint it here.

1. *Emporia (Kans.) News*, 17 May 1862 and 12 July 1862. See also William Connelley's interview with Eli Sewell, 7 July 1910, in the Connelley Papers, Box 13, Kansas State Historical Society and Charles Green, *Early Days in Kansas* (Olathe, Kansas: Charles Green, 1912), 1:48-51 for additional information on Baker's killing of William C. Anderson and the Anderson brothers' murder of Baker.
2. *Ibid.*
3. Green, *Early Days*, 1:48-51.
4. *Emporia (Kans.) News,* 12 July 1862; Green, *Early Days,* 1:48-51.
5. 1840 Marion County, Missouri census; 1850 Randolph County, Missouri census; 1860 Breckenridge County, Kansas census; *Emporia News*, 17 May 1862 and 12 July 1862; Connelly Papers, Box 13.
6. *Kansas City Journal,* 12 May 1888, statement of William H. Gregg.
7. *Lexington (Mo.) Weekly Union*, 7 February 1863.
8. *Boonville Weekly Monitor*, 11 June 1864. See also Henry C. Levens and Nathaniel M. Drake, *A History of Cooper County* (St. Louis: Perrin & Smith, 1876) 186 and *OR*, vol. 34, pt. 4, 235 and 238.
9. *OR*, vol. 34, pt. 1, 1001-1002.
10. *Ibid.,* 1007-1008.
11. *Carrollton Democrat,* 15 July 1864.
12. *CMS,* 5 August 1864.
13. Thomas Goodrich, *Black Flag: Guerrilla Warfare on the Western Border 1861-1865* (Bloomington: Indiana University Press, 1995), 137.
14. *CMS,* 12 August 1864 and *OR*, vol. 41, pt. 2, 479.
15. *CMS,* 12 August 1864; *Macon (Mo.) Gazette* 11 August 1864.
16. *OR,* vol. 41, pt. 1, 230; *Macon Gazette* 11 August 1864.
17. *OR*, vol. 41, pt. 1, 230.
18. *Ibid.*
19. *Ibid.,* 230-231.
20. *Ibid.,* 231. See also *OR,* vol. 41, pt. 2, 624-625, and *CMS,* 19 August 1864.
21. *CMS,* 24 August 1864. See also *OR*, 41, pt. 2, pp. 839, 840, and 880-881.
22. William Crump to Moses Barth, Rocheport, Missouri, 28 August 1864, in the Moses Barth Papers, Western Historical Manuscript

Collection, University of Missouri-Columbia. See also 1860 Boone
County census in which Turny is enumerated.
23. Charlie Meyer to his uncle Moses Barth, Rocheport, Missouri, 28
August 1864, in the Barth Papers.
24. *Ibid.*
25. *CMS*, 26 August 1864.
26. *OR,* vol. 41, pt. 2, 858.
27. *OR,* vol. 41, pt. 3, 111.
28. *Ibid.,* 276.
29. *OR*, vol. 41, pt. 4, 24; *KCDJC*, 11 November 1864 quoting the *St.
Louis Missouri Democrat*
30. *Kansas City Star,* 9 September 1928, quoted in the *Missouri
Historical Review* 23, no. 2 (January 1929): 344-345. See also the
Richmond Missourian, 22 May 1924, quoted in the *Missouri
Historical Review* 19, no. 3 (April 1925): 493-494.
31. *OR*, vol. 41, pt. 4, 607 and vol. 48, pt. 2, 45. See also John N.
Edwards, *Noted Guerrillas*, (St. Louis: Bryan, Brand & Company,
1877), 327-328.
32. *OR,* vol. 48, pt. 2, 45.
33. *OR,* vol. 48, pt. 2, 371.
34. *OR*, vol. 48, pt. 2, 342, 352, and 370; *KCDJC*, 10 May 1865; *Fort
Scott Union Monitor*, 18 May 1865.
35. *OR,* vol. 48, pt. 2, 342 and 354.
36. *KCDJC*, 13 May 1865.
37. *OR,* vol. 48, pt. 2, 371.
38. *Ibid.,* 599.
39. *Ibid.,* 587.
40. *OR*, vol. 48, pt. 1, 290-291.
41. *Ibid.,* 293.
42. *OR*, vol. 48, pt. 2, 668.
43. *Ibid.,* 738 and 785.
44. *Ibid.,* 528.
45. *Ibid.,* 546.
46. *CMS* 16 June 1864.
47. *OR*, vol. 48, pt. 2, 785 and 838.
48. *Ibid.,* 872. See also pp. 837 and 848.

49. Albert Castel and Thomas Goodrich, *Bloody Bill Anderson: The Short Savage Life of a Civil War Guerrilla* (Mechanicsburg [Penn.]: Stackpole Books, 1998), 136.

50. *KCDJC*, 16 February 1866.

51. Castel and Goodrich, *Bloody Bill Anderson*, 136-137; Donald R. Hale, *They Called Him Bloody Bill* (Clinton [Mo.]: The Printery, 1975), 87.

52. *Howard County Advertiser*, 15 March 1866; *CMS*, 16 March 1866.

53. *Ibid.*

54. *Macon Times* quoted in *KCDJC,* 8 April 1866.

55. *Howard County Advertiser* 15 March 1866; *CMS* 16 March 1866.

56. Thomas Clement Fletcher to an unnamed colonel, Jefferson City, Missouri, 19 March 1866, in the Thomas Clement Fletcher Papers, Western Historical Manuscript Collection, University of Missouri-Kansas City.

57. J. W. Buel, *The Border Bandits: An Authentic and Thrilling History of the Noted Outlaws, Jesse and Frank James and Their Bands of Highwaymen* (St. Louis: Historical Publishing Company, 1881), 110. Some accounts of Shepherd's separate acts of revenge on Jim Anderson and Jesse James for the killing of Ike Flannery say that Shepherd and Flannery were cousins, but Buel, whose main source for *Border Bandits* was Shepherd, correctly states that Flannery was Shepherd's nephew. Census data suggests that Flannery's mother, Sarah, was probably Shepherd's older sister. See the 1850 and 1860 Jackson County, Missouri censuses. See also in the 9 November 1879 *Galena (Kans.) Miner* Shepherd's statement to citizens of Galena immediately after his supposed murder of Jesse James that he had killed James to avenge the death of his nephew.

58. Buel, *Border Bandits,* 109-110. Shepherd's claim that Flannery had inherited the money from his father is belied by census records, which suggest that Flannery's father died (or else abandoned the family) before 1850. It's possible that the money was set aside for him at a young age and he had only recently been able to claim it, but it's more likely Shepherd invented the tale to justify Flannery's sudden wealth.

59. Buel, *Border Bandits,* 110-112.

60. *Ibid.,* 112 and 10 May 1867 *Jefferson City Missouri State Times* quoting the *Glasgow Times.*

61. U. S. Census, 1870, *FamilySearch,* www.familysearch.org, accessed 9 August 2014; Texas Marriage Records, *FamilySearch,* www.familysearch.org, accessed 9 August 2014; Baker, James R., Jr., Missouri Partisans, vol. 1, The Author, 2013.

62. Edward E. Leslie, *The Devil Knows How to Ride* (New York: Random House, 1996), 375 and 403.

63. *Kansas City Star,* 9 September 1928, quoted in the *Missouri Historical Review* 23, no. 2, (January 1929): 343-44.

64. William A. Settle, Jr., *Jesse James Was His Name* (Columbia: University of Missouri Press, 1966) 38-40 and 59-60.

Chapter Twelve
JOHN THRAILKILL: A DESPERADO OF THE WORST CLASS

1. CSR, M322, #8; *Marriage Records Early-1850 West of Mississippi River CD #227* (Automated Archives, Inc., 1994); 1840 Livingston County, Missouri, census; 1850 Polk County, Iowa, census; 1860 Holt County, Missouri, census. Others have suggested that Thrailkill's occupation was a painter (of houses), but his military service file clearly says printer.

2. CSR, M322, #8.

3. *Ibid.*

4. *Ibid.*

5. CSR, M322, #8; *OR*, vol. 22, pt. 1, 292.

6. CSR, M322, #8; *SJWH*, 23 July 1863; transcript of John Thrailkill trial by military commission, January 1864, File NN-1233, Records of the Judge Advocate General, Record Group 153, National Archives Building, Washington, D. C.

7. *SJWH*, 23 July 1863; Thrailkill trial transcript.

8. *Ibid.*

9. CSR, M322, #8; Thrailkill trial transcript.

10. Thrailkill trial transcript.

11. CSR, M322, #8; Thrailkill trial transcript.

12. *OR*, vol. 41, pt. 1, 57-58, and pt. 2, 137, 296. Exactly when Thrailkill reached Missouri is not clear; so it's uncertain whether he was also with Thornton and Taylor on July 7, 1864, when they raided the town of Parkville in southern Platte County and conscripted many of the Enrolled Missouri Militia there. It's also possible but less likely

that Thrailkill was with Taylor on July 4 when the latter skirmished with some Clay County militia under Captain William B. Kemper.

13. *OR*, vol. 41, pt. 1, 53, pt. 2, 292; *History of Ray County, Missouri* (St. Louis: Missouri Historical Company, 1881), 302; *Liberty Tribune*, 22 July 1864.

14. *History of Caldwell and Livingston Counties, Missouri*, 196-198; *OR*, vol. 41, pt. 2, 273.

15. *History of Caldwell and Livingston Counties, Missouri*, 199-201; *OR*, vol. 41, pt. 2, 273; *SJWH*, 28 July 1864.

16. *History Caldwell and Livingston Counties, Missouri*, 201-202.

17. *Ibid.*, 202-203, and *OR*, vol. 41, pt. 2, 318.

18. *History of Caldwell and Livingston Counties, Missouri*, 203-205; *OR*, vol. 41, pt. 1, 60-61, pt. 2, 317.

19. *History of Caldwell and Livingston Counties, Missouri*, 203; *OR*, vol. 41, pt. 1, 60-62. Although Thrailkill called himself a major during his 1864 summer campaign in Missouri, he had been listed as a captain in official Confederate records earlier in the summer.

20. *OR*, vol. 41, pt. 2, 341.

21. *OR*, vol. 41, pt. 1, 62, pt. 2, 341; *History of Caldwell and Livingston Counties, Missouri*, 206.

22. *History of Caldwell and Livingston Counties, Missouri*, 206-209; *OR*, vol. 41, pt. 1, 61; *SJWH*, 28 July 1864.

23. *SJWH*, 28 July 1864 and 11 August 1864.

24. *OR*, vol. 41, pt. 2, 507 and 562-563.

25. *OR*, vol. 41, pt. 1, 233, pt. 2, 572-573 and 622-623.

26. *OR*, vol. 41, pt. 2, 622-623 and 748; *History of Caldwell and Livingston Counties, Missouri*, 209.

27. *OR*, vol. 41, pt. 2, 748, 856-857, and pt. 3, 232-233.

28. *Liberty Tribune*, 23 September 1864.

29. *OR*, vol. 41, pt. 1, 425 and 429.

30. *OR*, vol. 41, pt. 1, 429.

31. *Ibid.*

32. *OR*, vol. 41, pt. 1, 425 and 429.

33. *SJWH*, 29 September 1864; *OR*, vol. 41, pt. 1, 415, 425, and pt. 3, 330-332.

34. *OR*, vol. 41, pt. 1, 415. Anderson is often credited with leading this attack, but the best evidence suggests that he was not present.

35. *OR*, vol. 41, pt. 3, 397 and 488. See also the Boone County history for an account of the Centralia Massacre and the ensuing battle.
36. *OR*, vol. 41, pt. 3, 670, 733, 841, 844, 890; *KCWWJC*, 29 October 1864.
37. *OR*, vol. 48, pt. 1, 1306, pt. 2, 9; *History of Caldwell and Livingston Counties, Missouri*, 209; undated clipping in Civil War Files (Quantrill's Men) at the State Historical Society of Missouri; www.worldconnect.genealogy.rootsweb.com.

Chapter Thirteen
SILAS GORDON: THE ONLY WHACKER OF ANY
PROMINENCE

1. Marriage Records: Southern States, vol. 1, CD #229 (Automated Archives, Inc., 1994); 1840 Clark County, Kentucky census; 1850 Platte County, Missouri census. Gordon's first name is sometimes incorrectly given as Cyrus. His first name was often shortened, but since the full first name was "Silas," the appropriate spelling of the shortened nickname was "Si," not "Cy."
2. James A. Price Papers, Folder 10, Western Historical Manuscript Collection, University of Missouri, Columbia.
3. *LDT*, 25 Dec. 1861.
4. CSR, M322, Reel #3; *OR*, vol. 3, pp. 33, 181, and 194-195; *OR*, v. 53 (Supplement), 444; *History of Clay and Platte Counties, Missouri* (St. Louis: National Historical Company, 1885), 695. Although later part of the Fifth Division, Thornton's battalion was attached to Colonel John T. Hughes's regiment of the Fourth Division at the beginning of the war. According to Hughes, the battalion rendered him "effectual and valuable service" at Carthage and "fought most gallantly." See the *CMS*, 26 July 1861, quoting the *Liberty Tribune*.
5. *History of Clay and Platte Counties*, 696; *LDC*, 2 November 1861.
6. *Ibid.*
7. *History of Clay and Platte Counties*, 697; *LDC*, 2 November 1861.
8. *History of Clay and Platte Counties*, 697; *LDC*, 3 November 1861.
9. *LDC*, 7 November 1861.
10. *LDT*, 8 November 1861.
11. *History of Clay and Platte Counties*, 695-696; CSR, M322, Reel # 3; *LDT*, 18 November 1861.

12. *LDT*, 27 November 1861.

13. *LDC*, 30 Nov. 1861; *LDT*, 30 November 1861; *History of Clay and Platte Counties*, 698.

14. *LDC*, 3 December 1861; 1860 Platte County census.

15. *LDC*, 3 December 1861.

16. *SLTWMR*, 13 December 1861.

17. *Ibid.*, 2 December 1861.

18. *OR*, vol. 3, 567; *LDC*, 30 Nov. 1861.

19. *LDC*, 6 December 61.

20. 1850 Platte census; *OR*, Series 2, vol. 7, 297.

21. *LDT*, 8 December 1861.

22. *History of Clay and Platte Counties*, 674-675, 698; *St. Louis Daily Missouri Democrat*, 13 December 1861, quoting the *Hannibal Messenger*.

23. CSR, M322, Reel #3; *History of Clay and Platte Counties*, 698.

24. *LDT*, 15 December 1861.

25. CSR, M322, Reel #3.

26. CSR, M322, Reel #3; *OR*, vol. 27, pt. 2, 733, 736, and 824.

27. CSR, M322, Reel #3; *Weston (Mo.) Border Times*, 16 March 1866; *History of Clay and Platte Counties*, 676; *OR*, vol. 24, pt. 3, 355; *LDC* 19 May 1863.

28. *LDC*, 16 May 1863.

29. *LDC*, 16 May 1863, 19 May 1863, 20 May 1863, and 24 May 1863. The account of the man being killed in Douglas County and the account of the man being wounded in the same county near the same time could have been two different reports of the same incident. This is not altogether clear.

30. *Wyandotte (Kans.) Commercial Gazette*, 20 June 1863. See also the *KCWWJC*, 23 May and 27 June 1863 for rumors of Gordon's activities in the Kansas City area during the spring of 1863.

31. Cutler, *History of the State of Kansas*, vol. 2, 1152. The post-war account in Cutler's history by W. H. Warner, post surgeon at Baxter Springs, identifies Gordon as a Quantrill man, but there appears to be scant evidence that Gordon rode with Quantrill during the summer of 1863 except during the Baxter Springs action. When Gordon reportedly first appeared in the Baxter Springs area (late September), Quantrill and his entire command were still in the Sni Hills of Jackson County, Missouri.

32. *Fort Scott Union Monitor*, 15 October 1863.
33. *LDC*, 28 October 1863 and 2 June 1863.
34. *LDC*, 7 November 1863; *OR*, vol. 22, pt. 2, 723.
35. *OR*, vol. 34, pt. 3, 776-777.
36. *Boonville Weekly Monitor*, 18 June 1864, quoting the *Jefferson City Missouri State Times*; *OR*, vol. 41, pt. 2, 762, 787-788, 794, and 807; *SLTWMR*, 26 August 1864.
37. *SLTWMR*, 26 August 1864; *LDC*, 21 August 1864; *OR*, vol. 41, pt. 2, 762.
38. *SLTWMR*, 26 August 1864; *OR*, vol. 41, pt. 2, 807.
39. *SLTWMR*, 26 August 1862; *OR*, vol. 41, pt. 2, 787-788.
40. *OR*, vol. 41, pt. 1, 441 and pt. 2, 824. It's not certain that the rifle beating and the fall from the horse happened during the same skirmish. They may have occurred during two different skirmishes near the same time.
41. *OR*, vol. 41, pt. 3, 233; *St. Joseph Morning Herald*, 19 September 1864.
42. *OR*, vol. 41, pt. 3, 521.
43. *Ibid.*, 733.
44. *OR*, v. 48, pt. 1, 1306 and pt. 2, 839; *Liberty Tribune*, 12 May 1865; *Branded as Rebels*, 169; and www.genforum.genealogy.com/gordon/messages/4731.html.

Chapter Fourteen
RUCKER, PULLIAM, AND COMPANY

1. 1850 Howard County census; 1860 Boone County census; Carolyn M. Bartels, comp., *Boone County, Missouri Marriages 1850-1872*, (n.p.). John F. Rucker is sometimes confused with John Fleming Rucker. It's easy to see how such an error happens. Not only were both men named John F. Rucker, but they also had several other things in common. Both lived in Boone County at the start of the war. Both joined Boone County military units, and both became majors in the Confederate Army. Both were born in Virginia, and they were probably related, at least distantly. However, they were definitely not the same person. John F. Rucker, the associate of Jackman, was living at Rocheport at the time of the Civil War and returned there after the war. John Fleming Rucker, who was about ten years younger than

John F., lived at Sturgeon before the war, and he became a prominent citizen in Sturgeon after the war.

2. CSR, M322, #96 and #189.

3. *OR*, vol. 8, 235 and 319; CSR, M322, #96.

4. CSR, M322, #137; 1860 Caldwell County, Texas, census; *Marriage Records Early-1850 West of Mississippi River*; and Elizabeth Prather Ellsberry, comp., *Will Records of Saline County, Missouri 1821-1863*, (n.p.).

5. CSR, M322, #122 and #137; *OR*, v. 13, 880.

6. CSR, M322, #96; *SLTWMR*, 4 August 1862; William Lay, comp., "Civil War Incidents in Howard County," www. rootsweb.com/ ~mohoward/cwpart1.html, quoting *CMS*, 8 August 1862 and 3 October 1862; *OR*, v. 8, 235, 319, and v. 13, 323.

7. CSR, M322, #189. Horace Rucker, also known as Harvey, joined Bill Anderson's band later in the war and was severely wounded in early September of 1864 when the gang fired into a steamer passing up the Missouri River and received return fire. He was identified as the "brother of Maj. J. F. Rucker, a noted guerrilla." See *CMS*, 9 September 1864.

8. CSR, M322, #189.

9. *OR*, vol. 41, pt. 1, 678, pt. 2, 23; 1860 Bates County census; Norton, *Behind Enemy Lines*, 143, 150.

10. *History of Boone County, Missouri*, 428-429; Norton, 152.

11. *SLTWMR*, 19 March 1863; Norton, 154-158. Jackman mistakenly recalled in his memoirs that the visit to Lyell's home occurred after the capture of General Bartholow (related later in this chapter) when, in fact, it occurred more than a month before.

12. Norton, 151.

13. *SLTWMR*, 28 April 1863; *History of Howard and Cooper Counties, Missouri* (St. Louis: National Historical Company, 1883), 286-287.

14. *SLTWMR*, 28 April 1863; *History of Howard and Cooper Counties*, 286-287; Norton, 153-154.

15. Norton, 153; *Louisiana (Mo.) Journal*, 9 May 1863.

16. *Louisiana Journal*, 9 May 1863.

17. *Ibid.*

18. *Ibid.*

19. *Louisiana Journal*, 16 May 1863.

20. *Ibid.*

21. *Louisiana Journal*, 23 May 1863.

22. *Ibid.*

23. *Ibid.*

24. *CMS*, 5 June 1863; *OR*, v. 22, pt. 1, 343; *History of Howard and Cooper Counties*, 284; *SLTWMR*, 6 June 1863; Norton, 165-166.

25. *OR*, 22, pt. 1, 344; *CMS*, 5 June 1863; *SLTWMR*, 6 June 1863; Norton, 167.

26. *CMS*, 12 June 1863.

27. *CMS*, 19 June 1863; *Louisiana Journal*, 30 May 1863.

28. *OR*, vol. 22, pt. 1, 373-374; *CMS*, 3 July 63; Fellman, *Inside War*, 45.

29. Norton, 170-177.

30. *CMS*, 3 July 1861.

31. *Ibid.*

32. *OR*, 22, pt. 1, 442.

33. *OR*, v. 22, pt. 2, 516; *SLTWMR*, 14 September 1863.

34. *OR*, v. 22, pt. 2, 516 and 521; *SLTWMR*, 14 September 1863; Norton, 177; Peterson et al., *Sterling Price's Lieutenants*, 113; Individual Citizens, Reel #F1396. "Manner Rucker" was probably meant as Minor Rucker, a name by which John F. Rucker was sometimes known. Rucker was very likely a nephew of Minor Rucker of Randolph County, Missouri (where several Rucker families had originally settled when they'd first come from Orange County, Virginia). This older Minor Rucker had a son who was also named Minor Rucker, but the son was not a notorious guerrilla. The wife of the older Minor Rucker was a sister or aunt of J. Drury Pulliam's mother; so Pulliam and John F. Rucker were perhaps related, at least by marriage. (Pulliam was also related to Sterling Price by marriage.) See *History of Randolph and Macon Counties, Missouri* (St. Louis: National Historical Company, 1884), 173.

35. *CMS*, 9 October 1863.

36. *Ibid.*

37. *OR*, vol. 41, pt. 1, 678.

38. Individual Citizens, Reel F1396.

39. CSR, M322, #189.

40. CSR, M322, #96; Individual Citizens, Reel F1396.

41. Individual Citizens, Reel F1396.

42. CSR, M322, #96.

43. Jean Boldt, http://genforum.genealogy.com/rucker/messages/ 864.html.

Chapter Fifteen
HOW MANY BOLINS ARE THERE?

1. Alf Bolin, a notorious bushwhacker who operated in the Taney County area south of Springfield, was very likely related to the Bolins of southeast Missouri. The incredible tale of Alf Bolin has been the subject of many articles during the past seventy-odd years. The short version of the legend is that Bolin killed forty or more men during the early part of the war, he himself was killed in a treacherous Union plot in early February 1863, and he was posthumously beheaded. Many of the details of the Bolin story seem to derive from one source: the 1885 statement of a former Union soldier who had been stationed at Forsyth at the time of Bolin's death. The soldier's account was apparently not widely known until it was published in the April 26, 1930, *Springfield Press*, and the original is now held at the Western Historical Manuscript Collection-Columbia.

Although the most sensational detail of the legend, the beheading of Bolin's body, appears to have some factual basis, the man's overall notoriety has almost surely been exaggerated. Alf Bolin is not mentioned a single time in the official records of the Civil War (although a lone reference to a horse thief named "Boler" operating in the area of Forsyth in the summer of 1862 might refer to Bolin). By comparison, the Bolins of southeast Missouri, who were not nearly as notorious (if the legend of Alf Bolin is to be believed), were mentioned in approximately thirty separate Union reports or communications.

For a long time, I suspected that the story of Bolin's beheading was likely a fabrication that arose as a befitting climax to the legend of his early-war exploits. It now appears that the opposite is probably true. Apparently the beheading of Bolin's corpse did, indeed, occur, and the earlier details of his career were probably embellished to justify the sensational circumstance of his death. I searched for a long time in numerous, Civil War-era, Missouri newspapers before finding any substantiation that Bolin was beheaded. I finally found a brief, passing mention in a long letter written from Springfield, dated

February 5, 1863, and published shortly thereafter in a St. Louis newspaper suggesting that such an incident did, in fact, occur.

"Last night, I am told," said the Springfield correspondent, "the head of a noted jayhawker was brought into town by some of our soldiers, dissevered from its body, and placed on a pole." The letter contained no further details, and it did not refer to Alf Bolin by name. Also, I have been unable to find any other contemporaneous account of Bolin's death. By comparison, the 1863 death, under less sensational circumstances, of Thomas R. Livingston, another infamous southwest Missouri guerrilla, was noted in Federal reports and in the Union press at least as far away as Kansas City.

The obvious conclusion to be drawn from all this is that Alf Bolin was probably not nearly as notorious in his own time as the present-day legend would have one believe. For instance, one of the atrocities usually attributed to Bolin is the murder of Old Man Budd in southern Christian County in September of 1861, but a first-hand account of this incident in the Individual Citizens file (Reel #F1477) suggests that Bolin played an insignificant role, if any, in the killing. The statement of Jacob Aleshire says the killing was done by about thirty men who'd formerly served under David Jackson (a Missouri State Guard captain who was killed in a skirmish with General Thomas Sweeny at Forsyth the previous July). Aleshire's statement says that the gang who killed Budd were now led by a man named Hilliard, and it makes no mention whatsoever of Alf Bolin. Although Bolin may have been among the gang, he was almost certainly not its leader.

So, while I briefly considered Alf Bolin as a subject for this book, I decided against the idea, because I did not want merely to repeat legends. I decided instead to concentrate on men whose stories could be substantiated by primary documentation.

2. 1850 Stoddard County (Mo.) census and 1860 Cape Girardeau County census.

3. Compiled Service Records, M322, #179, military service files of Nathan Bolin and Jesse Bolin. Although no Missouri State Guard service record for John F. Bolin has been found, other evidence suggests that he also served in Thompson's command, probably as a captain. See, for example, *OR*, Series 2, v. 1, 537.

4. CSR, M322, #17, military service files of John F. Bolin, Nathan Bolin, and Thomas Bolin.

5. *OR*, vol. 22, pt. 1, 466-467; *SLTWMR*, 14 August 1863.

6. *SLTWMR*, 14 August 1863. A Confederate report suggests that the guerrillas at Round Pond may have been led by Captain John McWherter of Colonel Solomon Kitchen's Tenth Missouri Cavalry and that Lieutenant John F. Bolin was only second-in-command, but Bolin was widely blamed by Federal officials for the attack.

7. *SLTWMR*, 14 August 1863; *OR*, vol. 22, pt. 1, 466-467.

8. *OR*, vol. 34, pt. 2, 243.

9. *Ibid.*, 74.

10. *OR*, vol. 34, pt. 1, 124; pt. 2, 243; *SLTWMR*, 8 February 1864.

11. *OR*, vol. 34, pt. 2, 243-244.

12. *Ibid.*, 244

13. *Ibid.*, 243.

14. *Ibid.*, 248.

15. James E. McGhee and James R. Mayo, comps. and eds., *Stoddard Grays: Confederate Soldiers of Stoddard County, Missouri* (Shawnee Mission [Ks.]: Two Trails Publishing, 1995), 5, citing the *Cape Girardeau Argus*.

16. *OR*, vol. 34, pt. 2, 248.

17. *Ibid.*, 253.

18. *Ibid.*

19. *Ibid.*, 254.

20. *Ibid.*

21. *OR*, vol. 34, pt. 2, 523, and pt. 3, 690.

22. *OR*, vol. 34, pt. 3, 690.

23. *OR*, vol. 34, pt. 4, 112. There are three separate locations in the boot heel region called "Horse Island," but this mention presumably refers either to the Horse Island near Kennett, Missouri, or to Horse Island Ridge in Greene County, Arkansas, rather than the Horse Island north of Cape Girardeau on the Mississippi River.

24. *OR*, vol. 41, pt. 2, 787 and pt. 3, 269.

25. *OR*, vol. 48, pt. 1, 129 and 475.

26. *OR*, vol. 48, pt. 1, 263, and pt. 2, 112.

27. *OR*, v. 48, pt. 2, 199.

28. CSR, M322, #54, military service files of Nathan Bolin, Thomas Bolin, and Jesse Bolin.

Chapter Sixteen
HILDEBRAND AND HIS GANG

1. In 1869, Colonel Chris Forrest published the first book about Hildebrand, entitled *Hildebrand the Outlaw: the Terror of Missouri*. It was a highly fictionalized account in the style of the dime novels of the era, and the selling price was, in fact, ten cents. Partly in response to the Forrest book and other embellished accounts of Hildebrand's exploits that were perpetuated after the war, the illiterate Hildebrand, supposedly to set the record straight, dictated his autobiography to life-long acquaintances James W. Evans and A. Wendell Keith. It was published the following year under the title *The Autobiography of Samuel S. Hildebrand: The Renowned Missouri Bushwhacker and Unconquerable Rob Roy of America, Being His Complete Confession Recently Made to the Writers, and Carefully Compiled*. The authors accepted Hildebrand's version of events without question and represented the book as the full truth, since their account of Hildebrand's story came from Hildebrand himself.

As one might expect, however, Hildebrand's side of the story is hardly more reliable than the dime novel that preceded it. In the Evans and Keith book, Hildebrand is represented as an avenging hero in much the same fashion that Edwards portrayed Quantrill and his associates. According to the autobiography, Hildebrand took up arms only because of great wrongs perpetrated against his family by the Federal government, and he is portrayed, in engagement after engagement, as fighting and succeeding at great odds against ruthless and treacherous Federal soldiers. While the Hildebrand family surely suffered at the hands of the Federal government, as many Missouri families did during the Civil War, Sam Hildebrand's account of events is just as surely one-sided.

Despite Hildebrand's exaggerated version of his life story, the autobiography has been the primary basis for numerous books and articles that have been written about Hildebrand during the succeeding years. Most authors have merely rehashed the legend that Hildebrand himself created. The main reason for this is probably the fact that there is a dearth of first-hand information about Hildebrand. Because of this void of material, if an author chooses to write extensively about Sam

Hildebrand, much of the information must come from Hildebrand himself.

Consequently, I have chosen not to write extensively about him. Rather I've limited my account of Hildebrand's activities mainly to those events that can be substantiated, at least in part, by sources other than the autobiography.

2. Walter A. Schroeder, *Opening the Ozarks: A Historical Geography of Missouri's Ste. Genevieve District 1760-1830*, (Columbia: The University of Missouri Press, 2002), 88; James W. Evans and A. Wendell Keith, *Autobiography of Samuel S. Hildebrand*, (Jefferson City, Missouri: State Times Book and Job Printing House, 1870), 22-23.

3. Evans and Keith, 30; 1850 St. Francois County census.

4. Evans and Keith, 67-73. See also Carl W. Breihan, *Sam Hildebrand, Guerrilla*, (Wauwatosa, Wisconsin: Leather Stocking Books, 1984), 5-25 and the 1850 St. Francois County census.

5. *OR*, vol. 3, 161.

6. *OR*, Series 2, vol. 1, 284.

7. Union Provost Marshals File of Confederate Individuals, #F1193 and Union Provost Marshals' Papers, Two or More Civilians, F1586, Missouri State Archives, Jefferson City.

8. 1850 St. Francois County census.

9. Union Provost Marshals' File of Confederate Individuals, Reel #F1193, Missouri State Archives.

10. *Ibid.*

11. *Ibid.*, and Breihan, 45 and 69.

12. Union Provost Marshals' File of Confederate Individuals, Reel #F1193.

13. *Ibid.*

14. *OR*, vol. 22, pt. 2, 665.

15. *Ibid.*, 679.

16. *Ibid.*, 683.

17. *Ibid.*, 715.

18. *Ibid.*, 740.

19. *OR*, vol. 34, pt. 2, 34. See also *Branded as Rebels*, 205.

20. *OR*, vol. 34, pt. 1, 875.

21. *OR*, vol. 41, pt. 2, 241; *St. Louis Daily Union*, 25 July 1864.

22. *OR*, vol. 41, pt. 1, 455-456 and 883.

23. *OR*, vol. 48, pt. 1, 129, 1069. According to Hildebrand, he operated closely with "Captain Bolin" throughout the war, and there is surely an element of truth to this assertion. However, the page 129 cited in this note is the only instance in the official records in which Hildebrand and the Bolin gang are mentioned together, and the connection between them in this instance is merely coincidental. Also, "Captain Bolin" is never identified by given name in the Hildebrand autobiography. Presumably Hildebrand was referring to Nathan Bolin, since John F. Bolin was hanged by Federal vigilantes in February of 1864. However, early in the war, John Bolin outranked Nathan Bolin and was the leader of the Bolin gang.
24. *OR*, vol. 48, pt. 1, 1170-1171.
25. *Ibid.*, 178.
26. *OR*, vol. 48, pt. 2, 28 and 45.
27. *Ibid.*, 207.
28. *Ibid.*, 207-208.
29. *Ibid.*, 496.
30. *OR*, vol. 48, pt. 1, 287.
31. See, for example, Breihan, 151.
32. Breihan, 167-169.

Chapter Seventeen
THE MISSOURI GUERRILLAS: WHO WERE THEY?

1. *OR*, vol. 8, 612.
2. John C. Moore, *Confederate Military History of Missouri* in Clement Evans, ed. *Confederate Military History* (1899; reprint, Wilmington, North Carolina: Broadfoot Publishing Company, 1988, Vol. XII) 186.
3. William E. Connelley, *Quantrill and the Border Wars* (Cedar Rapids, Iowa: The Torch Press, 1910), 299 and 316.
4. Fellman, *Inside War*, 251.
5. *LDC*, 5 April 1862.
6. Connelley, *Border Wars*, 304. See Chapter 2 in Edward E. Leslie, *The Devil Knows How to Ride: The True Story of William Clarke Quantrill and His Confederate Raiders* (New York: Random House, 1996) for a refutation of Connelley's charges concerning Quantrill's cruelty to animals as a child.

7. O. S. Barton, *Three Years with Quantrill: A True Story Told by His Scout John McCorkle* (1914; reprint, Norman, Okla.: University of Oklahoma Press, 1992), 9.

8. Fellman, *Inside War*, 137. Fellman is also mistaken in claiming that Quantrill's trip to Richmond seeking a colonel's commission was a mere figment of Edwards's imagination. Fellman says Edwards invented the incident and Quantrill's dialogue with the Confederate Secretary of War to advance the myth of "the guerrilla hero who had understood the true meaning of war." If only genteel Confederate officials would have allowed "real men" like Quantrill to conduct the war, Edwards tried to suggest, the South would have won. While Fellman is right that Edwards was advancing the myth of the guerrilla as heroic warrior and while he is also surely correct in assuming that Edwards invented Quantrill's dialogue with the Secretary, ample evidence predating publication of *Noted Guerrillas* exists to show that Quantrill did, indeed, make a trip to Richmond in the winter of 1862-1863. See, for example, Quantrill's military service file, microfilm copy at the Kansas City branch of the National Archives.

9. *Ibid.*, 107.

10. See, for example, the *LDC*, 5 December 1861, which mentions Hays, Renick (an officer in Hays's regiment), and Quantrill as the leaders of a late November foray into Independence. This was approximately one month earlier than biographers have generally placed formation of Quantrill's guerrilla band. This early association with Hays (an association that continued throughout the following summer) suggests that Quantrill may have been, like Renick, an officer in Hays' Missouri State Guard command.

11. *OR*, v. 8, 835.

12. Fellman, *Inside War*, 18-19.

13. *St. Louis Daily Missouri Democrat*, 30 November 1861, quoting the 24 May 1861 *St. Louis Morning News*.

14. *LDC*, 23 April 1863.

Bibliography

Books and Magazine Articles

Adamson, Hans Christian. *Rebellion in Missouri, 1861: Nathaniel Lyon and His Army of the West*. Philadelphia: Chilton Company, 1961.

Baker, James R., Jr. *Missouri Partisans: Their Deeds and Their Families*. The Author, 2013.

Barton, O. S. *Three Years with Quantrill: A True Story Told by His Scout John McCorkle*. 1914. Reprint, Norman, Okla.: University of Oklahoma Press, 1992.

Bevier, R. S. *History of the First and Second Missouri Confederate Brigades 1861-1865*. St. Louis: Bryan, Brand and Company, 1879.

Breihan, Carl W. *Sam Hildebrand, Guerrilla*. Wauwatosa, Wisconsin: Leather Stocking Books, 1984.

Britton, Wiley. *The Civil War on the Border* (2 vols.). New York: G. P. Putnam's Sons, 1899.

Brownlee, Richard. *Gray Ghosts of the Confederacy: Guerrilla Warfare in the West, 1861-1865*. Baton Rouge: Louisiana State University Press, 1958.

Buel, J. W. *The Border Bandits: An Authentic and Thrilling History of the Noted Outlaws, Jesse and Frank James and Their Bands of Highwaymen*. St. Louis: Historical Publishing Company, 1881.

Castel, Albert. *A Frontier State at War: Kansas, 1861-1865*. Ithaca (NY): Cornell University Press, 1958.

Castel, Albert. *William Clarke Quantrill: His Life and Times*. New York: Frederick Fell, Inc., 1962.

Castel, Albert and Thomas Goodrich. *Bloody Bill Anderson: The Short Savage Life of a Civil War Guerrilla*. Mechanicsburg, Penn.: Stackpole Books, 1998

Confederate Organizations, Officers, and Posts 1861-1865: Missouri Units. Springfield (Mo.): Ozarks Genealogical Society, Inc., 1988.

Connelley, William E. *Quantrill and the Border Wars*. Cedar Rapids, Iowa: The Torch Press, 1910.

Cornish, Dudley T. *The Sable Arm: Black Troops in the Union
    Army 1861-1865*. 1956 Reprint, Lawrence: University Press
    of Kansas, 1987.
Cutler, William G. *History of the State of Kansas* (2 vols.). Chicago:
    A. T. Andreas, 1883.
Eakin, Joanne C. and Donald R. Hale. *Branded as Rebels*. The
    authors, 1993.
Edwards, John N. *Noted Guerillas*. St. Louis: Bryan, Brand &
    Company, 1877.
Evans, James W. and A. Wendell Keith. *Autobiography of Samuel S.
    Hildebrand: the Renowned Missouri Bushwhacker and
    Unconquerable Rob Roy of America, Being His Complete
    Confession Recently Made to the Writers, and Carefully
    Compiled*. Jefferson City, Missouri: State Times Book and
    Job Printing House, 1870.
Fellman, Michael. *Inside War*. New York: Oxford University
    Press, 1989.
Forrest, Chris. *Hildebrand the Outlaw, the Terror of Missouri*. New
    York: Robert M. DeWitt, 1869.
*General Orders of the War Department, Embracing the Years 1861,
    1862 & 1863, vol. 2*. New York: Derby & Miller, 1864.
Gilmore, Donald L. *Civil War on the Missouri-Kansas Border*.
    Gretna, La.: Pelican Publishing Co., 2006.
Goodrich, Thomas. *Black Flag: Guerrilla Warfare on the Western
    Border, 1861-1865*. Bloomington: Indiana University Press,
    1995.
Green, Charles, ed. *Early Days in Kansas*. Olathe, Kansas: Charles
    Green, 1912.
"A Guerrilla's Diary." *Harper's Weekly* 9, no. 468 (December 16,
    1865): 790-791.
History of Boone County, Missouri. St. Louis: Western Historical
    Company, 1882.
History of Caldwell and Livingston Counties, Missouri. St. Louis:
    National Historical Company, 1886.
History of Carroll County, Missouri. St. Louis: Missouri Historical
    Company, 1881.
History of Cass and Bates County, Missouri. St. Joseph: National
    Historical Company, 1883.

History of Clay and Platte Counties, Missouri. St. Louis: National Historical Company, 1885.

History of Hickory, Polk, Cedar, Dade, and Barton Counties, Missouri. Chicago: Goodspeed Publishing Company, 1889.

History of Howard and Cooper Counties, Missouri. St. Louis: National Historical Company, 1883.

History of Lewis, Clark, Knox and Scotland Counties, Missouri. St. Louis: Goodspeed Publishing Company, 1887.

History of Linn County, Missouri. Kansas City, Mo.: Birdsall and Dean, 1882.

History of Livingston County, Missouri. St. Louis: National Historical Company, 1886.

History of Newton, Lawrence, Barry, and McDonald Counties, Missouri, Pt. 1. Chicago: Goodspeed Publishing Co., 1888.

History of Ray County, Missouri. St. Louis: Missouri Historical Company, 1881.

History of Vernon County, Missouri. 1887. Reprint, Clinton, Mo.: The Printery, 1974.

Leslie, Edward E. *The Devil Knows How to Ride: The True Story of William Clarke Quantrill and His Confederate Raiders.* New York: Random House, 1996.

Levens, Henry C., and Nathaniel M. Drake. *A History of Cooper County.* St. Louis: Perrin and Smith, 1876.

Livingston, Joel T. *A History of Jasper County and Its People. Vol. 1.* Chicago: The Lewis Publishing Co., 1912.

Marriage Records Early-1850 West of Mississippi River. CD #227. Automated Archives, Inc. 1994.

Marriage Records: Southern States, Vol. 1. CD #229. Automated Archives, Inc., 1994.

McGhee, James E. and James R. Mayo, comps. and eds. *Stoddard Grays: Confederate Soldiers of Stoddard County, Missouri.* Shawnee Mission, Kansas: Two Trails Publishing, 1995.

"Missouri History Not Found in Textbooks." *Missouri Historical Review* 19, no. 3 (April 1925): 493-494.

"Missouri History Not Found in Textbooks." *Missouri Historical Review* 23, no. 2 (January 1929): 343-44.

Monaghan, Jay. *Civil War on the Western Border, 1854-1865.* Boston: Little, Brown, 1955.

Moore, John C. *Confederate Military History of Missouri* in Clement Evans, ed. *Confederate Military History*. 1899. Reprint, Vol. XII, Wilmington, North Carolina: Broadfoot Publishing Company, 1988.

North, F. A. *History of Jasper County, Missouri, Pt. 2*. Des Moines: Mills and Co., 1883.

Norton, Richard L, comp. and ed. *Behind Enemy Lines: the Memoirs and Writings of Brigadier General Sidney Drake Jackman*. Springfield, Missouri: Oak Hills Publishing, 1997.

Pearson, William N. *Sherwood: The Forgotten Village*. The author, 1978.

Peterson, Richard C. et al. *Sterling Price's Lieutenants: A Guide to the Officers and Organization of the Missouri State Guard 1861-1865*. Shawnee Mission, Kansas: Two Trails Publishing, 1995.

Schrantz, Ward L. *Jasper County in the Civil War*. 1923. Reprint, Carthage, Mo.: Kiwanis Club, 1988.

Schroeder, Walter A. *Opening the Ozarks: A Historical Geography of Missouri's Ste. Genevieve District 1760-1830*. Columbia: The University of Missouri Press, 2002.

Settle, William A., Jr. *Jesse James Was His Name*. Columbia: University of Missouri Press, 1966.

Sistler, Byron and Barbara, comps. *Early Middle Tennessee Marriages, Vol. 1—Grooms*. Nashville, 1988.

Snead, Thomas L. *The Fight for Missouri*. 1886. Reprint, Independence, Mo.: Two Trails Publishing, 1997.

Supplement to the Official Records of the Union and Confederate Armies. Wilmington, North Carolina: Broadfoot Publishing Co., 1994.

Switzler, William F. *Illustrated History of Missouri, from 1541 to 1877*. 1879. Reprint, New York: Arno Press, 1975.

Thompson, Henry C. *Sam Hildebrand Rides Again*. 1950; Reprint, Walsworth Publishing Company, 1992.

Van Gilder, Marvin L. *Jasper County: The First Two Hundred Years*. The Jasper County Commission, 1995.

Violette, Eugene Morrow. *A History of Missouri*. 1918. Reprint, Cape Girardeau, Missouri: Ramfre Press, 1960.

Williams, Walter, ed., *A History of Northwest Missouri*. Chicago: The Lewis Publishing Company, 1915.

Unpublished Sources and Government Documents

Alexander, Peter Wellington. Papers. (Microfilm copy of original papers held at Columbia University, New York.). University of Arkansas Library, Fayetteville.

Barth, Moses. Papers. Western Historical Manuscript Collection, University of Missouri-Columbia.

Beilein, Joseph M., Jr. *"The Presence of These Families Is the Cause of the Presence There of the Guerrillas": The Influence of Little Dixie Households on the Civil War in Missouri*. Master's Thesis, University of Missouri, Columbia, 2006.

Civil War File. Quantrill's Men. State Historical Society of Missouri, Columbia.

Compiled Service Records of Confederate Soldiers Who Served in Organizations from the State of Missouri. Record Group 109. Microfilm copies at National Archives, Kansas City Branch.

Confederate Pension Applications. Records of the Missouri Adjutant General's Office. Microfilm copies at Missouri State Archives, Jefferson City, Missouri.

Connelley, William E. Papers. Box 13. Kansas State Historical Society, Topeka.

Fletcher, Thomas Clement. Papers. Western Historical Manuscript Collection, University of Missouri-Kansas City.

Missouri Adjutant General's Office Confederate Cards, Missouri Soldiers, 1861-65, War Between the States. Missouri State Archives. Jefferson City.

Missouri Marriage Records, 1805-2002, www.ancestry.com.

Missouri. Population Schedules of the Sixth, Seventh and Eighth Censuses of the United States. (Microfilm copies at the Joplin, Missouri, Public Library). Washington, D. C., The National Archives and Records Service.

Price, James A. Papers. Folder 10. Western Historical Manuscript Collection, University of Missouri, Columbia.

Regimental Letter Book, 1st Kansas Colored Infantry. (Microfilm M858, Roll 5). National Archives and Records Administration--Central Plains Region (Kansas City, Missouri).

Returns from Military Posts: Fort Scott, Kansas, 1859-1866. (Microfilm M617, Roll 1137). National Archives and Records Administration—Central Plains Region (Kansas City, Missouri).

Transcript. Trial of John Thrailkill by military commission, January 1864, File NN-1233, Records of the Judge Advocate General, Record Group 153, National Archives Building, Washington, D. C.

Transcript. Trial of J. W. Terman by military commission, July-August 1864, File NN-3087, Records of the Judge Advocate General, Record Group 153, National Archives Building, Washington, D. C.

Trego, Joseph Harrington. Diary. Microfilm #MS 1008.01. Kansas State Historical Society, Topeka.

Unfiled Papers and Slips Belonging in Confederate Compiled Service Records, National Archives Microfilm Publication M-347, Roll 335, online at www.Fold3.com.

Union Provost Marshals' File of Confederate Individuals, Record Group 109, microfilm copies of National Archive records, Missouri State Archives, Jefferson City.

Union Provost Marshals' File of Papers Relating to Individual Citizens, Record Group 109, microfilm copies of National Archives records, Missouri State Archives, Jefferson City, and online at www.Fold3.com.

Union Provost Marshals' File of Papers Relating to Two or More Civilians, Record Group 109, microfilm copies of National Archives records, Missouri State Archives, Jefferson City, and at www.sos.mo.gov/archives/provost/provostPDF.asp.

U.S. Civil War Draft Registration Records, www.Ancestry.com

War of the Rebellion: A Compilation of Official Records of the Union and Confederate Armies. 1880-1902. Reprint, CD-ROM, Oakman, Alabama: H-Bar Enterprises, 1996.

Weldon, Steve. Interview. June 29, 1999.

Newspapers

Baxter Springs (Ks.) News, 1 October 1931.
Boonville (Mo.) Weekly Monitor, 1864.
Caldwell County (Mo.) Banner of Liberty, 24 June 1864.
Carrollton (Mo.) Democrat, 1864.
Carthage (Mo.) Evening Press, 1938 and 1953.
Carthage Weekly Press, 19 October 1911.
Columbia Missouri Statesman.
Des Moines Daily State Register, 1862.
Emporia (Ks.) News, 1861-1862.
Fort Scott Union Monitor.
Fort Scott Western Volunteer, 1862.
Galena (Kans.) Miner, 1879.
Girard (Kans.) Press, 26 May 1870.
Howard County (Mo.) Advertiser.
Jefferson City Missouri State Times.
Joplin Globe, 11 February 1934.
Kansas City Daily Journal of Commerce.
Kansas City Daily Western Journal of Commerce.
Kansas City Journal, 1888.
Kansas City Weekly Western Journal of Commerce.
Leavenworth Daily Conservative.
Leavenworth Daily Times.
Lexington (Mo.) Weekly Union.
Liberty (Mo.) Tribune.
Louisiana (Mo.) Journal, 1863.
Macon (Mo.) Gazette, 1864.
Richmond (Mo.) Northwest Conservator, 1862.
St. Joseph Morning Herald, 1864.
St. Joseph Morning Herald and Tribune, 1865.
St. Joseph Weekly Herald.
St. Joseph Weekly Herald and Tribune, 1864.
St. Louis Daily Missouri Democrat, 1861.
St. Louis Daily Union, 1863-1864.
St. Louis Tri-Weekly Missouri Republican, 1861-1864.
Weston (Mo.) Border Times, 1864-1866.
Wyandotte (Kans.) Commercial Gazette, 1863.

Index

About the Author

Larry Wood is a retired public school teacher and freelance writer whose historical articles have appeared in popular magazines like *Wild West* as well scholarly journals like the *Missouri Historical Review*. His previous books include *The Civil War on the Lower Kansas-Missouri Border*, *The Two Civil War Battles of Newtonia*, *Civil War Springfield*, and *Ozarks Gunfights and Other Notorious Incidents*. Wood is a staff writer for *Show-Me the Ozarks Magazine*, and he maintains a blog on Ozarks history at www.ozarks-history. blogspot.com. He and his wife, Gigi, live in Joplin, Missouri.